PUBI
POLI
A CRITI
APPROACH

Mark Considine
University of Melbourne

MACMILLAN

First published 1994 by
MACMILLAN EDUCATION AUSTRALIA PTY LTD
107 Moray Street, South Melbourne 3205

Associated companies and representatives
throughout the world

National Library of Australia
cataloguing in publication data

Considine, Mark, 1953– .
Public policy : a critical approach.

Bibliography.
Includes index
ISBN 0 7329 1297 0.
ISBN 0 7329 1296 2 (pbk.).

1. Policy sciences. I. Title.

320.6

Typeset in Plantin Light
by Typeset Gallery, Malaysia

Printed in Hong Kong

Cover design by Maria Fontana

Contents

Preface

We live in an age in which social and political life are compressed between the giant treads of a global economy and the hard flat surface of mass culture, between things primarily instrumental and those increasingly narcissistic. For all their efficiencies and gratifications, in neither of these realms do we often find acknowledgement of the importance of public culture, and still less of the institutions which sustain it. Nor do the dominant economic narratives pay much attention to the simple fact that successful, innovative societies are built upon systems of social recognition and responsible trust, as well as upon order and control.

It was with these very rudimentary ideas in mind that I set out to write about the relationships and structures of policy making, mixing an interest in innovation and public culture with a number of contemporary institutional questions. I hope that others will find these issues to be as interesting as I have done, and that they, too, might be tempted to enter these debates and stake their own claims.

But first a word of thanks. Peter Beilharz, Ann Capling, Iva Ellen Deutchman, Harvey Feigenbaum, Bruce Headey, Rosemary Kiss, Michael Muetzelfeldt, John Murphy and Genevieve Timmons read various parts or versions of the manuscript and made helpful suggestions and useful criticisms. Jan Souter, Rita Corelli and Craig Lonsdale from the Department of Political Science gave invaluable assistance with the preparation of the manuscript, as did Peter Debus, Elizabeth Gibson and Diana

Giese from Macmillan. My thanks go to all these people and to the students in the Political Science Department at the University of Melbourne who endured my early experiments with this material.

Finally I dedicate the book to my children Kate, Tom and Patrick Considine.

Mark Considine, 1994

I

Introduction and Overview

This is a book about the way public policies are made and unmade. It seeks to explain how individual decisions and programs are shaped by the larger patterns of political life. The book does this by suggesting that policies emerge as the regular creations of policy systems. These systems are often invisible to outsiders, yet they account for much of what happens in public policy. Policy systems are the patterned relationships between key sets of social actors. To argue that policy is formed as a systemic process is to adopt a particular explanatory framework. The most common alternatives to it are theories of élite dominance, and theories of rational choice. As the book develops it will become obvious that certain of the propositions of these alternate accounts are being addressed, but in a way different from that suggested by their proponents. We should not discount the roles which élites play, since they are clearly important in many cases. Nor should we ignore the role of choice in many important policy episodes. But beneath the surface tension created by the leadership struggles and cost-benefit comparisons identified in these other accounts, we find continuing dilemmas and enduring responses. These reflect the character of institutions and the other structures which shape political interaction.

The book begins with some general propositions about these larger problems. It then spirals downwards to a consideration of specific policy cases or episodes. Its central claim is that policy emerges from identifiable patterns of interdependence between key social actors such as parties, corporations, unions, professions and citizens. It is suggested here that it is the character of these systemic dependencies which shapes behaviours, problems and solutions. Often these relationships are subject to significant dispute, instability and serious conflict. We cannot assume that those regularly involved in creating policy, or providing the services which result, are compliant or contented. The opposite is often the case. Conflicting interests are common. But when do these differences matter most? How can co-operation be achieved? Under what circumstances can systems create innovation? These are our key questions.

The significance of these systemic activities cannot be underrated. Public policy is one of the central processes through which our communities respond to major social, economic and environmental problems. They shape and determine the health, welfare, education and the developmental opportunities of every citizen. The flexibilty and creativity found in policy systems are therefore of interest and significance at every level of social life.

Policy

Policy is a deceptively simple term which conceals some very complex activities. All political actors espouse policies, decry the policies of others, or mutter in discontent at things omitted from what should have been. When governments announce a public stance in regard to some contemporary issue, they are said to have adopted a policy. As a result there are policies on homelessness, policies on South Africa, and policies about protection of the environment. Equally, any firm decision to grant entry to a program or turn off access to a valued good is rightly termed a policy stance. The admission of refugees and changes to pension entitlements are examples.

By the same logic, when public officials commit public resources to a program to support some members of society, these too are called policies. Thus welfare and the building of roads and new schools are important parts of policy. And when key institutions give legal force to the rights of some individuals and groups, these laws are seen as reflecting an important type of public policy. Affirmative action for women, Aboriginal land rights, ethnic cultural rights and entitlements to vote are examples of this type.

Policy, then, may be expressed as any or all of these three things:

- clarifications of public values and intentions;
- commitments of money and services; or
- granting of rights and entitlements.

What these very different actions have in common is that they are each part of the public exercise of power. They therefore yield to a common definition. We might call this the standard view: **A public policy is an action which employs governmental authority to commit resources in support of a preferred value**.

Because it says little about the origin and consequences of policy, this is an insufficient definition. The standard view is thus a staging post from which intellectual provisions may be drawn in preparation for a further journey. The first claim of this book is that the standard view is too instrumental—that is to say, too likely to see policy as a game to be assessed by a scoreboard rather than through an understanding of what happens on the field of play or, for that matter, in the audience. The instrumental view turns policy into a theory of choice and a study of costs (March and Olsen 1989).

The other thing to note about the standard view is that it is often antisocial, not just in being difficult to get along with, but in blocking access to bigger social questions. The policy world appears as a game played by a few specialists and their élite patrons. The social environments or contexts which give meaning and support to these players is often obscured, and regularly omitted altogether.

Developing a larger framework to challenge and amend the standard one produces dilemmas. The more conventional explanations do give us important insights. Prising these loose from unwanted assumptions takes considerable effort. It cannot be done by fiat, nor by simple choice, between Framework A or Framework B. The alternative is fundamentally concerned with process, with recipes rather than blueprints, with cooking rather than engineering. In a sense everything in the policy world is really just process, the movement of people and programs around common problems such as education, transport and employment. None of the initiatives in these fields stays fixed for very long because the problems themselves keep moving and changing. We cannot afford, therefore, to view policy as just a study of decisions or programs. The specific decisions which often interest us are merely important punctuation marks within this flow—not the thing itself.

The critical approach proposed in this book aims to uncover the streams of attachment and communication which inform decisions and explain innovations. The particular outcomes or 'resultants' (Allison 1972) which are routinely called policies will be viewed as episodes within these more continuous enactments. An alternate definition to the standard one might therefore be that **policy is the continuing work done by groups of policy actors who use available public institutions to articulate and express the things they value.**

Public and Private

At first sight it may appear that these two definitions rest mainly upon distinctions drawn between the public world of governments and bureaucrats, and the private or semi-private behaviours of individuals and groups.

This is neither a fair account of the standard approaches to public policy, nor to the critical alternatives being suggested here. The public and private spheres are entwined at every level, and this is always and everywhere the case. In conventional policy studies the behaviours and interests of groups outside the formal political system have long been acknowledged as important. Bentley (1908) made this clear with the claim that 'all phenomena of government are phenomena of groups pressing one another, forming one another and pushing out new groups and group representatives (the organs and agencies of government) to mediate the adjustments'.

This is no coincidence. In practice the resources and values which establish public policies are part of a capillary system spreading throughout the national and even the international system. These key resources and values flow into the public realm from outside but, once enacted, new policies have impacts on both the public and private lives of citizens.

For instance, in most liberal democratic systems the public lives of ordinary people are regulated in part by policies and rules governing the voting system, rights to form parties and associations, and entitlements to demonstrate, erect posters and publish social and political comments. Official policies enacted as rights and programs also regulate important public activities such as education and health, although clearly these two also begin to show the overlap between public and private impacts. Policies which seek to control abortion, contraception, drug use and the care of children also show how thoroughly entwined are the realms of public and private experience.

Is there no distinction worth making between the two worlds of public and private? Is there no difference between the way standard models and critical accounts explain this divide?

In this book it will be argued that the key to answering this difficult question lies not in differences in types of resources, nor in debates about markets versus bureaucracies, nor in philosophical discourse about self-interest versus altruism, nor in any of the other popular dichotomies found in the literature. There are two means to distinguish what is public policy and what is not. The first is to be found in an understanding of the particular role of authority within the public policy realm. Governmental authority is quite unlike that found in the private sphere for reasons which derive from the need for governments to gain continuing popular support for their actions. Authority is a specific form of activity in which those engaged in a relationship acknowledge the existence of legitimate power. When this source of legitimate power is invested in an institution it becomes a critical gateway through which values and resources must pass in order to survive or prosper.

The second, and related issue is one of values. In private transactions people may choose different values to guide them. Markets use money as the measure of value. In families and other close relationships values may be based on affection, common interest or beliefs. In the public sphere values must ultimately be located within a framework of rights. This is quite a different situation from that found elsewhere in society.

Values

Policy Actors

As a result of this intersection of public and private interests it is important to note that although policy is always an expression of governmental authority, policy makers may come from anywhere. **Policy makers are usually defined as those key politicians and bureaucrats who have command of the institutions which**

must give approval to any decision or program. Sometimes the textbooks also include the leaders of key interest groups such as business and trade unions in the category of policy makers. In our approach a more forensic view is proposed. Policy makers are described as actors, and they include any individual or group able to take action on a public problem or issue. Analysis must then define who has influence, who is excluded, and who achieves what they want.

This inclusive approach prevents an important mistake often made in commonsense discussions of policy making. The élite of government officials and their advisers may control the all-important institutions which can confer legitimacy, but they do so after a wide range of other groups have had their say. They must also do so in a manner which guarantees them continuing popular support. In practice the circle of policy makers is always much wider than a roll-call of elected and appointed officials. Political parties, the media, interest groups and social movements can be viewed as the virtual partners in a larger set of relationships which shape government behaviour.

The exercise of policy making power is therefore a shared or group activity, even though the ultimate outcome often appears to be the preference of a specific leader or party. Ours is a system which strives to personalise these activities, to make leaders the heroes and demons of the story. Leaders certainly participate in this deception, calling months of bureaucratic work on a new policy 'My plan for the future', or attacking an opponent's position as 'typical of his whole approach'. Without denying the importance of leadership it is worth pulling the camera back from the head-and-shoulders view of policy makers. This book attempts to sketch an outline of the social, perhaps even the anthropological character of the policy world. The accent is upon groups or clans, group processes, systems of groups and tribes linked together, and patterns in the ways they interact.

Policy Process

Another way to think about the distinction between the individual and the systemic is to separate official actions (and non-official ones) from the continuing process of which the action is a part. In most policy making, this book will argue, history, continuity and process are decisive. Sometimes a crisis will occur for which there is no precedent, no history and no prior values and assumptions. Indeed, some commentators have argued that AIDS and nuclear destruction involve exactly these kinds of unknown and unknowable problems.

More usually, however, policy approximates a struggle for certainty through regularity. Governments do not start and stop a commitment to a policy area; rather, they modify, prune and adjust. Key interests rarely leap from one ideological position to something entirely different. They amend, reorganise and reposition through smaller steps.

There are a number of reasons why groups and individuals behave in this fashion. These are discussed at length later in the book. The point worth making here is that each particular amendment and adjustment will make little sense to the observer until these are put in the context of the pattern and the process of activity (and inactivity) which precedes and surrounds it. This is true of policy speeches by Prime Ministers, of bureaucratic decisions and of interest group manoeuvres.

The metaphor which often appears in policy books is of the competitive game. Policy makers are often called players and researchers seek to understand the rules of the game, the goals and the penalty system. This is a useful introduction to the puzzle but it is an inadequate one. Unlike the game, policy making does not stop with the sound of a whistle. The process works through a continuing succession of episodes.

In making this key distinction between policies and the policy process, the policy analyst widens and changes the field's scope. Attention moves beyond the technical world of cost-benefit and takes on a political dimension. To examine policy as a purely technical matter, the analyst could simply seek to estimate the strengths and weakness of the available mechanisms for achieving a stated goal. For example, if the elimination of poverty was the policy goal, the analyst might compare the effects of a Guaranteed Minimum Income (GMI) approach with a job creation strategy, and investigate the effect of both on the material well-being of the target group.

These technical matters are not unimportant. Experts help shape the policy making process by forcing participants to consider the likely impacts of their proposals and by generating alternatives. But this alone cannot explain the choices ultimately made, or the means used to get there. Technicians and the expertise they deploy are but one element of the framework of analysis which must also include social and political matters. For instance, the most cost-efficient solution to the elimination of poverty might be the forced migration of the poor to other countries or regions. But such a strategy might well contravene international agreements, violate the law or be objectionable to key community groups whose support is needed.

Achieving effective policy outcomes will therefore require an understanding of the social and political context of policy making which shapes and often determines which options, goals and strategies will be available for consideration. Expertise is never free of these constraints. As well as being surrounded by highly political actors, expertise itself has its own vested interest in the advancement of its own techniques, position and power. This does not mean that those seeking to understand how policy is made should dismiss all participants as equally prejudiced or tainted, but rather that searching questions should always be asked. Finding the right questions involves mapping the roles and interests of all who have a stake in any given policy.

Policy Systems

How is this policy context made available to understanding and explanation? The first step is to acknowledge that every policy has some kind of history, and that this history is a story of deals, alliances and attempts at finding solutions. The groups and individuals who have created this context will usually be found to form regular patterns of communication and interaction. Very few policies happen only once, and almost none occur by the random collision of novices. Typically the key participants in a policy system are linked through institutions, groups, networks and other continuing relationships. **These are based on shared understandings, values, common sources of disagreement, and patterned interactions which can best be described as policy systems**.

These systems are built from two main dimensions—the material and the intellectual. In this book the material realm will be called the political economy of the policy system. The intellectual field is termed the culture of policy making. The first is primarily concerned with resources, and the second with ideas and values. As the analysis proceeds, it will become obvious that these two frequently overlap and intersect, but for now the division helps to pinpoint important differences.

Figure 1.1 The Structure of Policy Systems

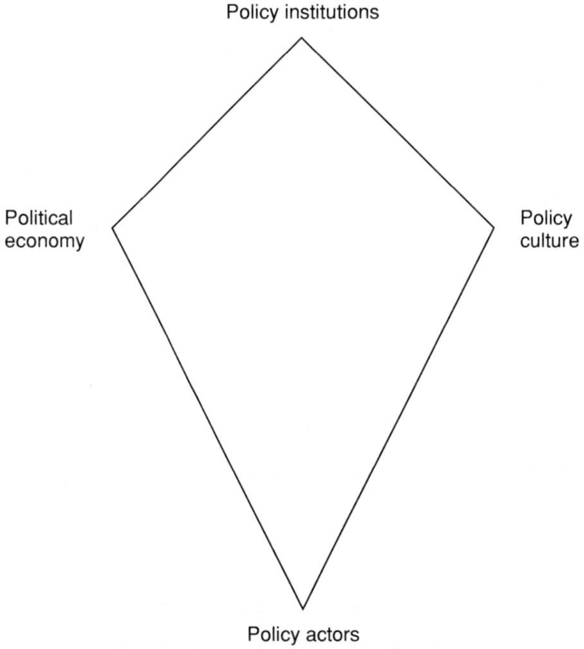

The housing policy system provides a useful illustration. If a political party or community group decides to do something about homelessness or urban crowding it must first seek to be informed about the existing state of play. This is first and foremost a practical, material question. What services are already being provided? Who provides them? Which kinds of people get access to current programs? Where do the resources come from? How do providers connect with users? What kind of regulation already exists to control the behaviours of these kinds of actors?

The answers to these kinds of questions quickly reveal that housing services are determined by banks and builders who are linked together by associations and interest groups. For the most part these housing interests will be seen to be private sector actors, but as the investigation is taken further, a range of public agencies will become visible. Governments at the federal level influence lending arrangements for house builders and the interest rates paid by householders.

State and local government authorities have roles as providers of rental accommodation and control the planning regulations which determine what may be built and where new development is permitted. Churches and philanthropic groups may also provide housing to a defined consumer group. Different types of consumers will also emerge through this analysis—some rich, some poor, some individual and others in families or groups. Resident associations and tenants unions may also be present within this policy system.

Political Economy of Policy

This existing structure of key relationships is called a political economy. All policy systems are defined by the particular political economy which has been inherited from the past. For simplicity's sake it is possible to identify four dimensions within each political economy:

- Provision: the relations between producers and consumers;
- Association: the links within each provider and user group;
- Intervention: the roles of public agencies; and
- Organisation: the prevailing techniques or technologies.

1. Provision

In every policy system there are several types of relationship between those who provide services and those who use them. In most cases there are also intermediary groups who distribute services which they do not actually control. It is important to appreciate that this arrangement of interactions provides a foundation for everything else in the system.

In our housing example, provider-user relations involve the buying, selling and renting of accommodation of different types and it will be important to establish who does what. Are the housing companies large or small? Do they service all groups or only some? Who supplies them with the resources and authority they need? How are the services distributed? What do consumers get from the system? How do they learn about their opportunities? What costs do they incur?

The pattern of service provision is typically the starting point for any proposal for new policy, whether this policy is to distribute new services, redistribute existing ones, or regulate some or all of those within the prevailing system. The kinds of questions which need to be asked of this prevailing pattern of service delivery include: Who benefits? What costs are imposed? Is it fair? Is it efficient? Could it be done better?

2. *Association*

Provider relationships and linkages among users come in different forms. Big trade associations at one end of the street face popular interests and movements at the other. This dimension of the analysis is primarily political in the sense that relations inside these interest groups help determine their ability to demand attention or to veto proposals. Affluent well-organised consumers can be expected to react very differently from poor, disorganised groups.

In the housing example it might well be that a small number of large organisations will effectively control the development industry in any city or region. Construction companies could be expected to be closely connected through a builder's association with its own lobby group and common political agenda. Banks and finance companies may own their own development companies. Firms of architects and planners might also be grouped into important guilds or unions, and some of them may also be involved in the development and sale of houses and apartments. Similarly, the political economy of this field will also involve resident groups, tenants unions and welfare housing collectives, all seeking to influence the distribution of services.

3. *Intervention*

Whether as providers, users or regulators, government agencies take a third, distinctive role. The prevailing forms of intervention in any system are likely to involve distribution, redistribution or regulation. Governments may provide services directly to people; they may use the tax and welfare system to shift resources between groups; and they may elect to impose behaviours on groups through the use of the law. In each case a different relationship is established between governors and the governed.

Relations between different governmental authorities will also often prove critical. These may be government agencies of the same level, or they may come from different ones. The tax system may give builders particular incentives or grant deductions to householders. The welfare system may provide relief for the poor or those on low incomes. Planning agencies will often set environmental standards and building codes. Agreements between federal and state ministries might also subsidise particular programs for new suburbs, slum clearance or accommodation facilities for the aged.

4. Organisation

As well as actors and the resources they share or struggle over, each policy system will usually be based on common forms of organisation. These are used to move resources around, to establish communication, and to help the participants to make decisions. The term organisation often implies the existence of a formal set of arrangements. This need not be the case. This aspect of the policy system includes both formal and informal patterns in the way the key actors relate to each other and to the wider social and material environment.

The two most common forms of organisation seen in policy systems are markets and bureaucracies. In the case of markets the key method of organisation is economic. Participants make judgements and follow pathways which are based on the search for profit and comparisons of cost. Providers seek customers who will pay directly for each service, and consumers make selections from a menu of alternative options based on information about price and quality. Markets need not only be private in nature. Municipal sports facilities and government-run child care facilities in Australia have a large element of market organisation in their method of linking providers to users.

In most cases, however, market systems are based on individual transactions in which the beliefs, needs and status of suppliers and consumers are of secondary concern to those directly involved. Money, price and questions of strategic advantage predominate.

Bureaucracy organises the system of service provision through a different set of expectations and relationships. In place of choice and price factors the bureaucratic method substitutes rules about entitlements, rights and standards of due process. These forms of organisation are characteristic of many public policy systems. Many education services are based, for instance, on principles of free and universal access.

In some academic treatments of this distinction between market and bureaucracy, analysts have sought to characterise the essence of the bureaucratic method as being the hierarchical nature of decision making (Williamson: 1975, 1982). While it is true that one of the key elements of bureaucracy is its commitment to an established code of rules, it is not always the case that these are hierarchically derived. For example, many community health centres seek to establish their rules of access and principles of entitlement through community consultations and the decisions of elected committees of management.

A variety of in-between mechanisms also exist in contemporary policy systems. Here are found combinations of some market principles alongside rule-bound mechanisms. Legal aid is such a case.

Those unable to afford expensive legal representation are provided with a subsidy which enables them to make use of lawyers in the regular marketplace. Rules governing the access to this subsidy reflect non-market principles of need and entitlement.

Similarly it is common to find policy systems in which some providers and users are governed by bureaucratic principles of organisation, while others with whom they interact obey market norms. In these cases an interesting set of hybrid arrangements often emerges to clarify and regulate the interacting of these two main logics of action. These various systems of organisation serve several important functions in the policy system. They help define the division of roles, they regulate the means by which transactions occur and they determine the character of the information being used. This part of the organisational system can be defined as the prevailing technologies of the policy system, provided we take care to allow the term technology to embrace both physical and social machinery.

A useful example of this technical element of the organisational system is the widely used arrangement of would-be users into queues or waiting lists. When the demand for a service is high and monetary qualifications are seen as insufficient or inappropriate, service providers and policy makers often seek to establish an integrated grading system.

This requires some device for gathering data about applicants, a means to store and analyse these data, and procedural rules for comparing the claims of the different categories of people in need. This complex arrangement of information technologies, rules and bureaucratic roles will have a powerful impact on the policy system, and will often come to dominate the judgements of policy makers seeking to improve or alter relationships within the system.

Policy Cultures

Once a map has been made of the different actors within the policy system and we understand the transactions which bind or divide them, much can be explained. One further step is still required, however. The pattern of roles and resource flows suggests a structure of power without revealing the values and priorities being advanced and contested. What do actors struggle to control? What do they value? How are these preferences created?

The particular culture or cultures present in a system describe this intellectual and emotional field. In many commonsense accounts of the role of culture there is a tendency to view established priorities and values as fixed or set. In using the term to describe and explain policy making it is important to take a more open, contingent view. Culture then becomes a means to examine shifting and contested patterns of belief and definitions of what is valuable to those engaged in policy making.

In seeking an understanding of the role of cultural factors we may think of five levels at which these kinds of issues are expressed:

- values
- assumptions
- categories
- stories
- languages.

Values are the building blocks of culture. From a potentially wide range of priorities and judgements available to them actors are found to favour distinctive ways of behaving and characteristic ideals concerning outcomes. Each of the five types of cultural effect described here are a part of the valuing process, or the system of evaluation. What policy makers call their values are in practice just the most open forms of evaluation. These values appear first as openly-stated agendas and manifestos. Leaders, agitators, officials and commentators engage in a continuous struggle to have their view of a problem accepted as valid. They also push others to take account of some underlying principle of policy action such as the need for fairness, equity or efficiency.

Supporting these visible values are a second line of judgements which might be termed key assumptions. Greater interpretive skill is needed to dig these out of the behaviours of key actors. Speeches, debates and submissions may omit direct reference to the key values being advanced, either because it is assumed that the audience is sympathetic, or because protagonists wish to avoid controversy. Equally, participants in a major policy discussion may be unaware of just how much their own position takes for granted by way of key assumptions. Gendered speech is now easier to analyse from this point of view because feminists have worked hard to draw attention to these kinds of unstated assumptions. Policy makers can no longer use terms such as 'the family wage' or 'voter preferences' without being forced to acknowledge that families and voters are terms which wrongly assume the existence of a standard, non-gendered individual.

Policy cultures link these kinds of values and assumptions together into regularly used categories. These provide the observer or analyst with important evidence of what is being communicated. Categories are the necessary shorthand enabling all those working in the same field to conquer uncertainty. Classifications such as 'the poor', 'the disabled' and 'ethnic communities' achieve a common meaning among those within the policy system, allowing them to move on to questions of strategy or preferred outcomes.

Like any accepted framework concerning practical decision making these cultural structures will often be communicated through common stories or vignettes which convey priorities and lessons without the need to argue explicitly in each and every case. In a Brisbane school where a colleague once taught, each new teacher was told a cautionary tale of a student who successfully brought a complaint against a teacher who had ridiculed the theory of creation contained in the Book of Genesis. The incident had not occurred at this particular school, and nor was it a recent event. The school principal used the story, however, as a device to curb liberal discussion of a variety of topics, and to initiate new teachers fresh from university into the accepted norms of the local secondary education system.

Anthropologists would call these stories myths and legends, but in everyday speech these terms imply a lack of truth or validity. In seeking to understand the discourse of policy making we require more openness than this. Stories may be both true and wrong if they are imported in an inappropriate way. Or they may be factually wrong but valid if the principle they advance is held to be helpful in dealing with persistent problems for which no official rule exists.

In many cases these basic building blocks—values, assumptions, categories and stories—are woven together into a characteristic policy language, sometimes called a policy discourse. Jargon, vogue terminology and favourite expressions are the hallmark of any policy language. How much these habits of expression convey and how much they conceal is a matter for investigation. The role of such a meaning system is rather more predictable. Special languages provide reassurance. They are a kind of safe haven for those who are under pressure or whose work imposes risks and doubts. These may be practical, empirical risks, or they may be psychological or emotional.

Doctors benefit from their special language in both these ways. The terminology helps reduce a mass of detail to standard words and expected responses. It also forms a soft barrier against patients or other professions who might be inclined to argue or attack the giver of unwelcome advice.

Special languages therefore abound whenever critical facts are uncertain, but where their personal significance is high. In military policy bombing raids become 'surgical strikes' and the killing of the innocent is called 'collateral damage'. In employment policy, giving someone the sack may be deemed a 'separation', while in family policy the difficulties of step-parents and step-children are moderated by terms like 'repartnering' and 'blended families'.

Policy insiders use special languages to shield themselves from outsiders. Also important is the internal work which languages do for participants who might otherwise succumb to doubt, or be tempted to exercise private judgement. These devices form an important part of the larger meaning systems which practitioners use to solve problems. Wherever constraints of time, information, skill or controversy deny actors the opportunity to engage in a more critical case-by-case appraisal, strong informal procedures tend to emerge.

In this sense the policy culture serves as a repertoire of preferred judgements and responses to be brought out whenever standard events or facts are present. In the occupational health and safety system, for example, key policy makers and practitioners regularly face cases of industrial accident or injury which do not fit easily into official definitions of merit and fault. Limited time and resources prevent them granting everyone the benefit or compensation they seek. As a result a series of informal judgement systems tend to develop.

These judgements combine fact and fiction in order to produce shortcuts for decision making which those in authority will accept. In this vein ethnic workers with back injuries are more likely to be dismissed as malingerers. The 'soft tissue' complaints of women employees are prone to be viewed as psychosomatic. Different classes of employer may be labelled careless or blameworthy if such a classification saves time and protects the system from expensive or risky investigation.

In some cases these devices are multiplied and extended beyond a specific policy problem, and take on systemic properties. Too little is known of the means by which this occurs but the phenomenon is nevertheless widely recognised. Deinstitutionalisation became a dominating cultural framework in many policy systems during the 1980s. In mental health, child protection, aged care and rehabilitation, officials and many community advocates came to share a common set of ideas about change.

In each of these very different areas a standard complaint about existing services emerged. Large institutions for the care of these people were criticised as expensive, inflexible, inefficient and dehumanising. The new values were concerned with returning people to the community, normalising their lives and granting them freedom from the order and discipline of institutions. Those opposed to these policies were categorised as out of touch, conservative or part of the old regime.

Once they have reached a high level of recognition we come to recognise the power of these frameworks by some guiding theme or purpose. Even if we do not fully participate or subscribe to them, we quickly know when we are hearing their message. Multiculturalism, economic rationalism and managerialism are cases in point. They have achieved a currency in contemporary Australia which makes them familiar outside the specific policy systems which spawned them.

These intellectual structures are a difficult matter for the observer. For one thing they are rarely written down or communicated in a manner which yields to measurement. Speeches and manifestos give us some points of ready access, but often these official pronouncements are crafted to reach beyond the realm of the insider to the wider audience of novices and dissenters. Interviews give greater purchase but are limited by the interviewer's status as an outsider for whom some form of translation is needed. Detailed observation and case study take the analyst closer to the issue, provided he or she is willing to stay long enough to learn the language without becoming seduced by it.

The other difficulty with this dimension of policy studies is that in clumsy hands the concept of culture easily gets overdetermined. Having found a value regularly expressed or a parable regularly retold, there is a tendency to think it decisive. Yet culture is much like all other elements of the policy puzzle. Its significance must be weighed against other actions and behaviours. A policy system entranced by a common intellectual framework in one period may be in ferment over competing approaches a year later. Still other systems may drift for long periods without any clearly resolved repertoire. Only critical examination can tell how far these intellectual structures have gone in prejudging what should have been done, or what might otherwise have happened.

Critical Method

In this brief outline the key elements of policy making have been laid out in straightforward fashion. This provides a practical starting point but an incomplete one. The remainder of the book will amplify and explain both the meaning of these factors and their differing relationships to the practical world of policy.

But it is also important to reflect upon the means by which

these elements are defined and used. This introductory summary of key factors has so far concealed some major questions about the weight to be placed on each, and the approach to be used in the evaluation of their impacts.

Mapping the key factors likely to be present in any story or policy episode is the beginning rather than the end of the analytical task. As well as description and narrative it is essential to make visible the dynamics, logics and main causes within these important processes.

Another way to think about the purpose of investigation (and any consequent advice or action) is to notice the difference between description, classification and explanation. Being able to describe what happens in a particular policy system is not the same thing as showing why it happens. Having an effective set of categories to study variables or factors is only a first step along the way to proposing a reliable account of why such elements are central.

The first rule of thumb is, therefore, to recognise in policy analysis that to explain is also to evaluate. This involves having a means or method to locate primary causes and distinguish them from the rest of the other detail. In the approach presented in this book, compelling explanations are viewed as outcomes not of a formula but of a certain process of critical thinking. This critical analytical method is part science and part interpretive craft. The ability to judge the boundary between the science and the craft is itself a matter of careful reflection and practice.

Four simple guidelines define this critical approach:

- The activities or phenomena must be clearly defined;
- The means for gathering evidence should be explicit;
- The criteria for judgement ought to be transparent;
- Specific episodes and methods should embrace larger theories.

Fortunately the first of these conditions is relatively easy to specify. Policy almost always has a practical, material manifestation, even if the underlying causes and debates over values are complex. Policy makers leave a trail of actions and behaviours which mark out a pathway. Even in cases where little official activity has taken place there will usually be some social problem or demand which leads the analyst to the location or starting point of the search.

Setting boundaries between what is being studied and what is background is more complex. There are no hard and fast rules. Employment issues flow over into welfare issues, into industry policy questions and back into national and international economic conditions. Defining the issue therefore requires some thinking about related problems. The critical point is to let the evidence also interrogate the critical framework. Where local causes appear weak, dig deeper. When deeper forms of specific knowledge yield little more, try wider. If breadth fails to turn up the guilty party, comparison with similar cases elsewhere may provide a testable account.

Sources of information about policy vary greatly and require judgements about desirable and feasible research strategies. A further guideline is therefore to seek a strategy of inquiry which is itself open to discussion, criticism and modification. Avoid circular arguments—that is, ones in which it is necessary to accept certain first principles before the logic can be appreciated. Knowing the limits of a particular approach need not restrict it. Rather, it might well open to view the benefits of using multiple techniques. Often the best inquiries are those which combine different kinds of sources and methods.

In-depth interviews with selected participants is often a good means for rounding up key issues or finding out 'who did what to whom'. Combining interviews with surveys or focus group discussions could then yield wider confirmations about the extent to which these judgements were widely shared in the community or among élite members too numerous to interview. Being critical about sources of evidence means questioning obvious interpretations to see if alternative explanations might also fit.

The extensive literature on policy evaluation provides a practical demonstration of these evidence issues. The science of evaluation has an impressive history. Using methods borrowed from the mainstream, social science evaluators have struggled to show how public programs achieve their results or fail in their endeavours. Careful identification of variables, the use of control groups and experiments, and the judicious employment of statistical techniques all assist this approach.

In theory it enables the evaluator to determine whether or not any given program produces the impact which it was designed to achieve. The real world of policy making and program implementation, however, often throws up conditions which resist these scientific methods. As Weiss (1972) argued after extensive experience with these techniques:

> What looks elementary in theory turns out in practice to be a demanding enterprise. Programs are nowhere near as neat and accommodating as the evaluator expects. Nor are the outside circumstances as passive and unimportant as he might like. Whole platoons of unexpected problems spring up.

In order to make good judgements about the effects of these 'outside circumstances', the evaluator requires well-developed political insight. Exposure to the field is a major part of this process. Involving oneself in it often means developing reflexive communication with key participants—that is, gathering information, developing impressions and judgements, then trying these out on critics, key players and other experienced analysts.

This kind of communicative strategy surrounds and informs the more formal aspects of evidence gathering and may be invisible to the novice. But 'learning the ropes' and becoming familiar with 'prevailing wisdom' is an essential part of analytical work.

The third part of a critical approach involves digging through the evidence and one's own methods in order to reveal the criteria used to make judgements. These take many forms. Sometimes participants declare themselves to be following a given path because they value some stated outcome. In these and other cases they make decisions which reflect a commitment to such values as tradition, peace or freedom. Equally, what is left out of a policy or strategy may speak volumes about what the key players wanted to avoid.

The values and preferences of the analyst are also a proper subject for this kind of critical investigation. The point has already been made in relation to evidence and sources. No part of the analytical task need be excluded from questions concerning the way choices have been made. Searching among alternative approaches provides a basis for this. So too does developing counter-scenarios in which hypothetical opponents are encouraged to mount critiques of one's own criteria, and counter-factual positions are considered as potential alternatives.

Finally, a critical approach is one in which the particular and the specific cases are tested against bigger theories. This assumes that the policy world contains some underlying regularities, something itself involving a certain outlook or perspective. This cannot be resolved in the abstract. Some events and outcomes may be random, eccentric or substantively unique. One's handling of evidence should leave open the possibility of reaching this conclusion. Without a theory however, even if it is no more sophisticated than a hunch, the analyst may see nothing but unique trees and no forests at all.

Both for academic and practical reasons it is important to test what we know about particular cases against more general ideas. In the study of policy making we see at close quarters the social problems, interest group struggles and government predicaments which shape the whole of our society and its future. Making sense of this always involves consideration of larger questions of equity, fairness, power and responsibility. Effective actors are those who can see the significance of the small things and place them in the context of larger movements and shifts. The same can be said for those wishing to refine our analytical skills.

References

Bentley, Arthur F. (P. Odegard, ed.) (1967) *The Process of Government*. Harvard: Belknap Press, p. 269.

March, James G. and Olsen, Johan P. (1989) *Rediscovering Institutions: The Organisational Basis of Politics*. New York: The Free Press

Weiss, C.H. (1972) *Evaluation Research: Methods for Assessing Program Effectiveness*. Englewood Cliffs, NJ: Prentice Hall

2

Policy Systems and Political Economy

Policy making is a significant human accomplishment. It may be less spectacular than rocket science, but it is no less complicated. Much of its complexity comes from the fact that new policy decisions are never written on a clean sheet of paper. Informing every policy episode is a particular history, a given time and a unique place. Even the most apparently independent and decisive actors, such as politicians and business leaders, who seem capable of turning the world with a single gesture, are always group performers. Their roles are both made possible and limited by the web of connections of a policy system.

The use of the term 'system' is much like the usage we find in common language. The health system, the education system and the welfare system all imply some level of concerted action across a known field. The term need not imply high levels of agreement about what is being done, nor great or detailed knowledge on the part of participants. And in our application it should not be thought that systems are defined by their common goals. Some systems have obvious goals and others do not. Most have purposes which are frequently the subject of deep disagreement.

To speak of a system is therefore to speak of groups of actors engaged in continuing, interdependent activity. One may be part of the electricity system without knowing much at all about the people who dig the coal and maintain the lines, and without consenting to the electricity board's employment policies or its attitudes to the environment. At a minimum actors within a policy system need only have in common their shared reliance on some part of the set of services which the system provides. Health, education and transport are cases in point. This shared reliance we will call dependency.

This leads us to two central claims: policies reflect the history and structure of the policy system in which they occur. And second, these systems are primarily driven by characteristic forms of dependence which link actors and groups (Downs 1972, Dimaggio 1983). What kind of dependency creates systems? There is no one answer to this question. In many policy systems the most obvious point of dependency will be material or economic exchanges. Welfare claimants depend upon the social security system for their material survival. Children depend on a school education so they may earn qualifications for the labour market. People depend upon others to help them attain these valued goods because they lack the ability to provide for them on their own. The degree of dependency will vary according to the resources each actor has in order to obtain what is valued. The very rich may provide their own education through private tutors but the poor will be more dependent on the state or the churches for their opportunities. These arrangements and relationships point to the practical dependency that in this book we will call the political economy of policy.

Non-material goods or relationships may also be a major source of dependence. For instance, neighbourhood residents may value a municipal improvement program because it offers them a chance to meet and express a sense of being valued and recognised. This may count more heavily for them than the dollar value of the road improvements or the local parks which are the substantive issues bringing them together. In order for there to be non-material dependency there must be some level of common language and similar preferences. This points us to the second part of any policy system—the policy culture. This is the cognitive or intellectual structure which enables participants to express emotions, to trust one another, to resolve disagreements and to repair damage done through conflict.

A good or service is a source of potential dependence whenever it is needed and can only be satisfied through some form of group interaction. This key proposition suggests that systems result from regular and co-operative action among those with a stake in a valued outcome, even where that stake is different from one actor to another. For instance employers and employees may see a job in totally different terms. For one it is a means to get work done and to make a profit. For another it is a means to earn income and use skills. Yet whatever their differences, the employer and employee are dependent on one another because both need the job to exist and to satisfy minimum needs for the other. In order to allow such difference to occur without damage to the system as a whole, patterns of trust, certainty and rule making must develop within the policy system to enable systemic interaction to continue. This in turn leads to the development of various kinds of policy making institutions, the subject of the next two chapters.

Figure 2.1 A Simple System with Input *a* and Output *b*

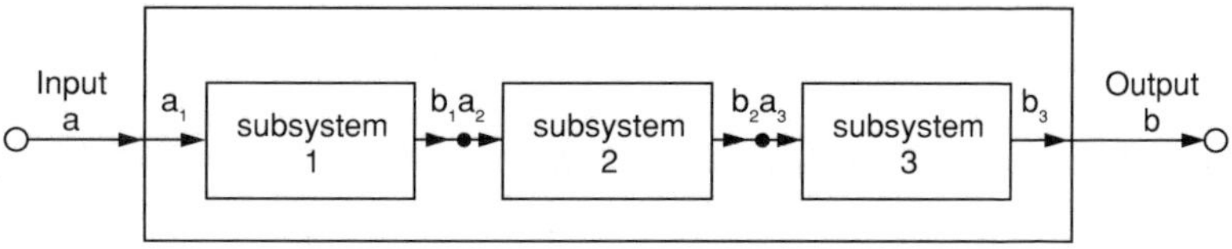

Figure 2.2 A Simple System with Feedback Loops

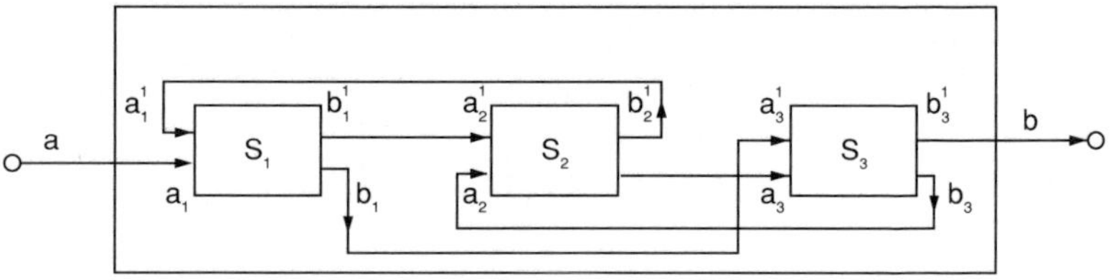

Figure 2.3 System Characteristics

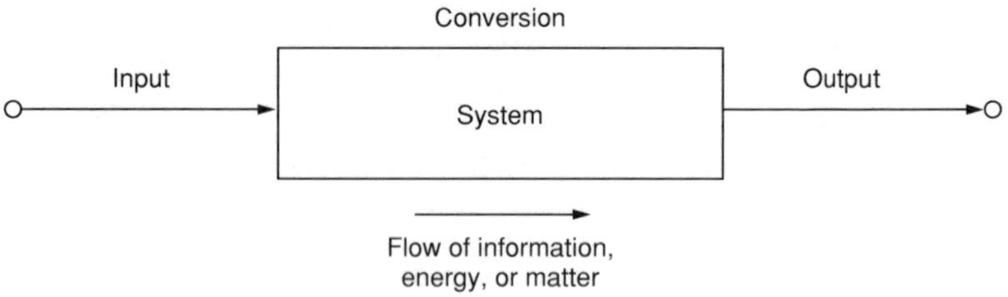

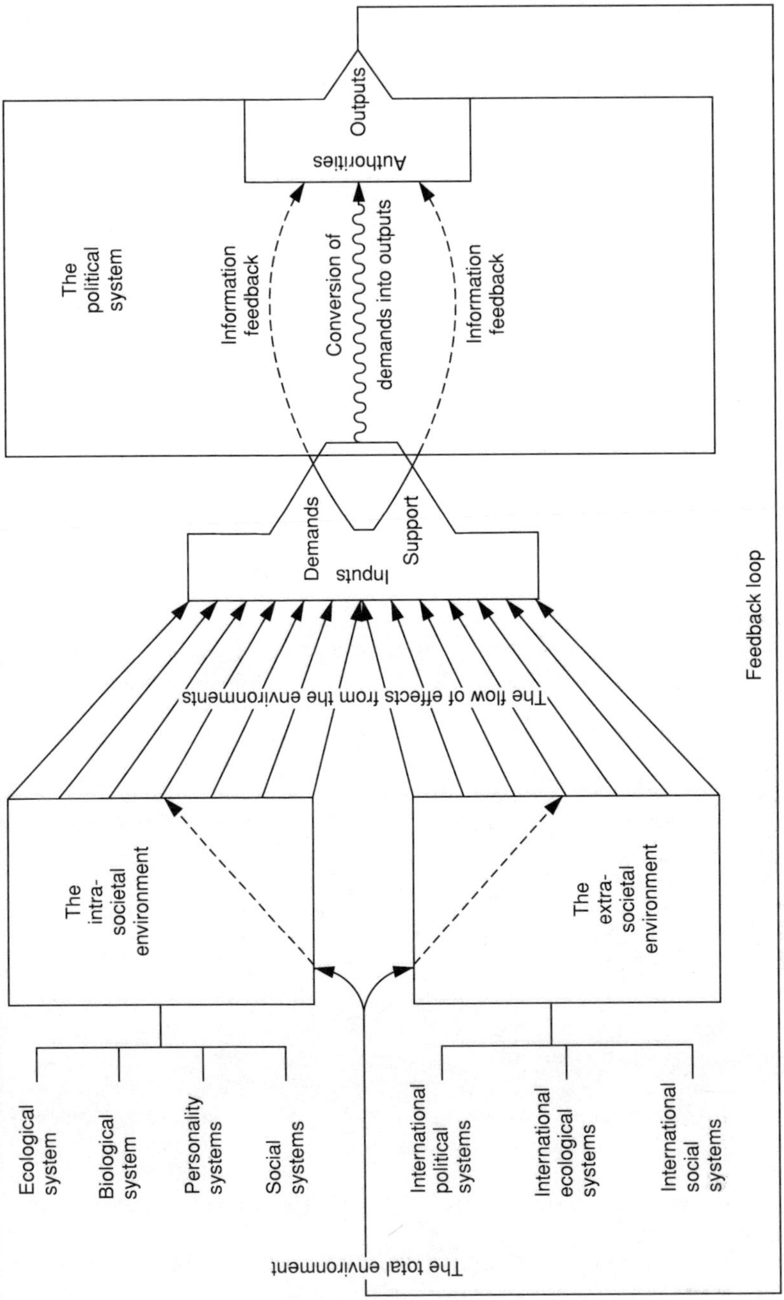

Figure 2.4 Easton's (1965) Dynamic Response Model of a Political System

Systems Theory

Our use of the term policy system needs to be distinguished from a number of other common uses found in the literature. Easton (1965) pioneered the application of systems theory to politics. He used what might be called an organic concept of the system in which politics was viewed as a 'conversion' process for turning inputs (demands) into outputs (programs). Like a biological organism, the political system was thought to interact with its environment in a continuous struggle to adapt to new pressures and opportunities. He called this a 'dynamic response model of a political system' (Figure 2.4). The chief attributes of the system Easton describes are environmental pressures and threats, program responses, information or feedback and effective adjustment:

> ...our analysis will rest on the idea of a system imbedded in an environment and subject to possible influences from it that threaten to drive the essential variables of the system beyond their critical range. To persist, the system must be capable of responding with measures that are successful in alleviating the stress so created. (Easton 1965: 33)

The key role given to regulating and dealing with demands is the distinguishing feature of Easton's system. Demand management takes the form of a sub-system of 'channels' and their 'gatekeepers' which both prevent the system becoming overloaded, and also select out those matters which are of vital importance to the survival of the system. Every political system 'incorporates such a demand network. It is a communication structure...through which demands are accumulated, interpreted, and then passed from one set of members or subsystem to another' (Easton 1965: 118).

The Easton system has much in common with the systems account provided by Parsons and his followers (Parsons 1951, Parsons and Smelser 1956). They too consider the primary virtue of systems to be their capacity to adapt and survive in the face of external pressures. Parsons gives a more general account of all human systems, defining them as having four common functions: adaption, goal attainment, integration and pattern maintenance. Adaption is the task of negotiating with the environment. Goal attainment involves mobilising resources in aid of a defined purpose. Integration is the function Parsons defines as control and co-ordination of the system. Pattern maintenance is his word for the means used to motivate actors to achieve common goals (Parsons 1956).

These standard works display a particular approach to the use of the systems concept which should be distinguished from the definition used in this book. First, the idea that success is in some respect a function of balance between what the environment dictates and political institutions give in response is highly problematic. Systems are not living things which can make choices about their circumstances. Any discussion of the way systems respond to pressures must, therefore, be broken down into more specific terms so that real actors can be identified. Similarly, the notion that systems seek their own survival is impossible. Actors within a system of relationships may seek to preserve certain aspects of these, but the system itself is merely a result: systems do not have goals, thoughts and strategies. These are properties of actors. Systems are the patterns of interrelationship between actors.

It is equally misleading for the systems concept to be used as a code or disguise for assumptions concerning social equilibrium. The Easton model and its Parsonian cousin suggest that system survival results from the possession of successful methods for balancing demands and outputs (Lockwood 1956, Burrell and Morgan 1980). According to the standard models the political process merely converts these ingredients: it does not create them. There is no particular reason, however, why political systems might not display quite radical forms of disequilibrium, upheaval and disorder. The fact that actors are dependent upon one another in some way should not be taken to mean that there is harmony or balance in the effects of this dependency. Indeed, where dependency generates hierarchy one might logically expect the system to endure persistent conflict over who is to be master and who servant.

Policy systems need have no inbuilt stability or consensus. They certainly require some clear pattern of interrelationship, based on material or normative dependency. But the extent to which this produces harmony, discord or indifference is open to question.

Public Goods

The things which bring people into co-operative liaison do not necessarily become the subject matter of public policy. What distinguishes the particular concerns of a policy system? Where is the policy system's boundary? This is a major question which has preoccupied political scientists, economists and political actors over the long history of the development of the modern state (Poggi 1978, Olson 1965, Mill 1964).

The first level at which it is possible to distinguish the policy system is to identify the unique nature of public goods. It may be argued that there are a number of important things which all citizens might be said to require and which are therefore of universal benefit. Protection from internal and external attack, a fair system of law enforcement and a means to enforce contracts between individuals and groups are the standard 'goods' described in this way (Samuelson 1954).

From here the policy studies literature divides between those who view the private market as the best means for producing and distributing all other goods efficiently (Mises 1962, Hayek 1935), and those who favour state provision for a variety of equity and effectiveness reasons (Lindblom 1988, March and Olsen 1989). In theory goods are deemed to be appropriate matters for public policy when:

1. The good or service can only be provided to whole groups rather than individual consumers (e.g. public parks);
2. Operating the system of provision as a private market would impose inefficiencies (e.g. tolls on highways);
3. Operating the system of provision as a private market would lead to the depletion of valued goods (e.g. air pollution);
4. Goods or services can only be efficiently provided by a monopoly (e.g. clean water);
5. Market-based incentives would be in conflict with cost containment (e.g. health care);
6. Market-based incentives would compromise ethical standards (e.g. universal welfare services); or
7. The process for creating the good is as important as the good itself (e.g. trials and legal appeals).

It will immediately be obvious that there are different criteria at work here. In some cases public provision of a good or service is preferred because public policy is seen as more democratic and therefore more ethically sensitive than private provision through the market. In other cases the resort to public provision is the result of market failure, as in the case of monopolies and the potential for exploitative behaviours. In a further set of cases goods are seen as part of the public realm because this is the only place where a universal system of distribution can be guaranteed.

It is also clear that policy systems vary in the way they define public goods. In some countries the communications system is viewed as a vital part of the public sector on democratic grounds.

Effective freedom of speech is thought to require open public access to television and radio. In other countries these services are left to private control through the market. This is not meant to imply that there are no settled principles for public intervention, only that their implementation in democratic systems will vary according to the strategic and ideological factors being discussed in this book. Put simply, the size and role of the public sector is the first battleground of public policy, and every policy battle contains elements of this long-term process of defining and remodelling the public sphere (Beilharz, Considine and Watts 1992).

The identification of key institutions and programs provides an empirical method of defining the subject matter of policy systems. What services are being provided? Who provides them? How are they funded? These questions begin to reveal the contours of the system. This is an internal view of the policy system, however. Sometimes policy systems are purely about internal regulation, but generally they are devised to help participants deal with some aspect of the world around them. So defining a policy system requires identification of the social problems or issues to which it is a response.

Poverty, homelessness, violence and ecological crisis are the kinds of shorthand terms which policy makers use to define these common circumstances. They are in no sense a fixed definition of the shared problems, for it will become increasingly obvious that the battle to enact policy involves a struggle to fix a definition of the facts which is consistent with the values of those who have a stake in these problems. We therefore acknowledge that any given policy system will contain the two elements already identified: a political economy and a policy culture. The remainder of this chapter and the next one is concerned with showing how these two elements shape any system and together define the problems which actors struggle to resolve. Before doing that one further element should be identified.

Policy systems are primarily composed of resources and values intertwined through institutions and habits. But this would be true of any co-operative system we could consider. A voluntary association or a group of friends sharing a house might fit this description. What distinguishes a policy system is the central role of government authority as a form of public power which can sanction and legitimise actions. This will be discussed at greater length below. Suffice to note for the moment that policy making must therefore be primarily concerned with the gaining and use of authority and with threats to the legitimacy of the policy making process.

Political Economy

Political economy means decision making about material conditions. There are two senses in which it is relevant to our concerns. Material conditions generate policy problems. Food, shelter and income are building blocks on which many other things depend. Not surprisingly, much public policy is directed at creating and sustaining these basic material conditions. This is the first sense in which policy is necessarily concerned with political economy. Zald (1970: 223) defines political economy as 'the study of the interplay of power, goals of power-wielders, and productive exchange systems'. Brown (1984: 14) identifies this as the way groups make a living:

> Except in a few places where it is possible for people, like the lotus-eaters of the old myths, to lie under palm trees and pick up the falling coconuts and bananas for food and drink and idly weave the leaves for clothes and shelter, human energy has to be expended to get a living; and not only by individuals but in groups. This requires some organisational structure...It also requires some cultural bonding to reinforce the structure. Today...the structure has become immensely and bewilderingly complex...nevertheless, it should be possible for us to sort out the several parts of the structure and to reveal their essential relationships.

In other words, we use political economy to refer to the basic mechanisms for providing for the material needs of a whole society. But a second sense in which it is used here is to refer to the particular arrangement of roles within a specific policy system.

The Political Economy of Policy Systems

Using the broader principles taken from wider social analysis we can identify the key components within a particular policy field such as the legal system. What forms of power are evident in the 'productive exchange relations' of a system of law enforcement and justice administration? First there are people or groups who experience problems which require police intervention. Their status as victims makes them the most vulnerable in this system, although one needs to distinguish within this category between those who experience violence and those who do not. Police interventions result in complex processes of investigation and then in the arrest of a prime suspect. From here the police role changes, their power diminishing in favour of lawyers and judges who, at the conclusion of a trial, give over their premier role to jailers, bureaucrats and parole officials.

The basic structure of this legal system is the practical world in which police, lawyers, criminals and jailers go about their daily tasks in pursuit of money, recognition and survival. The first level at which a policy system can be understood is therefore the level at which it arranges the distribution of roles and access to resources.

Resources

Resources are all those things in a policy system which can be allocated, bought, sold, exchanged or fought over. They include money, jobs, accommodation and status. To a large extent the material structure of the policy environment defines the struggle to control these scarce resources. Housing, food, education and transportation are the daily diet of governmental decision makers and interest group agitators.

But these resources are more than just the issues at stake in policy battles. They are also the means used to win. For instance, in securing an historic incomes Accord with the Australian union movement in the early 1980s, the Hawke Labor government needed an organisational capacity to research, consult and negotiate with unions, bureaucrats and business leaders. The resources at stake were the pay and working conditions of employees. The resources in play were the bureaucratic and political tools fashioned through the Economic and Planning Advisory Committee (EPAC), the Prime Minister's Office and the Secretariat of the ACTU. It would be tempting to distinguish between resources which are desired as an end in themselves and those which are simply a means to other things. In practice most resources serve both functions. Resources are sought after for their own value or for their capacity to deliver other benefits.

The resources which give character to the policy system come in three main categories: property, labour and technology. Policy makers at all levels seek to deploy the resources at their disposal so as to advance their own and the group's interest. The analysis of the means by which resources are produced, exchanged and valued has a long history which can be traced through the traditions of political economy as a field of inquiry. When John Stuart Mill published his *Principles of Political Economy* in 1848, the first great revolution in economic theory had not yet taken place. Political economy still referred to the production, distribution and consumption of wealth, and its practitioners concerned themselves with the social mechanisms for attaching value to these activities.

Social questions and their moral significance were still considered to be at the centre of the discipline of economics: in other words, economics had not yet declared itself a 'science'. As Black (1970) points out, the sharp distinction 'between the explanation of "what is" in an economic system and the consideration of "what ought to be", only came with the arrival of neo-classical economics and the idea that economics was a true science'.

By establishing the importance of the linkage between social resources such as wealth and the system of valuation developed to govern them, the original political economists provided a useful starting point for the understanding of public policy. Policy issues can be related to a particular form of production, distribution or consumption of social resources, and to some means for attributing value to them. The way these larger factors are arranged in relation to one another will often determine the possibilities for change.

The other key element to be derived from these early formulations is that labour or human effort was considered as the basis of value. This was where productivity, innovation and dynamism emerged, according to the first observers. It was therefore critical, in their view, that any analysis of groups or industries take careful account of the manner in which work was organised, divided and remunerated.

Thus for Adam Smith (1776), David Ricardo (1817) and J.S. Mill, the key to understanding the economic order of a system was the role and cost of labour. They sought to establish a theory of the objective value of labour which would explain all other transactions. The cost of all-important commodities was, in their view, determined by the objective cost of the human effort involved. In the works of radical political economists such as Marx and Engels, however, these links between economic activities and social conditions were viewed as historically conditioned arrangements, rather than as universal or objective truths:

> The Marxists did not shun the idea of universal truths but instead replaced the classical theory of value with a new universal, called historical materialism, in which class structure was used to explain important social conditions, although historical materialism's claims to offer a reconciliation between open and closed elements in the productive system proved inadequate. (Aronowitz 1990)

Marxism at least succeeded in establishing the idea that the struggle over labour power was, in industrial societies, a key source of social change.

Attempts to redirect and alter the basic resource structure of a system often require great effort. The particular pattern of distribution creates both winners and losers who will obviously react very differently to proposals for change.

Even before the decision to act is taken, however, it is necessary for policy makers to identify which resource issue is most important to the problems they wish to solve. It is not always obvious. For instance, in many modern societies large numbers of young people can be found living on the streets or in squatter accommodation. Closely associated with this problem is a subculture of unemployment, drug abuse and poverty.

In formulating responses, policy makers in government agencies, voluntary groups and among youth themselves must analyse the economic dimensions of the problems they face. This is not a straightforward matter. With limited resources to expend they must make difficult choices between competing forms of support. Should most of the available funds go towards good-quality accommodation? Or would it do more good to provide income assistance and allow these people to make their own choices about how they spend it? Or perhaps it would be more effective to spend most effort on programs of prevention which focus on job training and personal development among the school leavers not yet prey to these problems?

In devoting resources to this problem policy makers will also have to give attention to the means available to raise the necessary funds and implement programs. Which groups are to be taxed or denied the services they want in order to redistribute in favour of this group? What restrictions will resource providers place upon the programs they fund? Are there people and organisations available to carry out the tasks?

Policy systems are therefore a means for the generation, organisation and distribution of resources. Resources may come in a large number of forms. A convenient summary suggests that property, labour and technology are the ones typically available. These may be held in private hands or be controlled through public agencies. The way they are deployed or organised (the authority system used) will shape important opportunities for people to earn income, generate wealth, obtain housing or develop valued skills.

Property

All policy systems are based upon a characteristic distribution of property, and the first task of policy analysis is to understand what form of property is at stake. This may be as simple as money or income. Property can also, however, be expressed in the form of valued social goods such as education or health services. Ownership and control of such a resource will help determine access and opportunity. Analysis will therefore need to take account of the structure of supply and demand in each case. Health services provide a useful example of the structure of supply and demand for a service which policy makers often seek to influence. The range of valued resources includes simple matters such as access to clean water and adequate food, as well as opportunities to take advantage of complex procedures such as surgery in modern hospitals or the use of remedial drugs or rehabilitation services.

The distribution of these resources will depend upon the level of investment by the community in health services, how much consumers are required to pay for access, and the incentives for doctors and other service providers to make their products available. If health services are expensive or in short supply, their distribution is likely to be uneven. Income, locality or membership of class, gender or racial sub-groups is then apt to influence who gets a service and who does not. The policy system will then be shaped by the relative power of suppliers and recipients to get what they want.

Medibank

The property rights within the health system have frequently become the focus for policy, as was the case in the creation of Australia's Medibank system. In 1969 the then-Labor Opposition committed itself to the creation of a new health insurance plan. Their interest in reform was spurred by a number of traditional complaints about the existing health system. First, the costs of medical services were borne unequally by those at the bottom of the income ladder. They paid more than they could afford for a service which treated them poorly. Second, public funds were being spent on the costly exercise of developing new hospitals and new medical services without there being any certainty that the health of the community was improving. Third, the medical profession appeared to many to be a producer cartel which dominated the health industry in its own interest.

Labor won the 1972 election with a health policy which proposed some major changes but which stopped short of full confrontation with private medicine. A comprehensive public insurance system would be developed to replace the private voluntary schemes, access improved, costs controlled, and unfashionable areas of medical specialisation such as geriatric and community health care developed. The Medibank policy proved popular with the electorate and was a contributing factor to Labor's return to power after twenty-three years in opposition.

Between December 1972 and November 1973 the proposals and the ministers promoting them were subject to concerted attack by the private health insurance industry and the medical profession. The doctors, acting through the AMA, announced that they would have nothing to do with the scheme, and after issuing an attack on the evils of nationalisation, promptly broke off contact with the government.

In order to lure them back to the negotiating table Labor offered concessions, including the idea that private insurance might be permitted after all. In three months of negotiation in late 1973, the debate shifted from concern over the rights of the poorest, most vulnerable groups, to arguments about the rights of the more affluent to have their roles sanctioned by public authority.

By November 1973, the new government had reversed much of its original policy, agreed both to support and further subsidise the extension of private medicine, had rejected plans to expand the role of salaried doctors and the community health system, and had given up its commitment to a single health fund.

One of the crucial determinants of this change, and of the further changes to Medibank in subsequent years, was the fact that, at this time, the government lacked the resources necessary to combat the private health industry. Control of it was concentrated in the hands of a well-organised, relatively unified group of doctors and private clinics.

Because they effectively controlled the chain of service delivery from research through to patient care, doctors were well placed to veto proposals by others. Their strength was evident in the fact that their co-operation was required in order to make any health scheme work. This kind of strategic advantage is a direct result of the particular arrangement of the intellectual property we call medicine. The existence of a form of medical monopoly within the health system explains both the power of doctors and their capacity to act as a common interest group.

A further aspect of this relationship is the dependence which it creates for patients in regard to their doctors. Unable to survive without medical help, and lacking alternatives to the medial system controlled by doctors, the ordinary patient finds it difficult either to avoid or challenge the service being provided. In the Medibank case these relationships helped put the doctors and the private health industry in a position of great strength. Other important resources which can be identified in this case include the funds and material resources available to the doctors and the health insurers to support their public campaign against the government plan, and the organisational capacity provided by the AMA and existing health industry groups. These financial and organisational resources were available to these interests to assist them in their effort to change policy, and were not available to others, such as health consumers.

In this way resources are also part of a relationship between suppliers and consumers. Property rights inevitably create a system of power in each policy system. Limited supply, high cost and monopoly provision leads to concentrated power and strict limits on change and flexibility. Unless governments intervene, these relationships also lead to great inequality. Alternatively, where resources are plentiful and supply is provided by a range of different interests, power is likely to be more widely distributed and quite different patterns of access and entitlement are likely.

To, summarise, property may be said to exist whenever an individual or group establishes an exclusive claim over some good or service. The political economy of a policy system is therefore based upon the pattern of ownership or control of the key resources upon which participants are dependent.

The Division of Labour

Next to property the most important element in any policy system is human effort or labour. The nature of human contributions is determined in each case by the characteristic division of labour. We learn a great deal when we know who does what and at whose command.

At the heart of any policy system is a characteristic means for allocating tasks to individuals and organisations. Some supply basic materials; others turn these into standard products or particular services; and still others are engaged in researching, promoting or planning. The keys to understanding this set of roles is to identify major skills, forms of specialisation and systems of control.

Human effort may be organised in a variety of different ways. Large bureaucratic organisations may divide tasks among officials who each have a career commitment to the service, and who each undertake a specific part of the total process. Weber claimed that this legal-rational division of labour was the most likely outcome in societies which were highly complex, and in which work systems based on family affiliation or caste distinction were apt to be too inflexible. These bureaucracies would tend, he argued, to proliferate in both the public and private sectors because their technical efficiency would become attractive to business, government and the public. The division of labour found in any given policy environment can be identified through an analysis of the contributions which each group makes to the production and regulation of goods or services. Specialisation and skill provide the basis for these characteristic divisions. Some participants contribute basic materials, others combine these into identifiable commodities, while still more supervise and co-ordinate their distribution.

Example: Education

The education services of modern societies provide a useful example. In most cases these are divided into primary, secondary and tertiary sectors where different age groups receive their own service. Separate organisations deliver these programs, giving rise to unique careers for teachers and administrators. Primary teachers typically take a class of children for a year-long period of instruction in many different skills. High school teachers specialise in one or two fields of study so that a greater depth of instruction can be achieved. Consequently the high school system involves a complex timetable and a very different form of learning. Tertiary institutions such as universities and colleges require higher forms of specialisation to equip students for their very specific job choices. By this stage the intimacy of the primary school group has all but disappeared, and students move through their programs as individual consumers.

The human resources required to run a complex educational system are grouped in public and private schools and colleges which receive funding in quite different ways. Public schools are paid for by governments through tax revenue. They aim to give a universal service to all children. Private schools attempt to sell education to those who have the financial means to purchase it. Regulating these different forms of provision requires a further form of human effort and specialisation. Education ministries, educational research institutions, curriculum authorities, teacher registration committees and examination boards bring together experts with training and experience in each of these sub-fields. Although almost invisible to the individual student, these co-ordinating structures play a central role in determining what will occur inside the classroom. They also link the world of the student to the larger universe of the labour market. Education policy is an outcome of efforts spread across this entire system, and the specific actions of teachers and students are extensively shaped by the way these contributions combine into an interdependent whole.

Bailey argues that these methods of organising people involve both the capacities which they possess and certain assumptions about the way roles ought to be assigned;

> Every political structure has rules about personnel, which is to say what qualifications a man [sic] needs to occupy a political role. These qualifications vary: age, sex, colour, caste, experience in politics, wealth, education, and many others. . .personnel rules, therefore, define compatibility between political roles and roles which exist in other structures, or between two sets of political roles. (Bailey 1977: 23)

How does the form of organisation in a system influence policy? Organisation is the means for bringing together all those things which specialisation has divided. In each policy system we find different arrangements for co-ordinating effort. They usually involve payment systems, incentives, systems of supervision, performance monitoring and sanctions. Clearly these constitute a system of power, although they may not always have this function. If participants are paid a single rate for all the time they spend contributing to the system the payment system cannot be said to exercise much control. In each system it will be necessary to discern which particular methods are used to direct and motivate participants so that they contribute to co-operative effort.

Within the same system there will be different and sometimes contradictory steering or signalling devices. For example, in a welfare agency one can find ministers of religion operating according to theological motivations, social workers following professional codes, and clerical staff obeying the commands of their superiors and the logic of their pay packets.

These divisions between skills and roles may have profound effects upon the way an entire system is organised. A welfare system dominated by priests will be quite different from one run by bureaucrats. Often we find whole systems under the virtual dominance of a key group defined by their skill or professional orientation. More often a dominant group is flanked by competing parts of the division of labour.

Water Politics

The water resources policy system in Australia provides an example of this. In 1984 the Victorian state government passed legislation which aimed to reorganise its role in the control of the water industry, much of which was composed of local water boards and authorities. What those responsible for developing the new Water (Management Restructuring) Act 1984 found when they reviewed this policy environment was that there was inbuilt privilege in the way roles and activities were allocated. For example, most water supply agencies were owned and operated by local government authorities, and these were run by local municipal engineers. Although elected officials sat on the controlling boards, there was a tendency for all policy problems to be framed in the form of engineering issues. New policy demands therefore tended to result in engineering solutions. Increased demand for water resulted in the construction of new dams. Water quality issues were solved by technological devices to kill contaminants or put high fences around storage facilities.

The regulatory agencies at state and federal level were also dominated by an engineering orientation. A similar training and an interlocking career path encouraged a dominant policy orientation to develop among regulators and providers. This division of labour also had an impact on the way other groups participated in setting policy goals and in using services. Farmers and industry groups who used large amounts of water became the natural allies of local water boards and engineers, who saw most problems as being solved by increases in supply. Since the costs of these extensions were met by loan raising paid for by local taxes or rates, ordinary consumers were subsidising bigger users. Similarly, the large construction companies, consultants and construction trades associated with building and maintaining these facilities were well organised and competent to push the case for more and more dams or bigger treatment plants.

For a period a consensus developed between these organised interests and, although ordinary citizens benefited from plentiful water, other values were omitted from consideration. In its attempt to alter policy the government moved first to change the division of labour in this field. It began by restructuring its own departments. Tasks specifically requiring engineering skills such as design and construction were put together, and engineers allocated to these areas. Other tasks such as assessment, review and research were given to multi-skill divisions containing a new mix of staff. Economists were recruited to help establish the financial viability of investments in water storage and treatment, ecologists were employed to assess the potential for improving the use of existing sources and for protecting catchment areas, and inter-organisational collaboration was initiated to see how the investment in water storage could be used to the advantage of recreation, fisheries and wildlife interests. This brought botanists, zoologists and social planners into the arena.

With a changed skill base government agencies were able to provide different kinds of advice and policy. More importantly they could signal to others in the policy field that the values and knowledge to be used in making claims or mounting campaigns had changed. The effect of all this was to alter patterns of dominance away from engineers towards economists, also giving environmentalists a corner of the action, since they found common cause with economists in rejecting the building of large dams in sensitive natural environments.

As economists and accountants took greater control, a new orthodoxy developed and it became more difficult for local interests to mount bids for new dams or other capital works. A user-pays philosophy took root, and the government's supporters in the finance market pressed their claims for privatisation and reduction of public loan raising. In some cases this resulted in a decline in access to water by farmers and rural communities and an increase in breakdowns in the treatment and supply of water and sewage services in the cities.

The deployment of water resources, then, owed much of its character to the way the water sector was organised. The number and nature of local suppliers, the form of regulation, the role of dominant professions and the influence of industry and other interests, were all important.

The method used by governments to allocate responsibility for tasks between departments or ministries is also a key technique influencing policy outcomes. The decision to put an employment program for women in a department concerned with the regulation of the labour market may produce a different effect than a choice which locates the program in a welfare department. Part of the difference is that the two departments can be expected to have their own, distinctive internal divisions of labour, specialisation and policy techniques. A department of labour can be expected to have an internal allocation of tasks, a communication system and a relationship with its environment which is based on the need to regulate employment practices. It is most likely to be internally divided according to industry sectors and to have tasks developed around inspection, investigation, education and prosecution. The treatment of existing and emerging issues will often follow the tracks laid by these specialisations.

Technology

There are two senses in which we can speak of the technology in a policy system. The first is that each system has its characteristic tools. Buildings, computers, cars and telephones are the simple forms of these implements. The second type of technology refers to methods or techniques. In practice much of the work going on in a policy system is made up of both. For example, the immigration system uses a set of proscribed regulations to make decisions about visa applicants, refugees and new residents. These are implemented through a computer system which contains programs for gathering information, guiding choices by officials and checking the appropriateness and efficiency of decisions.

Every policy system has its own characteristic way of shifting resources around, communicating priorities and allocating costs and benefits. The tools or instruments used in a particular system help define the roles of those involved. In particular these devices pin the government and other actors to a firm set of obligations. Here are some of the main tools which can be seen in different systems:

1. Rule Making

Many things which governments wish to do are achieved by using the law to prohibit or restrict the behaviours of certain groups within the policy system. Road safety is a good example. Setting speed limits, prohibiting set levels of alcohol and making regulations for the construction and engineering of motor cars all involve the use of governments' rule making power. While it is true that some of these things then require the establishment of an apparatus to make sure rules are obeyed, the bulk of the work is done by legislation (Linder and Peters 1989).

The simplicity of this tool is also the best argument for its popularity. Governments will naturally prefer to deal with a problem by imposing a ban or issuing a legal restriction rather than by establishing elaborate programs or tax incentives. This is a tool which is low cost and quick. The basis of rule making is authority and although this is not a finite resource like money or staff, it is a limited one. Governments must negotiate their own constitutions with the Parliament and the courts in order to make the rule making instrument effective.

Within this general category of rule making we find several types of specific tools which governments have available to them. Bans and prohibitions have been mentioned. Laws may also be used to compel a given group to publish information about itself, to conduct elections for its office bearers, to keep its own funds in a desired form, or to allow employees or consumers certain rights. All these things are achieved by rule making and enforcement (Hood 1983).

2. *Direct Provision*

In many cases government agencies create and distribute goods or services through their own agencies and programs. They run electricity supply systems, give income assistance, run prisons and operate sporting facilities. All the investment, planning, distribution and funding issues are resolved inside the government agency.

To do this the government employs staff, builds facilities and creates a management system. In some cases boards of directors may be used to assist with this management role. In others the minister is the final authority for bureaucrats engaged to carry out the functions required. These direct services may be paid for through taxation, by grants from other levels of government, or by fees and charges.

As Williamson (1975) Rivlin (1977) and Salamon (1989) show, direct provision greatly increases internal control over the program, and thus over a large part of the policy system. Direct provision allows government to choose experts, control information and use the incentive system which it regards as appropriate. Because most decisions are taken internally, the direct provision approach allows for fewer delays and foul-ups, a fate which awaits programs which must negotiate several organisational boundaries.

Direct provision is also a means for government gaining economies of scale. A single system for paying social security benefits will normally be cheaper than several local systems. A related benefit is that direct provision allows standard criteria to be applied across the entire system. Finally, direct provision has the advantage that it 'establishes a more stable framework. . .for bargaining with external interests'. This has potential advantages for government and for interest groups. Trade unions may develop agreements which then apply across the system, consumer groups can take up their case with a single authority, rather than fighting every local office, and governments may settle these issues once and for all, if they wish to do so.

3. *Grants*

When not actually providing services itself, government engages in a variety of strategies to encourage others to do so. Indirect provision, or the giving of tied grants, is thus a vital tool for public policy making. Governments may choose to give money to a group or organisation for some purpose, or to provide loans.

Alternatively it can grant a subsidy or special licence for a specified activity, or it is able to use its role as a consumer to purchase goods or services. Each of these forms of action can be used to shape the policy system towards some priority or other.

These grants can be distinguished by two sets of factors: the extent to which government specifies a purpose, and the degree to which the grants form a continuing relationship. Grants given to relieve hunger, support flood victims or employ artists rarely specify exactly what the recipient is to do in return. It is assumed that the purpose is of high priority to both parties and the recipient is left to get on with spending the money. In other cases, however, governments make very specific demands of recipients. Performance contracts, audits and other techniques are used to make sure that grants produce the government's desired outcome. In these cases grant recipients may become an extension of government itself (Beilharz, Considine and Watts 1992).

Similarly, grants may be one-off forms of assistance (such as project grants), or they may be a regular part of resource sharing, as in the case of block grants and shared funding agreements with hospitals, church welfare agencies and private schools.

The rationale for using grants is their flexibility. This is a form of subcontracting where other organisations pick up the cost of finding clients and consumers, employing staff and worrying about long-term viability. Governments value this kind of tool because it allows them to vary the funding commitment very quickly. It also helps shield government from direct responsibility in cases where the service is controversial.

Grants and subsidies also permit governments to intervene in areas which might otherwise be difficult for them to influence. For example, the federal government in Australia has used grants as a means to assume control of the education system, one which in constitutional terms belongs to the states. Subsidies in the industry policy area allow governments to change the internal behaviours of private firms, something they would find hard to do by using more direct tools.

4. Taxes and Charges

Finally, governments may choose to organise other groups or individuals through taxing them in specific ways. Taxes are the other side of grants and are just as important. The way government prices its own services is a key means for influencing what is provided, who will get it, and how effective it will be in reaching desired outcomes. Individual income tax is clearly a decisive form of government policy making. Setting the levels of personal tax is the main opportunity governments have to influence the level of material equality in the community.

Indirect taxes, taxes on specific goods and charges for the use of government services are also valued tools. Where it may be impossible to prohibit a good, governments can make it less accessible by lifting the tax applied to it. Cigarette taxes are a good example. Similarly, governments can use revenue raising techniques to create incentives for individuals or groups to shift their own resources towards some project or value which government has deemed important. An example is tariffs on particular brands of imported cars, which create larger markets for locally produced models.

The great advantage to government of these techniques is their low cost. No major bureaucracy is needed and much of the implementation is hidden from view. The tax payer carries much of the burden of working out what should be paid, and in administering the paperwork.

In addition to these more obvious tools the analysis of policy systems also needs to pay attention to techniques. Methods for recording and publishing financial information, for example, rely upon standardised methodologies which are just as powerful in shaping the way work is done as are the visible machines of industry. Double-entry bookkeeping, stock exchange registers and the annual report formats of companies and corporations rely upon complex procedures which shape the storage and flow of information and its application to policy problems.

We can see which methods are most important in a system by asking how participants receive information and how decisions are made.

Markets are frequently used to mobilise effort and facilitate choice. They are therefore a key communication and allocation technique. Each market has its own character. Auctions differ from private sales, for example. Sale by tender creates different opportunities for participants to interact than sale via an advertised price. What these various market mechanisms contribute is an alternative chain of interaction and communication which will impose constraints on different parties in each case.

Standard operating procedures (SOPs) are another mechanism for ordering these interactions. In many policy environments people and resources are brought together through fixed sets of decisions sanctioned by authority holders. Hospitals will usually have a standard approach to the assessment of patients who attend outpatient or emergency wards. Counter staff will be required to gather common information from the applicant and to respond to this information with pre-arranged instructions. Taxation forms, applications for a telephone connection and registration for voting all involve decision making techniques which are inbuilt, or structured through standard operating procedures.

Plans are the other major technique used to create order in policy environments. Often involving several interests these authoritative directions give participants signals which guide their contributions. Local governments, for example will often publish statutory plans for urban growth or renewal which regulate diverse actors interested in conservation, traffic congestion, housing prices and the state of local shopping centres. The plans tell householders and investors where new development is to be encouraged, and which activities government will try to limit in the future.

Technologies and techniques such as those discussed here serve to focus, co-ordinate and amplify human effort. They also set a framework for the linking of one set of efforts to another—seller to buyer, applicant to service provider, and investor to producer. Changes in technology are among the most potent forces in policy environments because they make some forms of effort redundant and empower new actors to take up key roles. The development of new psychotropic drugs in the post-war period, for example, has enabled many severe forms of anxiety and depression to be controlled without recourse to placing patients in institutions. This has led to fundamental change in the provision of psychiatric services in most countries.

The explanation of policy change therefore owes a great deal to an analysis of the role and nature of prevailing technologies of both the material and organisational kind (Perrow 1986).

References

Aronowitz (1990) *The Crisis in Historical Materialism*. London: Macmillan

Bailey, F. G. (1977) *Strategems and Spoils: A Social Anthropology of Politics*. Oxford: Basil Blackwell

Black, R. D. C. (1979) 'Introduction' in W. Stanley Jevons (ed.), *The Theory of Political Economy*. Harmondsworth: Penguin

Burrell, Gibson and Morgan, Gareth (1980) *Sociological Paradigms and Organisational Analysis*. London: Heinemann

DiMaggio, Paul (1983) 'State Expansion and Organisational Fields' in Richard Hall and Robert Quinn (eds), *Organisational Theory and Public Policy*. Sage, Beverly Hills

Downs, A. (1972) 'Up and Down with Ecology—the "issue attention cycle"', *The Public Interest* 28: 38–50

Hayek von, F. A. (ed.) (1935) *Collectivist Economic Planning.* London: Routledge and Kegan Paul

Hood, Christopher C. (1983) *The Tools of Government.* London: Macmillan

Lindblom, C. E. (1988) *Democracy and the Market System.* Olso: Norwegian University Press

Linder, Stephen H. and Peters, B. Guy (1989) 'Instruments of Government: Perceptions and Contexts', *Journal of Public Policy,* 9: 45

Lockwood, David (1956) 'Some Remarks on "The Social System"', *British Journal of Sociology* 7: 134–43

March, J. G. and Olsen, J. P. (1989) *Rediscovering Institutions: The Organisational Basis of Politics,* New York: Free Press

Marx and Engels (1988) *Communist Manifesto*

Mill, John Stuart (1964) *Utilitarianism, Liberty and Representative Government.* London: Everyman's Library

Mises von, L. (1962) *Bureaucracy.* Westport, C T: Arlington House

Olson, Mancur (1965) *The Logic of Collective Action.* Cambridge, MA: Harvard University Press

Perrow, Charles (1986) *Complex Organisations: A Critical Essay.* New York: Random House

Poggi, Gianfranco (1978) *The Development of the Modern State.* London: Huntchinson

Ricardo, David (1962) '*Principles of Political Economy*', in Joan Robinson, Economic Philosophy. London

Rivlin, Alice M. (1977) 'Social Policy: Alternative Strategies for the Federal Government', in Robert Haveman and Julius Margolis (eds), *Public Expenditure and Policy Analysis.* Chicago: Rand McNally College Publishing

Salamon, Lester M. (ed.) (1989) *Beyond Privatisation: The Tools of Government Action.* Washington DC: Urban Institute Press

Smith, Adam (1910) *The Wealth of Nations.* London: Dent

Weber, Max (1968) *Economy and Society,* vol. 1. New York: Bedminster Press

Williamson, Oliver (1975) *Markets and Hierarchies: Analysis and Antitrust Implications.* New York: Free Press

Wiseman, H. V. (1966) *Political Systems; Some Sociological Approaches.* London: RKP

Zald, Mayer N. (ed.) (1970) *Power in Organisations.* New York: Vanderbilt University Press

3

Policy Systems and Policy Cultures

Most of the things which policy makers discuss and struggle to influence concern practical, material problems. These include health care, transport, environmental issues and poverty. But policy never merely allocates the things people want. We always find beneath the surface a battle to rank priorities, evaluate competing claims and define responsibilities. As a result policy systems need to be understood as complex structures for political learning and memory.

Having discussed the economic relations which determine policy systems, it is tempting to dismiss everything else that occurs within them as background. Most textbooks treat non-material matters in this way. However, as we have already noted, much of what people value about public policy making is the symbolic benefits it creates or sanctions. It is our contention that each policy system contains a culture of its own, made up of characteristic values, preferences and habits of interaction. These cultures may be seen as strong or weak according to the extent of participation, the number and range of arenas for involvement, and the amount of communication between sub-groups.

Putnam (1993) convincingly argues that culture amounts to differences in the 'social capital' available in a policy system, and that these will explain that system's capacity to develop, to manage change, and to engage in innovative activity. This has nothing to do with homogeneity. Systems which contain diverse and conflict-ridden values systems may be far more effective than those with low levels of disagreement. What counts is the underlying forms of engagement and solidarity.

Coleman (1990) has provided an account of social capital for societies as a whole, but it can quickly be seen that the principles apply also to sub-fields such as regions and policy systems:

> Like other forms of capital, social capital is productive, making possible the achievement of certain ends that would not be attainable in its absence. . .For example, a group whose members manifest trustworthiness and place extensive trust in one another will be able to accomplish much more than a comparable group lacking that trustworthiness and trust. . .

The mention of trust and culture immediately introduces a welter of issues so far left untouched in the analysis of political economy. How do actors within a system communicate and contest issues unless they have some means to agree on what is to be discussed and disputed? Policy systems are meaning systems. They contain means by which issues, problems and solutions are evaluated and valued. Actors develop elaborate meaning systems to allow them to explain their own behaviours and those of others. In policy terms much of the culture of these systems is concerned with explaining the nature of things and why they can or cannot be changed.

As March and Olsen (1989: 42) argue: 'Despite ambiguity and uncertainty, individuals interpret and try to make sense out of their lives. They try to find meaning in happenings and provide or invent explanations.'

In the practical world of politics actors can do nothing about the conditions they live under without a means to communicate ideas and emotions, and to identify and express values. All policy making involves explicit and implicit acts of judgement, preference and evaluation. Often the value at stake in a policy making episode is visible and acknowledged by all. Campaigners wishing to achieve pension increases know that they value improved living standards for social service recipients. But values may also be contained within the process of policy making, as well as in its overt decisions.

In her study of Vermont town meetings, Mansbridge (1980) noticed the impact of these process values. One of the things which had previously helped build commitment to the meeting system was the role it played as an important form of social interaction. Townsfolk looked forward to the March meeting as the end of the region's long, isolating winter. Formal processes such as distributing ballot papers also served as opportunities for enjoying group solidarity 'with the growing noise of scraping chairs, shuffling feet, hellos, jokes, and courtesies, most of the people in the meeting filed down each side of the hall to deposit their ballot. . .for ten minutes, the meeting became a party'.

Values

Values explain policy and invest all its ordinary practices with meaning. From the open declarations of intent in legislation, to the unspoken preference for one means over another, and on into the measure and evaluation of the actions which result, values are titanic and ubiquitous. To make a claim that people have certain needs or to assert that the state should intervene to protect its citizens implies a judgement based upon value. Political rhetoric is jammed with high-sounding values and anti-values: equality, freedom, development, growth and so on.

Values are first found within the language of policy actors. They express their preferences and explain their purpose in undertaking or refusing different forms of behaviour. Although purpose giving, values need not be articulate or even consistent. It is commonplace in policy making to find the same individual or group giving support to a position they do not fully recognise, or claiming inconsistent principles in support of a single outcome. Although much of the valuation of policy is done openly through language and action, some lies buried in the silences and implied exclusions which regularly dog policy work. A minister's speech on the importance of exports may say nothing at all about domestic markets and without uttering a single word she may signal a decisive shift away from support for local manufacturers, small business or the tertiary sector. Even the absence of a preference can be incorporated into a value-laden theory of inaction, alienation or exclusion.

Although values emerge in every conceivable situation they are not always decisive: that is, it is not always they which *cause* action. Action may often emerge as a result of chance, luck or coincidence. The winning side may claim that the result was perfectly consistent with their goal, but this simply shows that values may come after the event, not before. The linear connection between values and choices which is so strongly held in the rationalist's view of his or her own actions, is broken. Values may be the things that people employ in order to choose jobs, clothes and vacations, but they are also the affections, desires and commitments which result from situations where there is little choice.

Students restricted by their timetables are required to take subjects which they expect to dislike but may find valuable. An unplanned travel detour reveals countryside which the traveller may never have chosen but nevertheless finds attractive. Values identify and give meaning. This often motivates individuals to act, but between the motive and the behaviour there are other intermediate forces, which caution, interpret and seek to direct the individual towards outcomes which may be of decisive interest.

Individual Values

It is common in Western thinking to view values as the domain of individuals alone. Liberal political theory and social science generally respects a tradition of defining key values, called rights, as the inalienable domain of solitary actors. When stripped to their basics, these accounts turn out to be but one way to understand the origin and value of values, a view termed methodological individualism (Popper 1962, 1972). Other accounts prefer an explanation which locates values within the shared domain of individual and social actors such as professions, corporations, parties and bureaucracies (Kuhn 1962, Lakatos 1971, Hindess 1988). The reason the analysis of values itself provokes a dispute which is value-ridden is that preferences and evaluations bedevil both the ability of the observer to recognise what he or she is observing, as well as colouring the alternatives they regard as appropriate and feasible. Observation and description are never totally free of the preferred outcome or pet theory of the observer.

The vast array of value events involved in policy making may be seen to provoke three broad sets of problems for both observer and participant. Preferences and desires may be seen first of all to pertain to either individuals or groups. The relation between the two has to be investigated empirically. Second, values can be understood as voluntary and flexible, or as structured into habits of mind which stretch across the behaviours of many similar actors. This is a question of openness and its limits. Finally, values can be considered as relative statements of good and bad situations, or can be located within claims asserting that a fixed or absolute need or right exists. According to most analysts, some understanding of these problems is vital if policy is to make choices between different ideals of what is good.

Without rejecting the possibility that these philosophical aspects of the values problem may impinge directly on the perceptions of policy actors, in this analysis the issue is considered *in practice* to be largely a province of social, not individual determination. This is not a claim which renders all values relative to the situation in which they are expressed. Rather, the assertion that some ideals are absolute can only be demonstrated through a consideration of the way they assist or restrict real people in actual situations. This can be seen in discussions of the importance of equality, a value which most modern policy makers accept but which can give aid to an almost infinite number of programs and laws.

Example: Equality

Equality is shorthand for several complex virtues. Liberals support equality of opportunity and claim that this should be enacted through restrictions on any impediment or form of systematic discrimination. Civil rights legislation and education programs to assist minorities typically aim to give all citizens the chance to vote, speak and gain appointment to important social positions. But this form of equality stops short of considering how effective groups actually are in using these opportunities. Radical egalitarians define equality through a consideration of the actual life experience of different groups of citizens, and therefore often seek to redistribute income, jobs and other benefits to close the gap between the haves and the have-nots. Bureaucratic rules of equal treatment are different again, attempting to guarantee that public organisations provide every citizen with the same service, thus introducing a potentially different notion of equality to either of the two suggested above. Policy systems differ in their prevailing conceptions of which matters should be subject to its principles of equality and which should be left to other rules such as respect for difference, freedom of choice and autonomy from external coercion (Dworkin 1977, Rawls 1971, Okun 1975).

Categories

One of the most important ways in which valuing becomes a social, rather than a personal achievement is through the use of categories or names. Naming is the surface level at which systematic practices invest policy environments with meaning. Most organisations, for instance, will have favoured categories of explanation and action which are thought to be appropriate to certain situations. The expression and management of conflict are critical examples. There may be no rules governing these activities, but group members will feel the discomfort should they step outside accepted practice. For instance, subordinates will be shown how to behave in the presence of superiors, where to sit, whether or not to use first names, how much debate is permitted in regard to established policy, and so on.

Political commentator Richard Barnet gives the example of some of the language categories which influenced national security policy during the 1960s in the United States:

> One of the first lessons a national security manager learns after a day in the bureaucratic climate of the Pentagon, state department, White House or CIA is that toughness is the most highly prized virtue. Some of the national security managers of the Kennedy-Johnson era. . .talk about the 'hairy-chest syndrome'. The man who is ready to recommend using violence against foreigners, even where he is overruled, does not damage his reputation for prudence, soundness, or imagination, but the man who recommends putting an issue to the UN, seeking negotiations, or—horror of horrors—'doing nothing' quickly becomes known as soft. To be 'soft'—that is, unbelligerent, compassionate, willing to settle for less—or simply repelled by homicide, is to be 'irresponsible'. . .it means walking out of the club.

The first step towards an understanding of these issues can be taken by locating values within groups. In this account policy-relevant values are viewed as the property of particular social settings. Individuals may seek to amend or challenge such arrangements but when it comes to the making of policy this freedom is largely confined to changes which are made meaningful by their compatibility with the prevailing norms and preferences of the group. For example, any individual parent may desire to be valued and rewarded for their work with children, to be given a salary for housework, or to receive high social standing for their effort to raise their children well, but this can only be achieved to the extent that other actors and organisations are convinced to rate this activity highly. This will then emerge as policy to provide child care, to allow tax deductions for family expenditure or in facilities to promote maternity and paternity leave to employees responsible for the care of children. Needs therefore become recognised as rights through a process of active engagement. Another way to express this connection between the individual and the larger group is to say that policy making is a continuous process for institutionalising values.

Customs and Conventions

Customs are the habits and rules through which a society attempts to memorise what it has learned about itself. These regulate the meaning given to important transactions at the group level. Without such memory collective action becomes impossible. Every action and problem must be considered as a new puzzle and every solution must be rated as equal to every other. In place of this potential for chaos societies of all kinds seek to prioritise certain things they have learned in the past and to impose these on new situations. Often these institutional values are embodied in the routine practices of a particular formal organisation such as a corporation or a government agency. New employees are taught how to recognise categories of action: 'this is a legal problem', 'this is a case for the social worker', 'this question must be resolved by the manager', and so on.

Not all policy values reside within organisations, however. Just as frequently they are expressed through more complex sets of interactions such as those governing the granting of civil rights or those which define the authority of the family. Take income policy as an example. No single organisation controls the way a society allocates material benefits to its members. Family and kinship groups influence the material aid given to children and older people. Work organisations distribute wages in accord with their own standards of performance or merit. Markets reward producers through the prices they charge. Government agencies give welfare benefits and regulate superannuation. The law defines the right to property and inheritance. Each of these practices contributes to a total configuration of opportunities and constraints upon the access which any given individual has to gain money and other material income. To say that a society values paid employment is to recognise the interconnection of these organisations in jointly giving value to a particular method for generating and allocating rewards.

Customs mediate between natural and social environments and the individuals dependent upon them for survival or prosperity. The continued existence of these customs is largely determined by their capacity successfully to accommodate local behaviours to wider environmental problems such as economic survival and social peace. The way customary behaviour memorises the past is necessarily selective. This selectivity is largely the result of a history of pressure and agitation from groups of people wanting their needs noticed.

This results in great variation in the form which customs take. No two countries have exactly the same marriage laws or the same criminal code. It also produces substantial dynamism within institutions. One generation's routine behaviour in regard to work and leisure is often radically different to the next generation's method of organising its preferences. In their struggle to impose order on complex behaviours customs frequently resist change and punish deviance. The fact that they are required to alter their shape from time to time is testimony to the force of changing circumstances outside their direct authority or reach. External threat and internal turmoil keep customs in a ceaseless circuit of repression and adaptation, such that when peace breaks out it is seldom lasting.

Customs do more than coerce. In fact their legitimacy is rarely achieved by continuous use of force. Customary behaviour is secured through a combined strategy of compulsion and recognition. For example, even in that most oppressive of institutions—slavery—victims may be brought into subjection by affection as well as punishment. Status is the systematic recognition given to individuals by custom. For instance, the prestige granted to religious leaders and to occupations such as doctors and lawyers comes from a complex interaction of state and private institutions, including the labour market, the education system and the family. These forms of status confer special powers on the individual, but they are powers shaped by a web of social expectations governing the appropriate conduct of those who enjoy these roles. These forms of recognition 'place' both superior and subordinate groups. In seventeenth century Europe, for example, indigenous peoples were defined as 'natives' or 'noble savages' in order to allow respect to be accompanied by domination. Modern societies have often recognised motherhood as this kind of special category. It is so valuable that basic rights to work, earn income and obtain other advantages may be effectively suspended to accommodate it.

Customs govern the systematic allocation of value to tasks and roles. All systems require arrangements through which value can be attached to actions and resources deemed to be important. These are the signals which enable interests to interact in the absence of detailed information. These critical messages circulate through a population and establish priorities, regulate exchange and sanction group behaviours. They also provide some code or accepted practice for the management of conflict.

In policy making there are a number of customary forms which influence the options available to actors and shape the behaviours which are likely to be preferred. Economic customs are often of primary importance. They include sets of conventions and rules governing the making of contracts, the means for exchanging goods and services, the determination of investment and the training and sale of labour. The behaviour of formal organisations will be centrally involved in giving voice and action to these belief systems, but individual organisations do not control such customs. In fact they often take their roles through the script written by larger contributors to customary codes.

Example: Markets as Conventions

This can be grasped by looking again at the market. To create an effective market society must engage in complicated actions to limit some forms of behaviour and encourage others. The state must guarantee the money supply and teach participants to trust its role as both a store of value and a medium of exchange. Producers must also be trained to rely on the likelihood that buyers will attend, that their produce will not be stolen and that other sellers will not be permitted to conspire to defraud them. In other words, participants must be brought to value competition and at the same time to limit their competitive urge to acceptable forms of conduct. The natural scepticism of consumers will also take some overcoming. They must be brought to a minimum level of confidence that the goods available for sale are genuine and authentic. Who creates this complex set of expectations and understandings? Certainly no single group can do it. Societies evolve market systems after the fashion of their own economic and political predicaments. This is achieved through countless interactions between the participants which, over time, lay down boundaries and habits which allow co-operation.

We assume that a market is always the same phenomenon. Yet all markets depend upon, and are explained by, highly complex conventions concerning information, entitlement to act, price setting, the role of intermediaries, rules of exchange, rights to compensation and systems of redress. Pepper traders in southern India settle the price of a particular crop through a ritual in which the potential buyer places a given number of beads in the hand of the seller. Both hands are covered by a blanket, leaving enthusiastic middlemen to fret over the final outcome. In the Australian housing market a similar form of ritual is carried out at house auctions where an auctioneer leads potential buyers through a series of manoeuvres designed to convince them to make high bids. The buyers engage in their own theatre by looking disinterested, feigning disgust and pretending to have exhausted their reserves. Markets would not be possible without these elaborate meaning systems. Planning techniques, judicial systems and all other policy making arrangements also rely on such structured or shared behaviours.

The idea that the policy maker's world is sustained by conventions and other customs challenges the more voluntaristic view of policy making as the scientific selection of values. While it is certainly true that policy making organisations such as the Cabinet, Parliament and the Public Service gather information, weigh alternatives and decide policy outcomes, the recognition of conventions alerts the observer to the role which values play in pre-designing both problems and solutions. Prior to the eruption of a policy problem, actors are enmeshed in various kinds of convention building activities which shape their deliberations. Schutz (1953: 10) calls these 'a treasure house of ready-made preconstituted types and characterisations' which turn the variable and the unique into a common language of decision and action.

Customs are composed of three levels of complexity—conventional behaviours or habits, special forms of deliberation, and socially prescribed symbols or signs of success and failure. Anthropologists provide a rich source of data about the social role of conventions. Douglas (1987: 9) points out that the group behaviour upon which any society depends requires that individuals 'share the categories of their thought' and that these categories basically consist of the means used to classify and interpret the world around them. She terms these systematic categories 'institutions':

> Institutions systematically direct individual memory and channel our perceptions into forms compatible with the relations they authorise. They fix processes that are essentially dynamic, they hide their influence, and they rouse our emotions to a standardised pitch on standardised issues. Add to all this that they endow themselves with rightness and send their mutual corroboration cascading through all the levels of our information system.

What is meant by 'conventions'? How can this be applied to policy making? A number of important kinds of conventions or established ways of treating policy issues can be recognised. First, conventions give most policy systems a prevailing set of commonly used categories. Most often these concern the means for dividing work and allocating priority. For instance, policy makers place some issues in a category called 'welfare' and others under 'employment'. Some matters are classified as 'private' and others as 'public'. Ask politicians about the action that can be taken to solve problems of poverty or disease and they will immediately begin to justify the characteristic attention span of the system by recourse to accepted boundaries—'governments can only do so much', 'we are better off than most', and so on.

Names and Boundaries

Boundaries and demarcations are necessarily selective and partial. They are shortcuts which save time and bother. They impose non-rational certainties on otherwise disordered issues. They also reveal what is being valued. When policy makers declare something to be a 'women's issue', or a 'matter of national security', they give it a recognised stamp which will guarantee it a particular kind of priority in the minds of others. One need not suppose that these categories are entirely elastic in order to acknowledge that what goes into them is variable. One government's minor diplomatic incident is another regime's provocation of war, and so on. The interesting thing to note is just how often people in a particular field are able to agree on what belongs in each category.

A useful way to identify such categories and boundaries is to observe the effort which goes into developing, maintaining and modifying them. Election manifestos, statements to Parliament and replies to questions frequently show ministers working hard to establish where they stand in relation to conventional boundaries. Often such speech making is primarily concerned with claiming the authority of customary thought, and far less interested in substantive outcomes. Naming policy problems is therefore a critical means through which actors communicate their expectations. As Edelman (1977) argues, 'the name for a problem also creates beliefs about what conditions public policy can change and what it cannot touch'.

It is important to note that new policy is frequently a struggle to maintain or challenge these categories. When an Australian state government recently renamed its primary industry department the Department of Agriculture and Rural Affairs, it was doing far more than providing the minister with an opportunity to design new stationery. The manipulation of names was an attempt to widen the constituency, limit the control of farmer organisations, alter the policy interests of the department, and include the social and educational needs of rural communities.

Establishing boundaries and giving them names is a way in which actors are involved in 'making up' the policy world (Hacking 1985) they inhabit. This is undoubtedly one of the most important ways in which conventions define policies. The identification of categories therefore helps the observer sketch what might be called the 'cognitive map' of a given policy field.

Examining these names and categories, and the issues which fit within them, is the second aspect of this conventional world which participants need to understand. By fixing a label, policy makers and the reference groups they wish to address collaborate in signalling the value to be attached to any given issue or problem. As Edelman (1977) points out, the name given to a problem immediately elicits expectations about its causes and the conditions which can be altered in order to bring about change;

> When we name and classify a problem, we unconsciously establish the status and roles of those involved with it, including their self-conceptions. If the problem is an economic system that yields inadequate monetary and psychological benefits, then the working poor and the unemployed are victims; but if the problem is personal pathology, they are lazy and incompetent. . .How the problem is named involves alternative scenarios, each with its own facts, value judgements, and emotions.

The choice of labels not only signals a positive preference, but omits other possibilities. 'In a situation in which a person is making a public decision about the category membership of an object by giving the object a verbal label, he is selecting a term out of a set of alternatives, each with classificatory import' (Frake 1969: 33).

In observing the influence of custom and convention policy makers automatically take account of the classificatory system which underpins the observed process of decision making. This is the set of informal understandings which spell out important detail about who should get access to certain parts of the process, how different organisations should interact, and which of the available *techniques* of policy making should be used to address emerging problems. Some of the questions which expose these boundaries and classifications include:

- What is the problem being discussed by different interests? For whom is the problem a problem? How do the terms and names being used suggest or imply a preference?

- Who is presumed to be a participant in the policy area being defined? Who appears to gain automatic admittance? Who must make a special case in order to get access? Who, by inference, are the outsiders?
- How is authority named and how are roles allocated among participants? Are there clearly defined leaders who are expected to initiate action, chair meetings, keep records and define what is going on? Are there implied limits on their action?
- What boundaries are established for discussion and action? What is their basis: geographic, temporal, financial?
- Is there a group who are regarded as the objects of action? How are they named, and what characteristic is identified as a qualification for becoming part of the group ?
- What means for taking action are favoured from the outset? What strategies might one expect to find in this policy area? Are there obvious omissions? When participants interact do some strategies spring to mind more or less automatically? Are other options absent or regarded as virtually outside their terms of reference?
- What form of interaction do participants typically use? Do they favour formal meetings bound by standing orders, semi-formal discussion groups, commissions of inquiry, written memoranda or some form of arbitration?
- What outcomes do participants regard as possible? Have some options already been highlighted as worthy of special consideration? Are 'success stories' or 'horror stories' from other areas commonly identified as a means to direct attention?

Examples: Work Injuries and Poverty

Two illustrations of the valuing role of categories and conventions show how these questions bring to the surface a number of contradictions and ambiguities which policy making must then manage through standard definitions, names, symbols and myths. Industrial systems place employees in situations where they are highly likely to be injured or killed at work. Every year thousands are maimed by the machines used to produce goods and services and many others suffer long-term illnesses which result directly from the stress, noise and poisonous environments in which they earn their living. There are several ways in which these problems have been named and categorised by political leaders and the élites who have a stake in the policy making process. From each typification there follows a logical policy response. Once the definitions are widely accepted and taken into 'conventional wisdom', action is almost predetermined. For instance, employers often describe these industrial problems as accidents. They emphasise the randomness and inevitability of injury and compare life at work with the risks people take on the roads or in the sporting activities they undertake. This shifts responsibility away from the work system towards the individual. Two policy strategies now appear to be available. Individual workers can be given instruction to make them more safety conscious, or the accidents can be excluded from the policy makers' realm on the grounds that they are inevitable and impervious to change. Victims can now be classified as either ignorant and negligent, in which case they are undeserving of protection, or they may be viewed as unlucky, in which case some form of sympathy and welfare support becomes logical.

An alternative formulation of the problem of industrial injury and death regards these events as a form of violence and exploitation in which employees are forced to submit to risk in order to earn a living for themselves and their families. Now it is the work system which is blamed, and responsibility is shifted from the worker to the employer. In this typification the policy maker will be encouraged to punish and control those who establish factories and offices which are unsafe. Victims will be given rights to sue negligent employers and obtain substantial damages though the courts.

In cases of poverty and homelessness the same constructions occur. When significant proportions of a population are found to lack the means to clothe, house and feed themselves, policy actors search for explanatory categories which define the policy strategies available. Here the victims may be people who lack the skills and motivations to get jobs, in which case blame is directed back on to the shoulders of those in distress. In extreme cases they may be defined as lazy, incompetent or malevolent, in which case steps may then be taken to control their actions through welfare systems which require them to change their behaviour. Alternatively, the poor may be defined as hapless victims of an economic system which grants unequal opportunities and which exploits vulnerable groups by throwing them in and out of work according to the needs of the economy. The policy choices are likely to be directed at job creation, income redistribution and controls on the managers' right to hire and fire. Employers showing scant regard for job seekers become the object of blame, and the economy itself comes under attention.

In practice most policy problems contain several potential categories and a number of possible definitions of the difficulty at hand. Most of this work has been done before issues emerge as subjects for attention in the policy system. Because no single category fits the experience of all those involved, policy makers struggle to pin problems down. Custom and convention help by providing dominant explanations, but these rarely entirely succeed.

Languages

At the policy level, too, there must be some means for the various participants to communicate. General social norms may go some way towards providing the groundwork for this language, but in most cases a specific form of valuation will develop. The observer should expect this dialect or vernacular language to reflect the local experiences and histories which are common to the policy environment. There is always some established history in each field which consists of a mix of standard attitudes and beliefs, together with particular values and standard responses developed to deal with the issues regularly encountered locally.

Every policy environment has its own vocabulary and grammar. These express a distinctive, if changeable, value structure. Often this is most clearly visible in the jargon and terminology of practitioners. In this sense it often helps to be an outsider for whom words such as 'termination' or 'separation' and 'early retirement' are likely to be less easily accepted as descriptions of the loss of paid employment.

Pettigrew (1979: 575) helps ground this potentially metaphysical puzzle of different meanings by pointing out that 'words are part of action. Socially built and maintained, language embodies implicit exhortations and social evaluations.'

In the more determinist accounts of the process of valuation, ideas and values follow hard on the heels of material interests. Find out who controls an industry or service area, and one finds out who benefits from the prevailing 'ideas in good standing' (Brown 1986). Discover someone's institutional position and expect their values to reflect that situation.

This is clearly a limited proposition. Even a casual examination of the common values and beliefs in the major policy systems shows there to be both diversity and rapid movement. Although ideas may well be used as weapons and shields by interest groups, giving the impression that they are derived only for this purpose, often they circulate much faster and display greater novelty than would be expected if they were determined only by structural conditions.

Authority

Policy systems value certain services and also categorise particular behaviours. But what makes them different from other parts of society is that the actions being sought or anticipated depend on governmental authority. Ministers, bureaucrats, teachers and police are more than members of a particular occupation. They share a special form of recognition and power which flows from the state's democratic right to intervene in certain aspects of private life (Baumol 1965, Dunleavy 1991, Dworkin 1987).

Making policy always involves an attempt to mobilise resources and direct human effort. For this to happen, individuals and groups must exercise and sustain political power. Close relatives, power and authority are, however, distinguished by the fact that, when harnessed to a framework of obligations and rules, power achieves a recognisable legitimacy. The extent of this achievement varies a great deal.

At its most simple level authority is invested in recognised systems of coercion. When army officers issue commands they are backed by an organised assignment of rules which require subordinates to obey or face penalties. When a committee chairperson conducts a meeting he or she expects compliance from participants in accordance with accepted standing orders. Deviance invokes censure and exclusion. If employees are directed by a supervisor to carry out a work task they comply because they know they are being paid to submit. Refusal invites dismissal.

When the capacity to issue directions is backed by rules and obligations which are widely acknowledged by the group, random coercive power is transformed into a form of authority. Those subject to authority may not like it, and these arrangements may still be violent or unfair, but where any combination of traditions and rules force power to follow an expected path, it will be seen to have achieved some degree of legitimacy. In other words authority is power multiplied by legitimacy.

Authority is always limited, but is rarely fixed. For example, political parties grant to their elected leaders certain powers to select ministers. In the Australian case the Liberal leader may both choose the members of Cabinet and assign their portfolios.

Labor's collectivist traditions limit their leaders' powers to the assignment of portfolios after Caucus has elected the ministry. However, in both cases, the leaders' authority may wax or wane according to how well he or she performs during election campaigns and in managing faction bosses, coalition partners and other rival authority holders. So, after his remarkable win in 1993, Labor Prime Minister Paul Keating was able to use his enhanced authority to control ministerial selection as well as assignments. In doing so he not only altered the parameters of his own authority, but also established a precedent for future Labor leaders. The faction leaders who lost influence during this period immediately set about recovering lost ground. The Left-wing group moved to banish one of their members for his support for the Prime Minister's strategy. They did not expect to alter the existing allocation of ministries, but rather to 'reassert the authority of the faction' by showing that penalties could be imposed.

Members of a group will grant authority to a leader or institution in different measure, and there is always an element of contingency involved. In the case of tradition, compliance follows the practice of generations reinforced by education and peer pressure. The authority of parents over children is undoubtedly the strongest of these traditional ties. But in most groups some elements of traditional authority are present simply because the resort to history saves time and trouble. For example, in many town councils the mayorship is allocated according to the principle of rotation and seniority. This means that the incumbent only serves for one term, and is then replaced by the next most senior councillor. This way there need be no embarrassing and risky struggle over individual suitability. New members are simply told it has always been done this way, and can quickly see the benefits of a system which eventually rewards everyone.

All forms of authority limit both leaders and followers. While much of the conventional study of authority tends to focus upon the leader and his or her skill in building and using authority, it is also critical to understand the subject's perspective. For those subject to its power an authority system serves to allocate recognition and support (Hegel 1987, Benjamin 1988). It may also offer or promise efficiency (Lindblom 1977).

In traditional systems individuals question or resist accepted practice at peril of being ostracised or shunned. Authority based upon a contract, on the other hand, is supported by notions of utility, rather than by elaborate ideologies concerning the common good or the future of the fatherland. Unadorned by the polemics of the past, contracts achieve compliance by regularly making subjects offers which self-interest cannot refuse. These transactions take several forms but always follow an economic logic. Two interest groups will decide to join forces in a campaign if the individual advantages of joint action outweigh their loss of autonomy and exceed the increased co-ordination costs. Employees will accept unattractive directives from the owner of a firm if labour market signals indicate that there are no other jobs to take if this one is lost. Obviously as the freedom of the subject diminishes, so too does the value of their submission. Where compliance relies exclusively upon coercion there is no legitimacy to speak of, since legitimacy is the reserve of respect which allows leaders to rule without always resorting to violence or threats.

In making policy, leaders and institutions may simply enforce their will through the use of the coercive powers of the state. More common, however, will be the occasions on which they will have to rely upon an achieved quota of respect which allows them to expand their authority to the point where a wide range of other actors will submit and comply. For example, when the Nixon administration instituted an Environmental Protection Authority in 1969 there were few federal legislative powers available to the new agency. Through an adventurous campaign of high-profile law suits against pollutors, the EPA gained media, White House and Congressional support for increased resources and better legislation (Wiehl 1974, Lundquist 1980).

The strongest sources of authority are those which involve consent. Where free, informed actors choose to submit to the directions of others they will usually do so for reasons of efficiency. Permission is given to the authority holder because of an acknowledgement that they are more knowledgeable than others, or from the belief that by accepting his or her direction the group will run more smoothly and avoid the costs of chaos and internal upheaval. At its strongest this form of permission becomes moral consent: that is, those subject to authority willingly accept command because they share a common purpose and believe in the ability of authority holders to bring into being some valued outcome.

But whatever its source, authority is always and everywhere a system of regulation. The technique of control or co-ordination may mask its form but not its effect. Edwards (1979) provides three examples of workplace control. Simple or direct control consists of personal command and direct supervision. The master craftsman stands beside the apprentice and issues instructions and rebukes. Directions are backed by the power to punish. Technical control, on the other hand, is expressed through the organisation of work. The moving conveyor belt, the system of specialisation of work and the numerically controlled machine require specific responses from the worker. They limit, direct and pace the flow of work. Although human supervision is still required to support this technical process, most of the authority is inside the work system. Finally, Edwards points out that bureaucratic control occurs when the social structure of the workplace carries most of the responsibility for controlling and directing operations. Detailed job hierarchies supported by training programs, performance measurement and pay increments help condition employees to seek opportunities to comply with company policy. Standard operating procedures (SOPs) replace supervisor instructions.

When this analysis of the sources and forms of authority is applied to political organisations it becomes clear that authority is frequently defined as the form of power and influence used to regulate an organisation and to direct its attention to key tasks. Even a small local neighbourhood action group has a political order or polity. Someone calls and chairs the meetings. Some recognised procedure is used to admit members, decide the conduct of meetings and make decisions. Someone usually produces minutes, edits a newsletter or takes some other initiative to establish communication. Most groups also have some system to manage resources, to operate a bank account or organise fund raising. Furthermore, there is almost always some means by which the group's goals, values or ideology are legitimised and publicised. All these functions involve political structures which grant and define authority.

All organisations require a political order or polity. Their size and great range of interests will usually necessitate more elaborate rules and greater differentiation of official roles. Often there will be a formal constitution, memorandum of association, trust deed or charter. If conflict occurs over fundamental matters of ideology these larger groups will usually also have quite complex systems for inter-factional negotiation and mediation.

Mansbridge (1980: 44–45) describes the authority system or polity of a small New England town:

> Selby is small, and its citizens govern themselves by coming together once or more a year in a face-to-face assembly—the town meeting . . .the adult residents of the town are the legal repository of the town's powers. . .the Selby town meeting votes on the school budget, and can mandate the school directors in any of the other matters. [They] must decide how much money to spend on their roads. . .[They] vote on whether liquor can be sold within their boundaries. . .set their own zoning regulations; make provision for their own sewage and garbage; create their own parks, cemeteries, and hospitals; institute their own local celebrations; hire their own fire and police protection; and tax themselves each year to pay for all this.

Rayman (1984) provides us with an analysis of another form of political order or polity—the Israeli kibbutz. In this example an informal dimension of authority becomes visible. All member co-operatives in the regional grouping meet in general assembly to decide major policy. In addition there is an elected secretariat which meets every week, and local committees of workers which decide their own meeting times and have the right to control certain local issues. In addition there is a formal board of directors for the twelve-to-fifteen member co-operatives, meeting twenty times a year to decide overall strategies and to assure financial accountability and legality. Rayman says that in addition to formal structures there is a good deal of informal structure for 'maintaining contact and working out problems:

> We are not a mass but only 166 or so people. We know each other. When we eat lunch together we can settle problems. There is a committee of workers in the miloubar [feed mill]. If they have problems the manager of the branch can tell me, since we drink coffee together every morning at 6 a.m. (Rayman 1984: 414)

These routine exchanges of information, informal checks on operational details, and chats about future possibilities appear haphazard and lacking in the kind of structured purpose associated with an authority system. Yet this is every bit as important as a formal meeting of managers, because here the two aspects of authority, decision making and legitimising, coincide. The coffee ceremony links functional operatives into a social group capable of generating support and respect.

In the development of any analysis of policy systems, nothing will be more important than governmental authority. Whether held by government alone or shared with private associations through corporatist arrangements (Schmitter and Lehmbruch 1978), power harnessed by legitimacy flows through every other variable, making all relationships political ones and reorganising the boundaries between the private and the political.

Summary: The Case of Social Insurance

Authority, resources and the development of a special kind of policy culture can be seen in the emergence of social insurance as a framework for solving problems of poverty, unemployment and ill-health.

This example provides a powerful case of the importance of understanding policy systems as governed by both material and non-material arrangements. Social insurance is two things at once. It is a financial device for pooling small amounts of money to provide large payouts to occasional beneficiaries. It is also a concept or name which encloses within it several possibilities: support in times of hardship, self-help and mutual aid.

Britain, Germany and Belgium each developed their applications of this framework to social policy in the middle and latter parts of the nineteenth century. The case of workers' compensation in Britain is a useful case in point. Prior to 1840 occupational health was a small sub-category of the common law field. Workers injured on the job could only get compensation if they successfully sued their employers in the civil courts, and to do this they had to prove that the employer had been negligent. The law provided the employer with many defences against such claims, with the result that workers were frequently left crippled and destitute. For more than thirty years the various interests battled over this inequitable system. Workers and their supporters pressured governments to widen the provisions of the law to make it easier to sue employers. Employers resisted these incursions, using their considerable financial and political might to hold back reform. Despite the Gladstone government's efforts to widen the scope of the common law to grant workers greater protection, the new law was successfully evaded by many employers, who saw increasing damages claims as a threat to their international competitiveness and profits.

As a means to break this deadlock, the Chamberlain government seized upon the idea of insurance as a way to give both parties an important part of what they wanted. Employers would be obliged to insure themselves and workers would only have to show that their injury occurred at work in order to receive income support. The 1897 Act which established this system not only became the framework for similar workers' compensation schemes in Australia, New Zealand, Ireland, Canada and the United States, but also incorporated the idea of social insurance into the thinking of reformers working in other fields. Soon this concept had spread to the field of pensions and unemployment relief, where it assisted the development of the modern welfare state.

What made social insurance such an important concept was that it provided scope for specific reforms while protecting many of the values held dear by key interest groups in these policy environments. Insurance evoked principles of self reliance, personal responsibility and the sharing of burdens without any redistributions in wealth or change in property rights. It also provided for a limited extension of the role of government without proposing any decrease in the rights of property owners. Indeed, the private insurance industry would prosper under this new system of social assistance. All this was achieved because the idea of insurance conveyed to all participants a recognised system of values which they could accept, and which would address important problems which they saw as needing attention.

In other words 'insurance' involved a widely understood set of ideas, values and concepts which were able to draw together different and often antagonistic interests in a new, ordered relationship. This does not mean that insurance solved all problems. To establish this it would be necessary to look at the distribution of costs and benefits, and the impact particular insurance schemes had on each set of actors. But the idea and the language of insurance created a distinctive form of communication between groups, making the negotiation of new policies possible. It remodelled older, existing norms, gave renewed value to thrift and personal responsibility, yet sanctioned limited forms of new policy. In this way a pre-existing disposition or set of conventional entitlements was used to confront a political problem which had become too great to ignore. The insurance concept validated given forms of authority, while allowing change in the flow of important resources. It would now be the task of insurance companies and courts to sort out the specific forms of organisation, standard categories and rules of compensation which would henceforth govern the treatment of claimants of all sorts.

References

Age, 12 May 1993

Baumol, W.J. (1965) *Welfare Economics and the Theory of the State*. London: Bell and Sons

Benjamin, Jessica (1988) *The Bonds of Love: Psychoanalysis, Feminism, and the Problem of Domination*. New York: Pantheon Books

Brown, W. (1986) 'Professional language: words that succeed', *Radical History Review* 34: 33–51

Coleman, James S. (1990) *Foundations of Social Theory*. Cambridge, MA: Harvard University Press

Douglas, Mary (1987) *How Institutions Think*. London: Routledge and Kegan Paul

Dunleavy, Patrick (1991) *Politicians, Bureaucrats and Democracy*. London: Harvester Wheatsheaf

Dworkin, Ronald (1987) *Taking Rights Seriously*. London: Duckworth

Edelman, Murray (1977) *Political Language: Words that Succeed and Policies that Fail*. New York: Academic Press

Frake, C. (1969) 'The ethnographic study of cognitive systems' in S.A. Taylor (ed.), *Cognitive Anthropology*. New York: Holt, Rinehart and Winston

Hacking, Ian (1985) 'Making Up People', in *Reconstructing Individualism*. Stanford University Press

Hegel, G.W. (1967) (translated by J.B. Baillie) *The Phenomenology of Mind*, Harper and Row, New York

Hindess, Barry (1988) *Choice, Rationality and Social theory*. Unwin Hyman, London, 1988.

Kuhn, Thomas (1962) *The Structure of Scientific revolutions*. Chicago: University of Chicago Press

Lakatos, Imre (1971) 'History of Science and Its Rational Reconstructions' in R. Buck and Robert Cohen (eds), *Boston Studies in the Philosophy of Science*, Vol. VIII. Dordrecht, Holland: Reidel

Lundquist, Lennart J. (1980) *The Hare and The Tortoise: Clean Air Politics in the United States and Sweden*. Ann Arbor: University of Michigan Press

Mansbridge, Jane (1983) *Beyond Adversary Democracy*. Chicago: University of Chicago Press

Okun, Arthur M. (1975) *Equality and Efficiency: The Big Tradeoff*, Washington: Brookings

Pleck, Joseph H. and Sawyer, Jack (eds) (1974) *Men and Masculinity*. Englewood Cliffs, New Jersey: Prentice Hall

Popper, Karl (1962) *Conjectures and Refutations: The Growth of Scientific Knowledge*. London: RKP

Popper, Karl (1972) *Objective Knowledge: An Evolutionary Approach*. London: Oxford University Press

Rawls, John (1971) *A Theory of Justice*. Cambridge, Mass.: Belknap Press of Harvard University Press

Rayman, Paula (1984) 'Collective Organisation and the National State: The Kibbutz Model', in Frank Fischer and Carmen Sirianni (eds), *Critical Studies in Organisation and Bureaucracy*. Philadelphia: Temple University Press

Schmitter, P. and Lehmbruch, G. (eds) (1978) *Trends Toward Corporatist Intermediation*. London: Sage

Schutz, Alfred (1953) 'Common-Sense and Scientific Interpretation of Human Action', *Philosophy and Phenomenological Research* 14, September: 10

Wiehl, Peggy (1974) 'William Ruckelshaus and the Environment Protection Authority', Policy Case Studies, Kennedy School of Government, Harvard University

4

Policy Institutions

The set of relationships we have been calling the policy system is composed of several different kinds of actors and a number of formal and semi-formal organisations. Their joint identity as a system has been discussed in the previous chapters, where the policy system has been defined as the pattern of dependency between these actors and organisations. In addition to the specific and immediate benefits which they create for participants, these policy systems are maintained over time by the work of policy institutions.

One of the most important means which systems have for reducing uncertainty and promoting solidarity between these various actors is through the development of routines and standard procedures. When these settled sets of rules and codes become entrenched they form recognisable policy institutions such as parliaments, parties and bureaucracies. At their broadest these institutions are any standardised behaviours which are regularly represented throughout the political or policy system:

> . . .institutions accumulate historical experience through learning. The results and inferences of past experience are stored in standard operating procedures, professional rules, and the elementary rules of thumb of a practical person. (March and Olsen 1984: 745)

The importance of these means for settling and defining what has been learned cannot be overestimated. Without them any social group would be forced to keep rediscovering the simplest ways of organising themselves and dealing with the common tasks of survival. Durkheim (1915: 29) pointed out that these routines were the very basis of the group's existence: 'if [the group] do not agree upon these essential ideas at any moment, if they did not have the same conceptions of time, space, course, number. . .all contact between their minds would be impossible'.

In other words, as well as being practical devices for solving routine problems, institutions are the group's way of establishing priorities, fixing values and turning profound philosophical problems into simple routines. This may sound a rather exaggerated description of the matters we will deal with here—elections, Cabinet rules and bureaucratic norms—yet there is no doubt that in each of these cases quite significant value problems have been settled through adoption of some routine practice. How long the routine will hold is as important a question as asking what function the institution itself performs.

When applied to policy making we see these regulated behaviours in more formal terms. Policy institutions refer to the particular machinery of government which controls the authority and the resources needed to sustain policy. The objective of this chapter is to show how institutions influence what happens in a policy system. Because most of the institutions we wish to examine span the whole political system the discussion will need to be somewhat general. However it is certainly true that particular policy systems, such as urban planning, have specific institutions of their own as well. Particular laws, special tribunals and local habits of consultation and appeal mark out these planning institutions. We will therefore need to take an occasional detour to look at the institutions which have grown up in response to local issues.

The focus on governmental customs and rules excludes many important institutions which may well have important effects upon policy. Before proceeding to discuss government institutions it is worth pausing to recognise these other types.

In common usage we often describe such things as marriage and the family as institutions and these arrangements certainly have important influences on policy, especially in social fields such as welfare and education. Customs concerning the time of marriage, the size of families, the role of women and men in domestic labour and the rights of children can certainly be considered central to policy analysis (Batten, Weeks and Wilson 1991).

Similarly, we would want to include the labour market as another institution which establishes important relationships and problems to which policy must often respond. The labour market includes customs and rules concerning the appropriate age and qualification of employees, expectations about pay and conditions of work, and the rights of managers and employers to give orders and impose penalties (Hall 1986). Without doubt these social and economic institutions play a part in structuring policy systems.

Governing Institutions

If an institution is defined as 'an established law or custom', then governmental institutions might be described as the particular system of laws and customs used to control relations between governors and the governed. In functional terms these arrangements are often described as the strategy forming, or steering mechanisms of the system (Painter 1987). There can be no doubt that they are central to policy. Schattschneider (1960) puts it simply:

> In politics as in everything else it makes a great deal of difference whose game we play. The rules of the game determine the requirements for success.

Institutions not only provide a regulated structure through which new proposals travel, but confer advantage on some approaches and restrict others. Our inquiry therefore needs to pay attention to the evaluation of institutions, to understanding their limits as well as the uses they have for settling, calming and improving social interactions among actors in policy systems.

Government institutions not only impose constraints on policy systems, but also lay down pathways for action and send signals to actors about how to move forward. They both regulate and enable change. It is for this reason that we speak of institutions as having both a control and a learning role, two functions which are not always easy for them to combine, and which create problems for actual and potential policy makers.

The regulatory role of policy institutions can easily be seen. Parliaments, parties and bureaucracies are examples of dominant institutions which lay down strict codes by which actors and their proposals are structured. These sets of rules express a form of accumulated intelligence concerning appropriate ways to behave. Their long histories give these institutions the ability to define action pathways which individual actors cannot always comprehend but which communicate the experience of previous generations of actors in a simplified form.

This systemic memory clearly has many advantages. Without it every issue, whether threat or opportunity, would have to be considered afresh and no action could be contemplated until the most basic of decisions about how to proceed had been resolved. In short, there would be no machinery with which to confront current concerns. These institutional short-cuts and ground rules have their problematic side, however. Because such regulatory mechanisms carry past practice into present circumstances they represent a constraint on change. Routines work precisely because they socialise for conformity and restrict the attention span of actors to those things previously found to be appropriate. If circumstances change, institutions may be found clinging to routines which solve problems which no longer exist. For example, parliaments which were developed during periods when interstate differences were a key form of social division often defined their upper houses as state chambers composed of equal numbers of representatives whose actual electorates were numerically unequal. As social changes replaced state differences with new forms of distinction (e.g. race, gender, ethnicity) these upper houses ceased being institutional innovations and became chambers of resistance and inflexibility.

Because they apply a brake to current pressures and force actors to follow established patterns of behaviour, the adaptive skills of institutions are highly variable. In periods of rapid social change these devices become the object of policy change, a practice which institutions themselves are apt to resist, at least in the short term. Institutional change is not uncommon but it is rarely the result of simple, rational deliberation by those affected. Four main types of change are found in the case literature and in each instance the evidence records the institutions as somewhat resistant to the pressures put upon them. Standard practices may change through *variation and selection* when rewards flow to those whose modified procedures meet with continued success among a critical audience of funding agencies, managers and clients (Pfeffer and Salancik 1978). New rules may also emerge as a form of *problem solving* if institutions receive irresistible pressures which simply cannot be answered using existing procedures (Lindblom 1959). Evidence exists to show that institutions may also alter their operations as a result of *contagion* (Benveniste 1987): that is, when neighbouring systems adopt new routines which are successful, similar institutions in the local system will be more likely to succumb to pressures to do likewise (Kingdon 1984). These mechanisms may also change as a consequence of *turnover* if newly arrived leaders or agitators bring with them a knowledge of alternative procedures which have been successful elsewhere or which provide a means to respond to the unmet demands of key groups inside or outside the institution (Boston 1991).

The range of devices and regulatory regimes which come under the heading of governing institutions is both wide and deep. Every political system is make up of a complex mix of institutions which define the use of public power. There are literally hundreds of such devices which may be considered important. Five types of institution can be identified and their impact sketched to show a general pattern of effects. They are:

- executives and legislatures
- legislation
- elections
- budgets
- intergovernmental structures.

Detailed discussion of bureaucracy, the professions and public managers will be left until later chapters. It should at least be noted here, however, that they, too, are institutions which figure prominently in this story.

Executives and Legislatures

There are two main types of legislative institution in Western societies: the parliamentary model and the presidential system. Although most readers of this book will be concerned to understand parliamentary arrangements, some comparative discussion will serve to highlight the policy making significance of the major institutional practices which are otherwise taken for granted.

In presidential systems the executive role is separated from that of the legislature and as a result the responsibility for running programs is kept apart from the work of considering which laws and policy decisions to adopt. In the parliamentary system the executive is established inside the legislature, in the popular house if there are two houses of Parliament, and both policy and implementation may be subject to direct intervention by legislators.

Since their tenure in office is entirely dependent upon maintaining the support of the legislature, members of the parliamentary executive (i.e. the Cabinet) have powerful incentives to keep close control over the proceedings of the legislature, and its independent review and representative functions are therefore more constrained than in the presidential system.

From the point of view of policy making capacities the parliamentary system presents a strong case of centralisation of authority and accountability. It is also true that as a result of this centralisation parliaments are thought to be able to perform a greater range of policy making tasks, to be capable of better policy choices, and to be able to make sure that these choices materialise as consistent programs and outcomes (Eckstein and Apter 1963, Weaver and Rockman 1993).

One of the reasons that parliamentary institutions are thought to possess this form of effective centralisation is that they informally promote the development of strong parties. Without a party system capable of maintaining a stable majority in the popularly elected house, the governing role becomes problematic. So even though their constitutions give no special status to parties (and often make no mention of them), parliamentary institutions create pressures against the development of independent action by individual legislators. This form of party or Caucus discipline protects the executive from threat and also establishes a shield for members of Parliament who wish to ignore or contradict the specific demands of their constituents (Rose 1974, Olson 1980).

In policy making terms this institutional arrangement alters the role of the elected member. He or she is forced to become a team player in the parliamentary system and strict rules of obedience and accountability are enforced through party preselection rules, Caucus regulations and through the functions of the party Whip, who is the parliamentarian responsible for ensuring that the wishes of the executive are carried out during voting and speech making, and in committee work. This can be contrasted with the functions of legislators in presidential systems, where the institutional separation of the executive role frees elected representatives from strong party control and encourages them to build their individual profile among constituents, interest groups and the media.

The policy making role of ministers in parliamentary institutions is also distinctive. The fact of their recruitment from among the ranks in the legislature and their necessary subservience to the collective interest of the Cabinet means that they are more apt to be policy generalists than specialists (Hawke 1979). This generalist background makes ministers heavily dependent upon the bureaucracy for policy advice. Even in those cases where ministers develop an expert personal staff to check the power of their own bureaucrats, the bulk of policy development and almost all the work of implementation and evaluation comes through the Public Service departments over which the minister rules (Headey 1974, Weller and Grattan 1981).

Comparisons of parliamentary and presidential institutions provide a rich source of evaluation concerning the policy implications of these particular arrangements. Lijphart (1992) and Weaver and Rockman (1993) provide some general propositions and case study evidence on this point. Parliamentary systems are better able to impose losses on particular groups because party discipline prevents rebellion by affected MPs and because the collectivist nature of the system reduces the number of 'veto points' at which outside interests can intervene. This advantage may well become a liability, however, when Cabinet is composed of coalition partners and vetos thus become institutionalised. The electorate may also be more punitive in a parliamentary system because the collective responsibility of Cabinet requires the executive to carry the blame for everything that occurs within the Parliament.

Although they have greater authority to act than their presidential colleagues, executives in the parliamentary system are sometimes thought to be less able to innovate. This is a result of the system's tendency to be highly centralised and therefore less open to new issues flowing in from outside the executive. In single party governments, this restriction also applies to the institution's capacity to act as a source of social cohesion. Because those not represented in the governing party are denied access to power, the tendency for them to become alienated will be higher than in a system which allows a more diverse approach to representation. The other side of this coin is the one already mentioned: that is, that presidential systems may purchase their representative function at the cost of increased veto and in extreme cases of policy gridlock, where no proposal can be implemented.

Although it is widely assumed that executives in the parliamentary system may be less available to innovative ideas flowing in from outside, this does not mean that Parliament itself is resistant to change. Considine and Deutchman (1992) show that compared with presidential systems, parliaments provide greater opportunities for women representatives to achieve leadership roles, and are less likely to produce a clear gender divide in committee assignments. Strong parties appear to be the explanation for this greater readiness to include new groups.

What we are calling the parliamentary system is in practice a collection of things which may vary in type and extent. Parliaments may contain more than one house, parties may be stronger or weaker and governments may be composed of one or more parties. These contingencies affect policy making opportunities and styles. In the strongest cases, such as New Zealand and Queensland, a single house ruled by a single party with a secure majority, wide ranging reform programs are able to be quickly implemented. Conversely, changes in government may produce extreme variations in policy and programs with a very real possibility of stop-start commitment and instability. Vogel (1993) and others also show these stronger types of regime to be vulnerable to being too insulated from public opinion and thus prone to getting out of step with popular sentiment.

These patterns of institutional policy capacity are also evident in local government systems. In the Australian case such local authorities are based upon a single chamber of locally elected councillors, who together constitute a combined executive and legislative institution. The key points of variance in these systems flow from the extent to which the role of mayor is separated from that of ordinary councillors and the degree to which these elected representatives are bound together in party collectives. Separately elected mayors, as in the Brisbane case, provide greater incentives for the development of a co-ordinated policy program and election mandate. This offers a brake on the tendency for local ward issues to overwhelm larger strategic ones. It also strengthens the capacity of part-time, amateur politicians to control the town hall bureaucracy and to negotiate successfully with other, professionalised levels of government.

Party groupings at the local government level further enhance this opportunity to develop cohesive and long-term objectives. As with other party consolidations, however, this development restricts an important part of the local representative's role. Party machine priorities may limit the willingness of councillors to defend local interests against the Caucus majority view, with a consequent loss of innovative capacity and legitimacy. Party Caucus activity, whether formal or informal, enhances the legislative competence of the Council to the extent that it allows specialisation. If Caucus members are able to rely upon their party colleagues to keep them informed of their specialist responsibilities, the Caucus may act as an effective division of labour in which councillors match the knowledge of their opposite numbers from the town hall bureaucracy.

Legislation

These different capacities have their most obvious effect in the creation of new laws or the amendment of existing statutes. Most, but not all, major policy initiatives involve new or revised legislation. Policy makers inside and outside government must push and cajole various other formal participants, bringing them into sequence at just the right time in order to enact a new law. This is no small matter. Many a brilliant policy initiative has been left languishing on a parliamentary committee agenda or has been so poorly drafted that the need for subsequent amendments has destroyed its credibility. Frequently the new legislation which a department requires in order to commence a program already promised by the government cannot be brought forward because of low commitment by other agencies which must give their clearance.

From the perspective of community groups with an interest in a given policy area, new legislation is also vitally important yet inherently difficult to influence. Departmental officers with whom they may have had dealings will not be able to control this process. Politicians with no previous interest suddenly become critical actors. Technical issues to do with law and administration loom, and often overshadow substantive goals and objectives. A new mix of horse trading and gunboat diplomacy dominates several further rounds of negotiation.

While much of this intimate detail passes the average informed citizen by, for advocates and proponents of reform this stage of policy development is almost always critical. There are two levels of complexity to comprehend, a vertical flow of sequential stages which shows the order of things, and a horizontal cast of the characters who figure in the drama at each point along the way.

The first stage we can identify is the initiation of new legislation. All new laws start out as proposals developed by one of a relatively small number of agencies. Parliamentary systems exhibit a common pattern of access and opportunity at each of these.

1. Initiative

A common source of initiative for new policy which is to be enshrined in law is the ministry or department responsible for the policy field in which action is required. It is as well to discuss the internal workings of these agencies in greater detail later under the heading of 'bureaucracy', for there are important differences in the way bureaucracies relate to the policy making process.

Strong ministers or ministers with strong personal advisers also play a key role in this initiating stage. Since the early 1970s all Australian governments have strengthened the role of the minister's private office by incorporating policy specialists into the political support role of this office. Ministerial advisers are often chosen for their ability to develop new proposals or to obtain from the bureaucracy the kinds of initiative which the minister or the government desires. Complex unwritten conventions govern the relations between ministerial advisers, ministers and the senior bureaucrats who have formal responsibility for policy development.

Advisers have functions other than assisting with the development of legislation. The extent to which these other duties overshadow the legislative function appears to depend upon the specific skills of each adviser, the extent of their party affiliation, party faction obligations of the minister and adviser, and the degree to which the minister is able to find sympathetic support within the mainstream of the department (Walter 1986, Polis 1991). There is also some indication that adviser roles may vary with the life-cycle of the government, with policy duties being greater in the early period in office and less salient after control over the bureaucracy has been firmly established (Considine and Costar 1992).

Other than the ministry responsible for the portfolio in which a new initiative is to be proposed, the most common alternate sources of proposals are special inquiries established by the government, statutory commissions such as human rights commissions or equal opportunity boards, and parliamentary committees. Many important welfare reforms in Britain and elsewhere have originated from Royal Commissions established to inquire into social problems.

Although they cannot demand parliamentary attention as a right, such inquiries carry significant authority and can rarely be ignored. Statutory offices such as the Ombudsman also regularly make suggestions for change, some of which emerge as new laws. But these offices carry less weight. Their attention is spread across a multitude of issues and, unlike high-profile special inquiries or commissions, they are soon regarded as an institutional vested interest. Their ability to claim space on a busy government agenda is limited.

Parliamentary committees vary in their impact according to the particular system in which they are located. In presidential systems and in simple congress systems, such as are usually found at local government level, committees are a most important source of new proposals. Parliamentary committees are traditionally more enfeebled by party discipline and executive domination of the legislature. Some issues are referred directly to a committee with an invitation for members to research policy options and propose action, but this is not common. Ministers and their departments prefer to keep such questions in the executive family. The exception to this general rule is the bicameral Parliament in which opposition or corner parties are able to use upper house committees as a means to develop significant amendments to government programs. In the Australian case ample evidence of this type can be found in the national Parliament during both periods of post-war Labor government and during the period of the Fraser coalition government (Lucy 1993, Weller 1989).

Since these parliamentary committees generally lack the research resources of government departments, corporatist institutions or Royal Commissions, the cases where they make a difference are often explained by the fortuitous alignment of a number of factors: the particular expertise of their leading members, the quality of proposals put to them by outside interests, and the weakness of the agency responsible for the particular policy field. A long-serving parliamentarian, armed with research provided by an articulate lobby group, campaigning for an initiative which lies outside or to the edge of the interests of existing agencies may have success, but the odds against remain formidable.

Any one of these formal agencies may initiate a broad proposal for legislative action. This will set out the problem at hand, the state of play so far as existing programs and laws are concerned, and a general argument in favour of the strategy being supported. There may as yet be no costing or consideration of possible opposition, and there will rarely be any detailed evaluation of alternative means. Yet this is often the most crucial stage of preparation. If this proposal strikes a chord with other policy makers, if the issues being addressed have been a source of concern among interested players, or if a public crisis establishes a requirement for urgent action, a significant and lasting commitment can be established at this early stage. If an election campaign or budget round occurs at this stage the difference between a broad proposal and a firm commitment may all but evaporate (Whitlam 1985).

2. Clearance

The second stage of consideration concerns the vetting of proposals in order to obtain permission or clearance to proceed further. No matter which agency or authority initiates a proposal for new legislation, there is always a demand that other authority holders be given an opportunity to check, modify or veto new policy. Ideas which have originated outside will be referred to the responsible department for detailed comment. Most initiatives will also be referred to the Attorney-General to check that what is being attempted is within the bounds provided by the Constitution and the common law. All proposals which involve new expenditure will also be sent to the Treasury, and those which create positions or alter conditions of employment will also often be sent to the Office of Personnel Management or Public Service Board. Some governments have a policy review office located in one of their central agencies. Their role is to see that the government's philosophy and strategy are being implemented across the whole administration and they may also demand to see new initiatives and to check them against their own priority lists.

A further layer of review is provided by the party policy committees of the incumbent government and by Cabinet sub-committees. In the former case ministers or other proponents of a new initiative may seek to increase their support during pre-Cabinet manoeuvring, or quell potential opposition, by discussing their intentions with the party policy committee. Composed of parliamentarians and elected members of the party, these groups have a variable impact. A key determinant of the significance of this impact is the internal party constitution and tradition which governs the Caucus role.

The Australian Labor Party and the Australian Democrats possess strongly entrenched habits of party committee authority which allow MPs to develop expert involvement in policy development and review. Caucus rules allow these committees to establish policy guidelines and to present their findings to authoritative Caucus meetings. Ministers therefore have strong incentives to co-ordinate the work of their respective party committees and to use the combined power of ministerial block voting in Caucus to restrain committee independence. However when party committees are able to build alliances with key groups within the party constituency (trade unions etc.) they can force the party leadership to modify proposals or adopt policies which are developed through this channel.

The experience of the federal Liberal party committee responsible for the development of the *Fightback*! program suggests that this party has also allowed authority to be shared in this manner. Sub-committees of the Cabinet can be drawn into the vetting process where an existing Cabinet procedure requires certain issues to receive such review, but it is also common to find sub-committees involved after Cabinet has had its first examination of the proposal.

3. Consideration

This third stage involves substantive consideration of new legislation. This step sees ministers deciding whether or not to grant permission for the proponents of the new initiative to proceed with a formal proposal or draft Bill and to engage in consultation with affected interests. This in no way guarantees the ultimate outcome, but it does allow proponents to develop a more detailed case and to draw on new institutional resources, since the executive is now openly committed to some form of action. Costs of withdrawing from action are high at this stage and the wider access of affected interests necessitates a willingness to make firm commitments. Agencies which had until then been resisting the proposal will be forced to offer some form of co-operation or justify their opposition in a detailed manner.

In deciding whether or not to allow the initiative to go beyond this stage, ministers employ a variety of standards. Much, as has already been noted, may depend on whether or not an election or budget process is on their minds. In some cases Cabinets act reactively, grasping at policy options which appear to relieve pressures foisted upon them from outside. This appears to have been the case with the Chifley Cabinet decision in 1948 to nationalise the Australian banking system. With their preferred proposal for stronger central control of credit apparently thwarted, the Labor Cabinet seized on nationalisation as a powerful strategic and symbolic initiative and with almost no preparation, costing or discussion, they decided to go ahead (Crisp 1961).

More commonly, this early consideration of an initiative will consist of checking that the actual proposal will work in practice, making sure that there is no major opposition from inside the government, and ascertaining what costs, both financial and political, might be expected. Media reaction to the initiative is most decisive at this point, with ministers and bureaucrats now being forced to take public positions on the problem being addressed and to defend the legislative option being proposed.

This stage often involves elaborate policy consultation. It is quite possible that until this point the proposal has been seen by no more than a handful of officials and a few interest groups, and has little more to support it than a few pages detailing general aims and alleged benefits. Even where the originating agency has undertaken a more detailed analysis, prior to getting Cabinet clearance it will normally have been difficult to undertake community consultation, interdepartmental negotiation or public debate.

As well as testing the original proposal for defects, this development stage will be concerned with attempting to forecast the likely impact of the initiative by seeking further information about similar initiatives elsewhere, or by inviting responses from experts in the field.

The means to be used to implement any new initiative will also come under scrutiny at this point. Which agency should administer it? How will resources be obtained? If new legal entitlements are proposed, how will the judicial system react? If a new program is anticipated, which organisations and professions are to be used? Questions of co-operation with other levels of government, including their financial contributions, are also likely to enter the public debate at this juncture.

Finally, this is the point at which those groups directly affected by the proposal will normally take up firm public positions. Shrewd governments will obtain gestures of support. The terms of this involvement may range from a perfunctory letter from the minister asking them if they will accept the proposals, to the establishment of joint management arrangements which guarantee their commitment. Where serious interest group conflict emerges at this point, a number of more elaborate consultation devices can be brought into play. These include further inquiries which legitimise interest group involvement in policy design and the use of skilled third party negotiators to iron out differences.

4. Decision

This point is reached when proposals are framed as a Bill for an Act and are presented to Parliament. Much now depends upon the extent of political control available to the Cabinet or executive. In the most straightforward cases the minister responsible for the proposal is able to call upon his or her party colleagues to show party discipline and vote the new measures through. The steps in this legislature process are described in Figure 4.1, below, which is taken from the Australian Parliament's code of practice. The first reading of the new Bill in the lower house simply involves the presentation of the legislation to members of Parliament for their information and for circulation among interested parties.

The second reading stage sees the legislation receiving substantive consideration in the form of an official debate. The speeches of the minister and shadow minister which are delivered at this point will set out the substantive justifications of the measure together with arguments for and against its enactment. The Bill now moves to the committee stage, during which all MPs sit as a working group to consider each clause of the Bill. The measure then travels to the third reading state for a conclusive vote after which it is sent to the upper house for passage through a similar set of steps.

In many parliaments the upper house is not controlled by the governing party. This allows the opposition and the minor parties to force hostile amendments or vetos and special rules apply to resolving disputes between the two houses. It is difficult to overestimate the significance of these upper house stages of decision making. The formal process of separate speech making and votes is typically accompanied by backroom negotiations between the responsible minister, his or her staff and the party leaders of both houses—all of whom now assume decisive control over the fate of the new measure. Party Whips, shadow ministers and party strategists enjoy great but temporary significance where the two houses are not controlled by the governing party.

At this point any number of issues relevant to the proposal may be raised and renegotiated. Furthermore, considerations which are quite separate will often be brought into play as the government seeks to trade its way towards a successful outcome. In explaining the final outcome it will therefore be necessary for the observer to appreciate the total configuration of government, opposition and minor party agendas and vulnerabilities.

Elections

The electoral system is undoubtedly the formal institutional framework which has the most dramatic affect on policy making. Elections focus attention on alternative policy packages and ideologies and deliver decisive authority for all new plans and proposals. Each type of electoral system delivers a different set of policy opportunities and constraints.

All democratic political systems require a specific institutional practice for deciding who shall become the popular representatives, which leadership élite will obtain executive office and what form of party majority will hold power inside the legislature. It is useful to think about elections as windows of opportunity as far as policy is concerned, for once an election has been called a wide variety of proposals begin to gain access to the formal institutions of government. It is also important to view elections as forms of issue structuring, since the type of practice used to conduct and decide the outcome of the election will influence the kind of policy debate which will take place (Taagepera and Shugart 1989).

Electoral systems combine with patterns of social cleavage to produce different forms of representation. These often prove to be the most decisive factors in explaining the policy making capabilities and styles of the entire system of government. Like all institutions these electoral arrangements set in place patterns which may be quite resistant to change. Lipset and Rokkan (1967) and

Figure 4.1 The Making of an Act of Parliament

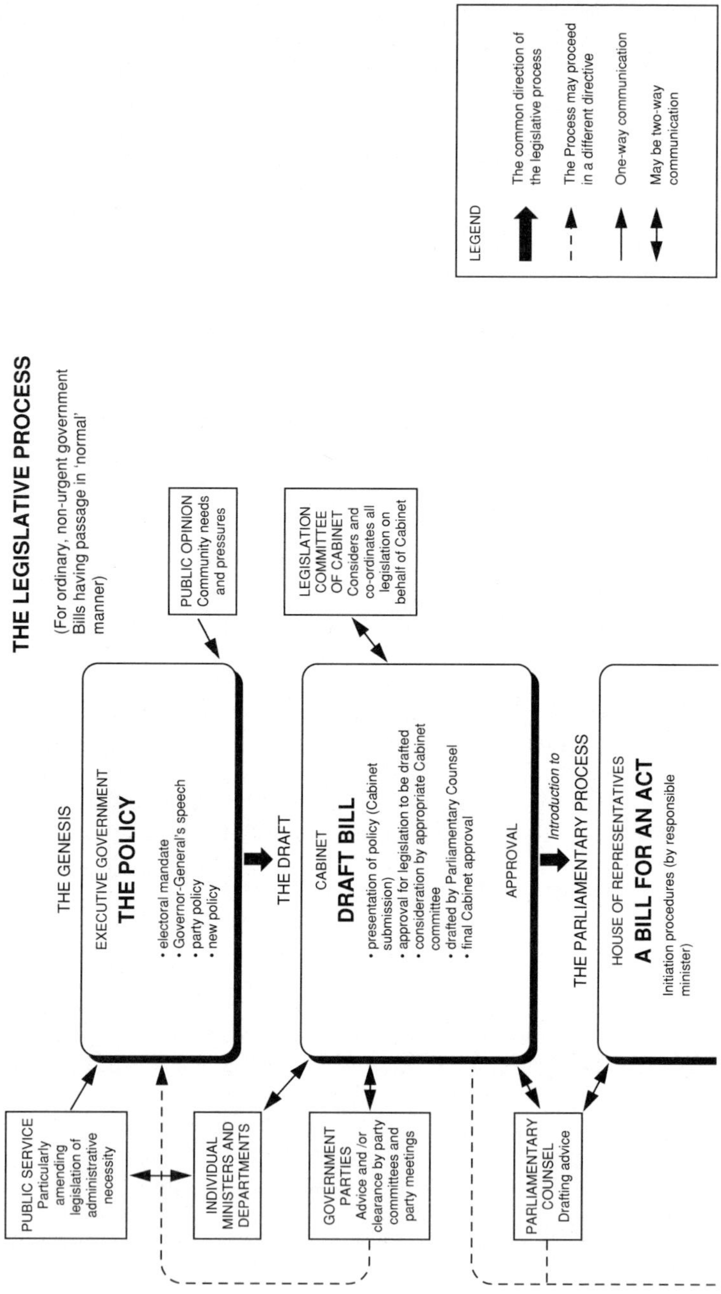

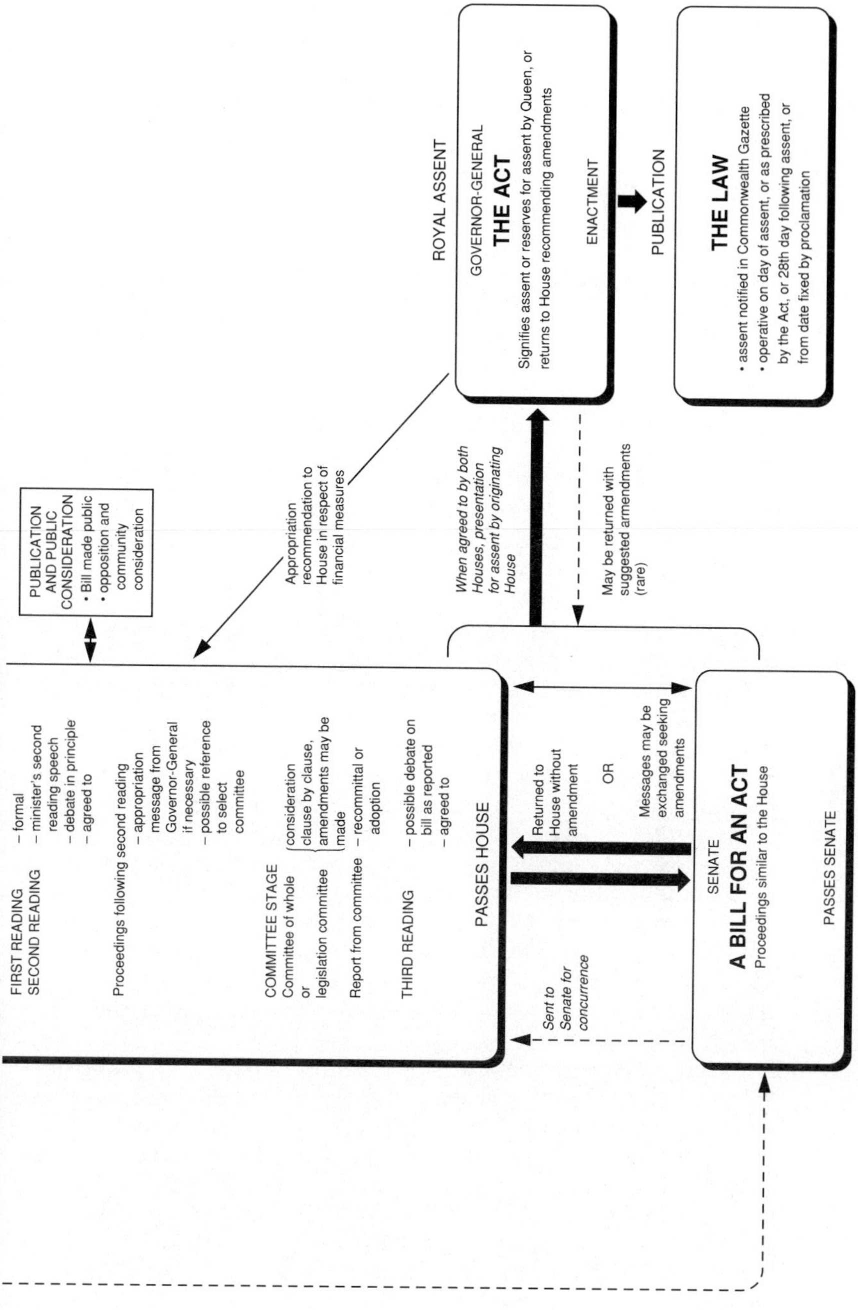
FIRST READING – formal
SECOND READING – minister's second reading speech
– debate in principle
– agreed to
Proceedings following second reading
– appropriation message from Governor-General if necessary
– possible reference to select committee
COMMITTEE STAGE
Committee of whole or legislation committee
consideration clause by clause, amendments may be made
Report from committee – recommittal or adoption
THIRD READING – possible debate on bill as reported
– agreed to
PASSES HOUSE
PUBLICATION AND PUBLIC CONSIDERATION
• Bill made public
• opposition and community consideration
Appropriation recommendation to House in respect of financial measures
Sent to Senate for concurrence
Returned to House without amendment
OR
Messages may be exchanged seeking amendments
SENATE
A BILL FOR AN ACT
Proceedings similar to the House
PASSES SENATE
When agreed to by both Houses, presentation for assent by originating House
May be returned with suggested amendments (rare)
ROYAL ASSENT
GOVERNOR-GENERAL
THE ACT
Signifies assent or reserves for assent by Queen, or returns to House recommending amendments
ENACTMENT
PUBLICATION
THE LAW
• assent notified in Commonwealth Gazette
• operative on day of assent, or as prescribed by the Act, or 28th day following assent, or from date fixed by proclamation

March and Olsen (1989) point out, for example, that the European parties of the 1960s were based upon the social cleavages which had existed in the 1920s. Similar claims have been made about the Australian party system (Connell and Irving 1980).

1. Electoral Rules

Important sources of difference in electoral systems include the use of preferential or proportional voting, single versus multi-member constituencies, and the length of the term of office between elections. In each of these areas the rules of election structure the kind of policy environment which actors must confront.

The form of representation which an electoral system sanctions always acts as a special institutional force for the development and structuring of policy issues. For instance, new social movements find it easier to gain a voice in systems which have proportional representation (PR). Katz (1980) shows that PR will lead to greater variety and to what he calls extremism. He follows Downs (1957) who asserted that parties in preferential voting systems will often converge in a two-party contest with the result that the range of issue differences will contract over time. In these cases parties will have strong incentives to concentrate their attention on 'median voters' who have no firm attachment to ideology or policy and can thus be bought off with short-term election promises.

On the other hand, PR will have a greater tendency to encourage multi-party activity because the method of calculating votes allows candidates to win seats with relatively small proportions of the total, regardless of how the rest of the votes are cast.

Paradoxically, smaller parties may tend to lock up or monopolise the issues with which they have obtained electoral success. They are also vulnerable to the charge that they render the system ungovernable which, as Schoonmaker (1988) has shown in the case of the West German Greens, may lead dissatisfied supporters to return to mainstream parties without a major gain in the policy area at issue.

Another important effect of elections is that depending upon the system used, encouragement is given to candidates to focus on local questions or to ferment internal party differences over policy questions. Tasmania and the Irish Republic both elect their lower houses using a multi-member electoral system, Hare-Clarke in the former case and STV-PR, or Single Transferable Vote/Proportional Representation in the Irish case. This means that up to seven candidates are elected from each single district and the allocation of seats is in order of the number of votes cast for each individual, rather than according to simple party affiliation.

The effect of these practices is that certain kinds of policy will be more likely to receive attention during election campaigns and between them. The voting system requires a high level of candidate specific voting. That is, each individual candidate must cultivate a personal following, regardless of party and to do this they strive to present separate policy profiles and promises. Parties respond rationally to these incentives by attempting to nominate candidates who have a strong local following, often the result of non-political notoriety achieved by being a sports star or media personality. The election campaign therefore takes on a distinctive character and politicians win and lose their seats according to how well they have been able to service their local support base through the gaining of government contracts, improvements to local services, and so on.

Under this form of voting, parties do not know how many seats they can win in any given multi-member electorate. They therefore run more candidates than will normally get elected. Because voting is not preferential, candidates from the same party are competitors. So, for example, in the Irish general election of 1982, seventeen of the twenty-five Fianna Fáil Party parliamentarians who lost their seats did so to members of their own party (Bowler and Farrell 1990). In this situation ministers have limited opportunity to enforce the party platform. They must take care not to upset local interests, especially in areas where their party is strong. It is obvious that under this form of election members of the same party will often have an incentive to express divergent opinions about policy and to attack policies suggested by their comrades.

This localism can be seen as an institutional logic which works as an advantage to those policy issues which can offer an immediate benefit to those voters within the candidate's support base but which may limit the capacity of the system to focus attention on larger, strategic issues which influence whole populations. Electoral systems which encourage this close relationship between candidate and constituency decrease the cohesion of the governing élite and make factionalism more likely, especially factionalism based on patronage rather than ideology. Prime ministers and other leaders will find it more difficult to take the lead on major issues under such circumstances and local party chiefs outside the Parliament may become the decisive policy makers. Japan provides a further example of this tendency (Weaver and Rockman 1993: 26).

Preferential voting systems allow parties to aggregate the national vote with the use of strictly managed how-to-vote cards. Individual candidates are therefore dependent on the party leadership for the swing necessary to get elected and to form a government. Stable patterns in the composition of the ruling parliamentary élite are therefore common in these systems, and even the use of coalitions is apt to produce quite stable governments. This is the case in Australian federal politics.

The ability of party leaders to resist the pressures of key interest groups is also higher in such electoral systems. Median or swinging voters play the decisive role in determining outcomes, and local politicians have little to offer interest group leaders because centralisation of the party platform is a precondition for electoral success, a factor which gives control to central party élites. When interest groups become involved in electoral politics in these systems they have incentives to maintain stable, non-opportunistic relations with the party they wish to support. Hence we find unions, business groups and farmers locked into long-term affiliations with particular parties.

Multi-party coalitions of the European type result directly from electoral systems which reward vigorous competition among several parties at election time. This increases the range of policy issues likely to be promoted by parties and interest groups. It also allows greater shifting of support on the part of interest groups seeking maximum advantage. Since they are unlikely to be punished by a single winning party after the election, these interests will behave less predictably than in the two party model. Party élites will therefore have strong incentives to constrain their maverick behaviour through the development of corporatist institutions and other means for drawing key interests into a predictable policy making role (Lehmbruch and Schmitter 1982).

In local council elections, similar effects are evident. The traditional pattern in Australia has been for councillors to be elected for three-year terms, staggered to allow an electoral rotation of one-third or so of their number each year. Preferential voting for a minority of the Council at any single election insulates the Council as a whole from major voter swings. This in turn diminishes the incentives for the formation of strong parties with specific platforms. Any mandate obtained at a particular election binds only a minority of those in the council chamber and weakens the policy claims which councillors can make on town hall bureaucrats and fellow councillors elected in other years.

The clear advantage of multi-party systems and those which allow high levels of local candidate initiative is their capacity to represent well. Electoral institutions which encourage real and active competition among candidates and which allow smaller groups to share in the spoils are clearly more able to contribute to social cohesion and solidarity.

2. Election Campaigns

The approach of the election period is itself a critical time for policy making in which executive control and bureaucratic dominance are temporarily suspended. Incumbent leaders search for a means to justify their rule and in so doing give special publicity and legitimacy to existing programs which may have been languishing for lack of interest. They also encourage their staff to bring forward any proposals which they might be able to include in their manifesto, opening the way for hitherto unrecognised issues to receive attention. These issues can travel very quickly while the system is in the grip of election fever, and if attached to a value position which can be made publicly appealing, may turn quickly into new policy regimes.

The institutional system itself influences the conduct of these campaigns, thereby structuring opportunities for participation and policy effectiveness. Several of these issues have already been raised. Voting systems shape party contests which in turn shape the kinds of campaigns that are fought. Preferential systems of voting for parliamentary representatives encourage aggregation. This creates strong incentives to run campaigns directed at a national audience and to select swinging voters for decisive promises.

Elections alter the opportunities for participation and, for a few weeks, change the relationship between the governed and the government. Depending upon the party system and the method of election, this period may see the mushrooming of new candidates with novel policy proposals, or the boiling down of issues into one or two themes around which two dominant parties organise themselves. This in turn will alter the role of the election manifesto. In multi-party contests some form of post-election bargaining is expected. Promises made during the campaign must be compromised in negotiations over coalition formation and the distribution of ministries. Manifestos or policy speeches are therefore less likely to become an institutionalised part of the policy making process.

In two party systems the manifesto quickly becomes an authoritative document which the future government expects to wield in the Parliament, with interest groups and inside the bureaucracy. Commitments made 'in the policy speech' therefore take on great significance. Policy actors, advisers and party officials who are able to influence the content of the leader's election policy speech have great, if temporary, power to direct the future attention of the government.

The press and rival leaders will, during this period, take interest group spokespeople more seriously, thus granting a public audience to those who would otherwise be excluded. Issue constituencies not previously organised may suddenly find the incentive and opportunity to form themselves into pressure groups or action associations. Established organisations also find election time an auspicious moment to consider forming coalitions, popular fronts and so on.

It is obvious that this shifting and reorganising of the terms on which individuals and groups participate in politics will always have a momentous impact on policy. It has been common to assert that these impacts fall mainly on what is called the agenda formation part of the policy making process, and there is much commonsense in this observation (Kingdon 1984). New groups and old ones with new ideas certainly push forward with items or issues which they want addressed. But the chance to get things on the agenda is only part of the opportunity structure provided by elections. This is also a time when administrative issues bubble to the surface, implementation questions receive attention and financial considerations are addressed.

The final point to note about election campaigns is perhaps the most important. Each system has its own rules concerning the calling of elections, and their frequency. The longer the period between elections the less can be expected from campaigns and manifestos. Within a year or two circumstances will have changed so dramatically that much of what was said will be forgotten. Long terms in office are also likely to change interest group behaviour. When the government is to be in office for five or six years (as in Britain) the stakes are very high and interest groups will need to find other ways to influence policy. Election campaigns will therefore be less important than where representatives face the ballot every two years (as in the United States).

Budgets

The most decisive formal process used to allocate funds to programs is the government's annual Budget. The policy significance of this cannot be overestimated, even in systems such as Australia's where the political executive controls this process and works hard to limit access by outsiders:

> The budgetary process offers a prism through which to distinguish underlying values—political, economic and social—in so far as they are reflected in specific decisions about the raising of revenue and the distribution of expenditure. Cash values reflect political values.
>
> (Wallace 1980: 13)

Budgets are two things rolled into one. They are the annual appropriation needed to run public programs and they are the government's major opportunity to signal its plans for the coming year. The comments made earlier about election policy speeches apply with equal weight to Budget making. Those able to set the spending and taxing priorities of the government have unique power to shape its policy agenda.

1. Process

In Westminster-type systems such as those in Australia and New Zealand, the Budget originates from a two-axis negotiation between politicians and bureaucrats at one level and between different ministers at the other. In its first stages the draft Budget will contain estimates made by departments. These include the proposed costs of continuing existing programs plus bids for new initiatives supported by the senior staff of the department. The minister and his or her advisers work through these bids, adding priorities of their own and scaling down programs no longer viewed as important.

At the central level a department of Finance or Treasury will collect drafts of the departmental budgets (sometimes called estimates) and filter them through the overall grid of available resource constraints and the government's economic strategy. Departments may be required to cast their bids in terms of centrally-determined priorities—for instance, only a 2 per cent increase may be allowed; programs may be required to emphasise employment growth; new initiatives may need be internally funded, and so on.

Most parliamentary systems now include intensive Cabinet sub-committee involvement in Budget preparation. Following the preparation of estimates by departments, these sub-committees take advice on the economic outlook of the country or state, the major policy demands being considered by ministers, and the effects of elections past and future.

The Budget process usually extends over several months and moves from wide-ambit bids towards actual decisions by a number of steps. In most systems a Cabinet committee will attempt to set general guidelines and to review the bids of big-spending organisations. Once the Budget has been approved by Cabinet it is brought forward by the Treasurer and presented to Parliament and the public in the form of an Appropriation Bill. Now a further set of pressures emerge and both existing and new programs are subjected to scrutiny.

Interests which feel themselves disadvantaged by program changes or new taxes now mobilise to have minor amendments imposed. It is generally the case, however, that once framed by Cabinet a Budget will become a symbolic test of strength, and governments will fight off attempts to reorganise expenditure and taxing priorities.

2. Policy

The practical policy significance of the Budget is fourfold. First, at the formulation stage inside departments, choices are made about which programs are to be cut and which are to continue. Organised interests arranged around any given program must fight hard at this point to preserve their advantages. The items deemed vulnerable to Budget pressure will signify the local priorities of management and the minister. In most organisations it is relatively easy to identify the current list of 'core' and 'peripheral' programs by finding out whether or not they are considered for possible cuts at Budget time.

Second, the extent and manner of external pressure on the departmental Budget will throw light on the political economy of the organisation. Which groups of clients or beneficiaries lobby hardest for their program? Which succeed without apparent effort?

Third, the nature of new Budget initiatives or at least bids for such initiatives, will represent current thinking inside the organisation concerning priorities for action. In a logical-rational process these initiatives will be seen to follow an orderly process of policy development. Just as frequently an externally-determined edict will suddenly declare new funds to be available under a broad policy heading, and officials will scramble to build a case for their favoured area. How departments handle this process of program initiation is critical to program and policy outcomes. Are existing programs being starved for funds in order to pay for new initiatives? Or does the Budget base, made up of existing commitments, tend to be left unexamined while new proposals are exposed to extensive cost-benefit analysis?

Lastly, policy significance is also attached to the relationship between the organisation and key external resource providers.

During Budget preparation, Treasury assumes a critical role in the assessment of departmental priorities, and the distinction between a policy issue and a resources issue fades. This is a critical time for program managers, since their areas of interest and expertise become exposed to a variety of external pressures including:

- Cabinet expenditure review committees
- Treasury officials
- Key economic interest groups
- Federal and state funding bodies
- Parliamentary critics
- Interstate and local competitors.

Budget politics is a process which has its own literature and its own techniques. For the policy maker the particular institutional rules of budgeting will prove important. Different techniques provide groups with varied access to decision makers. They also convey different values around which bids must be mounted. These rules vary the scope for change at any stage, limit access to information, and guide decision makers towards some ultimate agreement or compromise.

In most systems the annual Budget cycle is governed by strict timetables with clear deadlines. By forcing policy makers to behave in a carefully prescribed manner and to obey general rules of conduct, Budget systems hope to limit individualistic behaviour and special pleading. 'If we do it for you we have to do it for everyone' is the commonsense logic which propels this set of routines (Wallace 1981, Hennessy 1986).

These rules are enforced by various institutional regulators. The Finance minister or Treasurer is a pivotal player during Budget time. Budget sub-committees vary in scope and impact. Observations in individual case studies suggest that committee effectiveness results first of all from élite cohesion, which in turn follows from electoral laws and the other institutional constraints discussed above. Much also depends on what is at stake. Second, institutions are strengthened during periods of constraint. Governments which need to cut their Budgets and restructure their resources frequently invest heavily in strong rules and elaborate committees.

Campbell and Halligan (1992: 137) report favourably on the Hawke government's Expenditure Review Committee (ERC), because they see it as having carried out a 'public choice approach to fiscal issues' at a time of 'severe economic pressure'.

The particular technique used to formulate the Budget also has an influence on policy and participation. Traditional line item budgets which grant large sums to departments under vague headings privilege existing programs but expose new bids to extreme pressure from above. They are somewhat conservative in policy terms because they conceal much of the policy intent of the Budget—even (perhaps especially) from politicians.

Program budgets favour activities currently in harmony with management and political priorities, but may reduce organisational flexibility. This is true wherever policy objectives cannot be clearly quantified, or where they are apt to cause controversy (Corbett 1992, Considine 1990).

Zero-based budgets force managers to explain the value of existing commitments and to measure their success against proposals for change. They are, however, exhausting, and prone to over-simplifying the effects of programs. Strategic or action budgets prioritise a small group of issues and enable rapid improvements in resource allocations to designated areas. Their disadvantages include a tendency to subject other programs to insensitive allocation restraints such as staff ceilings or productivity cuts.

Budgets are an institutionalised means for providing ordinary resources and managing the housekeeping of government, and in this role they appear to offer the policy analyst little joy. But as a continuous process of valuation and evaluation of policy, they are unsurpassed as a window for observation and influence. The rules used, the structures developed and the techniques adopted all affect the policy competence of politicians, bureaucrats and interest groups.

3. Budget Theories

Given its centrality to the policy process it is no surprise that budgeting attracts great interest in the research literature. The Public Choice group led by Tullock (1976), Buchanan (1986) and Niskanen (1975) have mounted a detailed critique of bureaucratic dominance of the Budget process in the United States, and this has become a key plank in the radical liberal attack on the public sectors of most Western democracies. Their claims are simple. Bureaucrats have a vested interest in increasing Budgets because they get jobs, promotions and status that way. They are also protected from the political costs of such increases. So too are politicians who find strategies to defer the costs of Budget increases by pushing them on to future generations through loan raising and deficits. Interest groups who develop lasting ties with the bureaucracy also benefit from this expanding expenditure, with the professions, teachers and other service delivery agents high on the list of offenders.

A great deal has been written for and against these propositions and the core of the debate appears to be that the central proposition cannot be empirically tested. Miller and Moe (1983) show that it is not possible to specify the so-called extra units of supply which these interests have produced because of their Budget-maximising activities. This does not rule out bureaucrat and interest group politics as a key element in budgeting. Rather it undermines the establishment of a general theory which rests upon their self-interest. The institutional framework in which the Budget is set may instead be expected to vary according to the kinds of regulatory factors discussed above.

Intergovernmental Structures

In most policy systems there are important institutions which regularise the relations between national and sub-national governments. In those such as trade and development there are also such structures linking national and international authority holders. To illustrate the policy importance of intergovernmental institutions we will confine our attention to the impact of federalism. These regulated forms of power sharing differ widely. In some cases the sub-national government is little more than an agent for the national. In others the two levels share the same authority and must co-operate as full partners. In a third type the two levels operate in different policy fields, overlapping only at the edges. These differences may be found between countries (e.g. Germany, Canada and Australia) and they may also be found between policy systems of the same country (e.g. Health, Transport and Defence). In some cases we also find these different divisions of authority within the same policy system, as is the case in Australia, where state governments control primary and secondary education and the national government controls the tertiary system.

The policy relevance of federal structures can be described first in some general propositions. Federal systems increase the number of political actors in any policy system. This has immediate consequences for those seeking to influence policy and those wishing to hold the line against outside pressures. Interest groups and community activists benefit from federal systems because they always have an alternative élite to whom complaints or counter-strategies may be taken. These alternative élites have a vested interest in taking up arms against their federal colleagues. State government officials and parliamentarians always need to prove their relevance, while their opposite numbers at the national level must fight off complaints that they are remote and careless in regard to local issues. These tensions are made stronger when different parties are in government at the two different levels in the federal system. The more mixed or ambiguous the division of powers between the levels of government, the more incentives there will be for this kind of competition.

In general, federal systems are characterised as ones in which authority is devolved to sub-units which have varying degrees of autonomy from central control. One of the great advantages of this devolution is its capacity to place responsibility for program delivery at a local level and to grant provincial authorities a strong role in tailoring such programs to local needs. Typically, federal systems give national governments most external powers and standardised programs such as welfare benefits, while local authorities have responsibility for human services. This promotes local adjustment to, and some forms of program innovation in those policies which need to be sensitive to particular needs in order to be effective.

In federal systems such as Australia and Canada where both levels of government must agree before major policy and program development can occur in key areas such as welfare, transport and education, the demand for joint action increases the complexity of the system, as well as multiplying the number of levels at which initiatives may be vetoed. By increasing the number of players whose co-operation is necessary before success is achieved, federal systems undoubtedly reduce the capacity to innovate. That they may also make it more difficult for any single government to enact obnoxious reforms or to repeal valued measures, is some consolation.

A key factor governing these outcomes is the nature of constitutional authority in each specific case. Policy making authority may be allocated specifically to one of the two levels of government, it may be given explicitly to them both, or there may be no clear allocation. Where one level has a clear constitutional mandate the policy significance of federal institutions turns on the nature of principal-agent relations. This is most often the case with state governments carrying out federal programs. When they act as agents of a program over which they have no independent rights and for which they have no responsibility, states have incentives to bend and amend guidelines to introduce goals of their own. Detailed scrutiny by the national government authority may be made difficult where programs are run from within a complex state department which is also implementing programs of its own.

Federalism is also a key institutional force in the policy system when federal divisions correspond to regional and ethnic cleavages. The Canadian province of Quebec is only the most extreme form of this condition. Most federations contain sub-units which have very different economic and social characters. Indeed, this is perhaps the most likely source of federal institutions (Madison 1966). The improved representation of these institutions may result in deadlock unless rules and routines for compromise develop. In all federations such devices are evident and policy making effectiveness is always heavily dependent upon these intermediate institutions. Australia's Loan Council is an example. Ministerial Councils also debate and authorise joint policy initiatives. Intergovernmental committees and working parties undertake evaluation and policy development roles. Annual Premiers' Conferences and the federal Grants Commission also carry out resource allocation functions. Each have their own rules of access, routines for consideration of claims, and standard ways of making decisions.

Conclusion

This discussion of the force of institutional pressures upon policy making has not been an exhaustive one. Our intention has not been to survey the field but to point to critical factors which are likely to impact upon policy. Two critical cases have been omitted. Tribunals and other courts have a central role in policy matters. Bodies such as administrative appeals tribunals (AATs) and the various Ombudsmen's offices hear complaints and establish 'case law' through which policy is made and changed. Also of increasing importance are boards of inquiry and Royal Commissions, both of which have their own routines for influencing policy. They bring new forms of expertise into policy debates; they shield politicians from controversy; and they create particular opportunities for interest groups to mobilise on current issues (Glezer 1982, Capling and Galligan 1992).

Our point has been to show the types of policy influence which these kinds of institutions may be expected to have. The critical factors which must be acknowledged include: effects upon élite solidarity or division, participation opportunities for citizens, access for interest groups, and impediments to successful implementation of policy intentions. Frequently, we find that institutions have their most powerful effect when their rules or routines combine with other institutional mechanisms. The relationships between parliaments, electoral systems and parties are a good example of this contingent effect.

Policy makers have limited control over these effects. The creation of institutions is always in large part a designed impediment to quick and radical change. Understanding the logic of any specific policy system is therefore dependent upon a careful analysis of how and why previous generations of policy actors have been successful in structuring their priorities into a regime of rules and conventions which others must negotiate before their own values and proposals can be implemented.

References

Bartrip, P. W. J., and Burman, S. B. (1983) *The Wounded Soldiers of Industry*. Oxford: Oxford University Press

Batten, Robyn, Weeks, Wendy and Wilson, John (eds) (1991) *Issues Facing Australian Families: Human Services Respond*. Melbourne: Longman Cheshire

Benveniste, Guy (1987) *Professionalising the Organisation:Reducing Bureaucracy to Enhance Effectiveness*. San Francisco: Jossey-Bass

Boston, Jonathan, Martin, John, Pallot, June, and Walsh, Pat (eds) (1991) *Reshaping the State: New Zealand's Bureaucratic Revolution*. Auckland: Oxford University Press

Bowler, Shaun, and Farrell, David M. (1990) 'Voter Behaviour under Proportional Representation by Single Transferable Vote: Solving the Puzzle of the Irish Party System', Paper given to annual meeting of the American Political Science Association, San Francisco, CA, August-September

Buchanan, J.M. (1986) *Liberty, Market and State*. Brighton: Wheatsheaf

Capling, Ann, and Galligan, Brian (1992) *Beyond the Protective State*. Cambridge: Cambridge University Press

Connell, R.W., and Irving, T.H. (1980) *Class Structure and Australian History*. Melbourne: Longman Cheshire

Considine, Mark (1990) 'Managerialism Strikes Out', *Australian Journal of Public Administration* 49 (2)

— (1991), *The Politics of Reform: Workers' Compensation from Woodhouse to Workcare*. Geelong: Deakin University Press

— and Costar, Brian (eds) (1992) *Trials in Power: Cain, Kirner and Victoria 1982–92*. Melbourne: Melbourne University Press

— and Deutchman, Iva Ellen (1992b) 'The Gendering of Political

Institutions: A Comparison of American and Australian State Legislatures', Paper presented to the Annual Meeting of the American Political Science Association, Chicago
Corbett, David (1992) *Australian Public Sector Management.* Sydney: Allen and Unwin
Crisp, L. F. (1961) *Ben Chifley: A Political Biography.* Sydney: Angus and Robertson
Downs, A. (1957) *An Economic Theory of Democracy.* New York: Harper and Row
Eckstein, Harry, and Apter, David (1963) *Comparative Politics: A Reader.* New York: Free Press
Glezer, Leon (1982) *Tariff Politics.* Melbourne: Melbourne University Press
Hall, Peter A. (1986) *Governing the Economy: The Politics of State Intervention in Britain and France.* Cambridge: Polity Press
Hawke, R. J. L. (1979) *The Resolution of Conflict: 1979 Boyer Lectures.* Sydney: ABC
Headey, Bruce (1974) *British Cabinet Ministers: The Roles of Politicians in Executive Office.* London: Allen and Unwin
Hennessy, Peter (1986) *Cabinet,* Basil Blackwell
Katz, R. S. (1980) *A Theory of Parties and Electoral Systems.* Baltimore and London: Johns Hopkins University Press
Kingdon, John W. (1984) *Agendas, Alternatives and Public Policies.* Boston: Little, Brown and Company
Lindblom, Charles E. (1959) 'The "Science" of Muddling Through', *Public Administration Review* 19: 79–88
Lipset, S.M., and Rokkan, S. (1967) *Party Systems and Voter Alignment.* New York: Free Press
Lucy, Richard (1993) *The Australian Form of Government: Models in Dispute.* Melbourne: Macmillan
Madison, James, in M. Farrand (ed.) (1966) *Records of the Federal Convention,* Vols 1–2. New Haven: Yale University Press
Miller, G. J., and Moe, T. M. (1983) 'Bureaucrats, Legislators and the Size of Government', *American Political Review* 77: 297–322
Niskanen, W.A. (1975) 'Bureaucrats and Politicians', *Journal of Law and Economics* XVIII (3): 617–43
Olson, David M. (1980) *The Legislative Process: A Comparative Approach.* New York: Harper and Row
Pfeffer, Jeffrey, and Salancik, Gerald R. (1978) *The External Control of Organisations.* New York: Harper and Row
Polis, Ann (1991) 'Ministerial Advisers in the Victorian Labor Government 1982–91', Master of Arts (Public Policy) Thesis, Department of Political Science, University of Melbourne, November

Rose, Richard (1974) *The Problems of Party Government.* London: Macmillan

Schattschneider, E. E. (1960) *The Semi-Sovereign People: A Realist's Guide to Democracy in America.* New York: Reinhart and Winston

Schoonmaker, Donald (1988) 'The Challenge of the Greens to the West German Party System', in Kay Lawson and Peter Merkl (eds), *When Parties Fail: Emerging Alternative Organisations.* New Jersey: Princeton University Press

Taagepera, Rein and Shugart, M. S. (1989) *Seats and Votes: The Effects and Determinants of Electoral Systems.* New Haven: Yale University Press

Tullock, Gordon (1976) *The Vote Motive.* London: ILEA

Vogel, David (1993) 'Representing Diffuse Interests in Environmental Policymaking', in Weaver and Rockman

Wallace, Helen (1980) *Budgetary Politics: The Finances of the European Communities.* London: George Allen and Unwin

Walter, James (1986) *The Minister's Minders.* Melbourne: Oxford University Press

Weaver, R. Kent, and Rockman, Bert (1993) *Do Institutions Matter? Government Capabilities in the United States and Abroad.* Washington DC: The Brookings Institution

Weller, Pat, and Grattan, Michele (1981) *Can Ministers Cope? Australian Federal Ministers at Work.* Melbourne: Hutchinson Australia

Weller, Patrick (1989) *Malcolm Fraser PM: A Study in Prime Ministerial Power in Australia.* Melbourne: Penguin

Whitlam, Gough (1985) *The Whitlam Government 1972–1975* Melbourne: Penguin

5

Actor Networks

The enduring sets of relationships within policy systems can involve thousands of clients and hundreds of governmental and non-governmental agencies. Their patterns of interaction, co-operation and dependency frequently become institutionalised into standard programs, the procedures and regulations for which may run to several volumes. We have discussed some of the major attributes of these systemic linkages in previous chapters, under the headings 'political economy', 'policy cultures' and 'institutions'. These larger structures do not account for all that occurs within these regions, however. Individuals are also linked and grouped through sets of associations which we will call **actor networks**.

Actor networks are the informal and semi-formal linkages between individuals and groups in the same policy system. They may be based on strong shared commitment, or on a loose common concern to share information. Network participants attempt to define their own identity as advocates of some issue or new problem. The inter-organisational character of networks gives them a dynamic quality which often places them at the centre of processes directed towards innovation and systemic change. When viewed as a total pattern of involvement and participation, actor networks constitute a key aspect of the social capital of the policy system, helping us to distinguish the dynamic from the static systems, and those with robust potential from those likely to collapse under pressure.

The different forms of association typical of the actor network have been variously described in the policy literature. Interest group theory, pluralism, corporatism, policy communities and policy networks each convey a different account of the role of this middle layer of activity which lies between the institutional realm and that of the solitary citizen. What we will call actor networks are in practice the evolving communication mechanisms which enable sub-groups within the policy system to develop shared policy preferences and common methods for representing these interests. These devices typically reach across organisational boundaries and persist beyond any single policy episode.

Emery and Trist (1965) describe these kinds of interaction as forming a characteristic 'causal texture', or a system of connections which is independent of the prevalent system of exchange, provision or regulation. This causal texture is based on the way groups and individuals are clustered and linked. This system can often shape the kind of action available to participants and can establish a characteristic kinetic property, by which they mean the degree of dynamism or inertia in the sector. This kinetic property is visible in the forms of action which participants see themselves as having available to them.

In this account we will rework the more usual concept of the policy network to include a more explicit acknowledgement of the roles of action and power. Without a clear understanding of the part played by action, the network idea may lose vitality and become little more than a description of interest group links. With a focus upon action we can seek explanations of actual behaviours and strategies and the ideas which inform them. In the framework being presented here, actor networks play a key role in our understanding of how policy systems learn, innovate and in other ways act upon themselves (Dluhy 1981). They form a capillary system through which major interests and institutions are drawn into common cause with other regular and irregular participants. But first, two preliminary points concerning the different levels of analysis through which we are moving.

The idea that policy is made through systematic co-operation and conflict, and that these systems are built from political, economic and cultural structures is a true but incomplete picture of the world of policy making. There is no system without participants and there would be no conflict, nor any need for mediation if these participants were not powerful actors in their own right. The first preliminary point to be made is, therefore, that policy must be viewed as the accomplishment of real people and actual groups. Larger structures and historical patterns inform policy making through the actions of actual decision makers who take these constraints into account, regard them as important and feel obligated by this inheritance.

Actors therefore perform two roles. They carry forward the routines and habits of the past, and they make up new or modified strategies for dealing with present and future circumstances. The scope for change cannot be predicted by an analysis of the larger structures of policy systems alone. Strategic assessments must also be made about the calibre of activists, the extent of mobilisation among those affected by policies, and the outlooks or ideologies of the many partisans who populate these systems. Clients may form themselves into neighbourhoods or self-help collectives with a policy change agenda. Professionals employed by government may elect to support the interests of clients and campaign against official policy. Public managers in service delivery agencies may decide to contest the priorities of their own government's central agencies by enlisting other service providers, academics and media comentators. Churches, trade unions and philanthropic organisations may join together to push values which promise quite different programs from those currently provided. Each of these forms of advocacy opens the door to new visions of the way policy should be organised.

These actions or behaviours are not independent, solitary choices of the type often described in theories of rational action (Allison 1971, Elster 1993). Instead they must be viewed as group achievements which reflect the character of received wisdom and the negotiations of interdependent individuals, none of whom have full control over the knowledge and the resources needed to create programs, decisions or other outcomes. This is not to deny that rational calculations exist and often influence private choices about such things as who to vote for, what car to buy, and which leisure activity to select. But when it comes to making and remaking policy, it is the inherited perceptions of needs and preference which also count decisively.

The second preliminary point is therefore a recognition that policy is only possible because individuals find ways to act together. Although conflict-ridden, policy is primarily a joint action among a complex range of actors. Government officials, business leaders, trade unionists, doctors, teachers and neighbourhood activists each communicate back and forth in a ceaseless effort to secure support, apply pressure and achieve some common purpose. Tracing the lines of joint effort, including those which fail, reveals a dazzling array of manoeuvres. Tight consensual bonds between key actors in one policy system can be contrasted with open, competitive associations in others. In either case, and in the many variations in between, the character of the associations between these critical actors will be important.

Actors

When we set out to describe policy making as the accomplishment of real actors we are setting ourselves against two important traditions in policy theory. The first is the one which views policy as always the manifestation of some predetermined historical pattern. Social theories defined in the literature as classical Marxism, structural functionalism and critical theory each present fixed social structures as the major source of policy outcomes (Parson and Smelser 1956, Ham and Hill 1984). They differ only to the extent that the individual is viewed as a beneficiary or victim of such structures. The second tradition seeks to push aside the achievements of institutions and other systemic influences, and to claim sovereignty for the individual (Olson 1962). Rational choice and individual preference are taken to be the foundation of all important social and political achievements. Neo-classical economics has legitimised this view, placing the market at the centre of all discussions of effective co-operation among individuals. The Australian and New Zealand policy regimes which have been formed from these materials are labelled 'economic rationalist', although paradoxically they are ideologies born within government rather than within the private sector (Pusey 1991, Boston 1991).

In contrast, the concept of action being advanced here originates with Durkheim (1893) and the radical interactionist sociologists such as Sennett (1970) and Strauss (1978). A comprehensive account is also to be found in the work of Touraine (1977, 1981) and Melucci (1980, 1985), whose discussion of the impact of social movements has transformed the sociology of action by replacing the older concerns with a new problem of order with the organising concept of conflict.

Policies are results. They emerge from the interplay of individuals and groups who seek to alter and confirm the rules and the programs organised by government. No single group or individual achieves exactly what they set out to get from these interactions. Instead the contests and negotiations which take place serve to define what will emerge. Learning, innovation, compromise and surprise invest these relationships with possibility. Another way to express this proposition is to view these participants as being involved in continuing relationships with one another. In all relationships, no matter how unequal, those involved have a say in what will be achieved.

The term 'actor' is a way of confirming that all of the systems and sub-sytems we have been describing depend upon the direct contributions of those involved. Even passivity or compliance is a type of contribution which has to be produced; it cannot simply be assumed. The concept of action as an evolving communication demands that we recognise power is always present in these relationships. Power is exercised every time a group is dependent upon someone else for the carrying out of a task or role. Leaders and followers, managers and employees, teachers and pupils, bureaucrats and clients exercise power through the forms of co-operation and conflict they enact. Giddens (1979: 93) confirms this relational view when he acknowledges that power is always a two-way process 'even if the power of one actor is minimal compared to another'.

The various systems and institutions described in previous chapters establish patterns and pathways through which these actors are encouraged to move. The incentives to conform are strong but not irrestistible. At the very least the policy actor must update and modernise the inheritance he or she has been given. Action is therefore a double deal. On the one hand these various forms of dependency put pressures on actors to conform to established routines in order to receive the resources or recognition which these rules provide. On the other, all actors retain the capacity to do otherwise: to push for concessions, to challenge the terms of their involvement, and to organise relationships alternative to those currently in place.

Actors come in various forms and every system seeks to define which type of actor it prefers to acknowledge. Individuals, citizens, consumers, interest groups, classes, ethnic communities, youth, women and clients are all terms which define a certain type of actor. In the same way that policy is the result of actor relations, the definition of the actor is a consequence of conflict and negotiation within the policy system. Today's 'in group' will be different from tomorrow's because new issues and contests will encourage the emergence of an amended list of key players. Policy systems which have very centralised power relations, where key resources are dominated by a cohesive group and where institutions effectively block outside pressures, will show less rapid alteration in the cast of actors than more disordered or devolved systems. But even in heavily regulated systems the potential for change remains great. Changes in the external environment, the inflow of ideas and demands from neighbouring systems, changes in technology, and the persistence of social inequalities regularly open the door to new actors pushing new agendas.

In this sense we can consider individuals to be actors in certain cases while in others key organisations will undertake important actions. Trade unions, hospitals, local government authorities, the Cabinet office or the Chamber of Commerce might well be the key actors in one case, while in another the occupational health officers who work in each of these locations may undertake the critical actions. Actors cannot be isolated by categories such as organisations, interest groups or formal associations. Instead the purpose of the activity, the ideas which inform it, and the systems of communication which make it possible will define the actors in each policy system.

Networks

In the account we have given in previous chapters, individuals and groups are related to one another through functional roles. This functional dependency is the prime source of the policy system. Patients depend upon doctors, who depend upon nurses and administrators, who depend on government funding institutions, and at the end of this functional pattern we see the emergence of the health policy system.

Networks may have functional attributes, but they also span a much wider universe of actions. They are a capillary system of inter-group, inter-interest co-operation which provides possibilities for repeated, regular activity. This recurrent character of the network distinguishes it from single policy campaigns and other temporary episodes in which groups collide and collude. Networks provide the possibility of communication between different actors on a continuing basis. The network may be composed of formal organisations, different government agencies, local activists and international support groups. It may have individual subscribers as well as group members and there may be several layers of activity. Some may use the network only for information, others may employ it as a means to obtain services, while still others will use the network to plan joint initiatives.

Studies of networks in the policy field include a wide range of issues. For some writers the network is an effective form of control in which interests capture government agencies and secure benefits for themselves at the cost of clients and taxpayers (McConnell 1966). Typically this kind of relationship occurs when a high level of functional dependency exists between a government agency and a well-organised interest group such as employers, doctors or media owners.

Figure 5.1 Perrow's Imaginary City Health Network

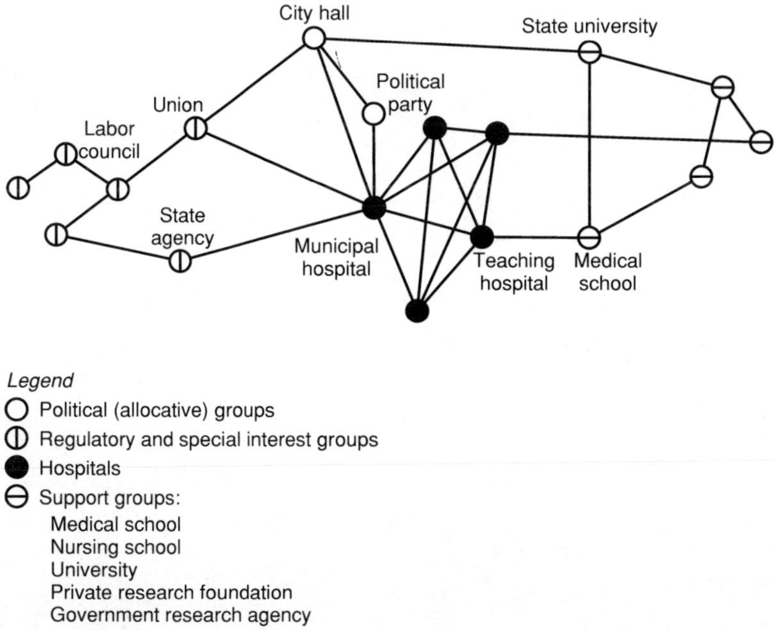

Source: Charles Perrow (1986) *Complex Organisations: A Critical Essay*. New York: Random House, p 196

The networks which develop from these functional ties are often viewed as private and self-interested. Government agencies comply with the demands of producers and politicians in an 'iron triangle' of stable, privileged interests. Peters (1986) defines this relationship as one based on functional dependence: 'Each actor in the iron triangle needs the other two to succeed, and the style that develops is symbiotic. The pressure group needs the agency to deliver services to its members. . .the agency needs the pressure group to mobilise political support for its programs.' The politicians need both to secure their legitimacy and re-election hopes.

The other standard works on network power come from those interested in coporatist policy making. In this case the network is composed of a small number of producer interests which share authority with government. Together they and the government representatives plan and execute policies. Schmitter (1970: 93) points out that in these cases the network is in fact a type of

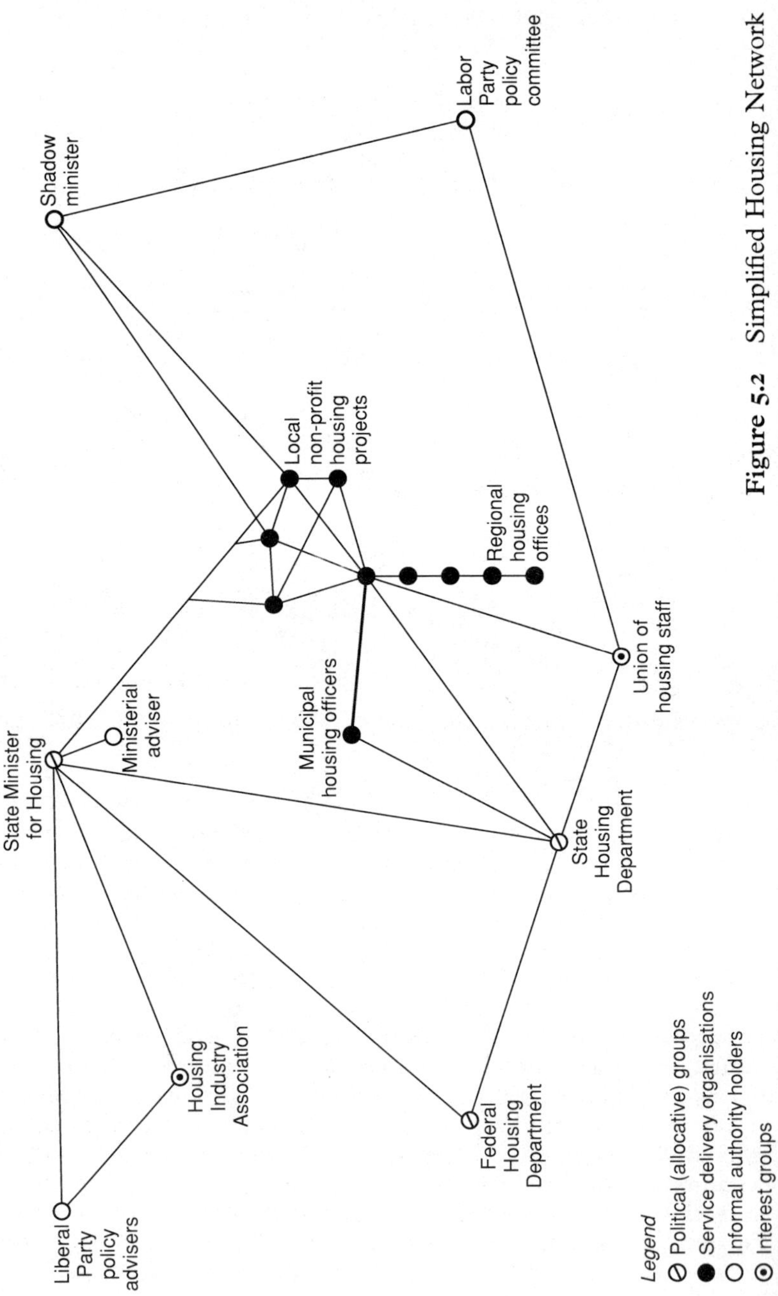

Figure 5.2 Simplified Housing Network

'representational monopoly', in which the state shares its authority in return for interest group support. The northern European states, Belgium and the Netherlands, and certain policy systems within the German state have displayed corporatist styles of policy making at various times in the post-war period. Typically, governments employ such arrangements in areas such as industrial relations, industry policy and social security where employer and union support is critical to policy stability.

The Australian arbitration system and the industries assistance sector has demonstrated some corporatist characteristics in this period, but the Australian habit of entrusting real decision making authority to courts and tribunals has limited the scope for formal power sharing (Mcintyre and Mitchell 1989, Rattigan 1986, Carney 1988). Instead the network patterns in these policy systems have retained a more fragmented character with employer, union and expert groups interacting through overlapping and complex local arrangements.

Rhodes (1981) leads the field in studies of policy networks, an approach which builds upon previous studies of policy communities. Here a limited number of key administrative, political and interest group leaders come frequently to interact and to develop shared values. Rhodes amends this approach by suggesting that interpersonal contacts are actually built upon functional ties. Engineers in local government, health administrators and town planners all interact because they share a common relationship with central governments which control their budgets or their statutory rights. For Rhodes and his various co-researchers the network springs from resource dependency (Marsh and Rhodes 1992: 10).

Benson's (1982) essay on inter-organisational networks must be acknowledged as the source of much of this research. It was Benson who first pointed to the fact that policy organisations were frequently clustered together according to resource dependencies. Rhodes has elaborated this into a series of network types in which highly dependent arrangements are taken to be more integrated and less restricted. Less dependent forms of association are viewed as loose and less stable. His five types include:

1. Policy communities in which relations are stable, membership is restricted and a common service is being provided;
2. Professional networks, where a particular form of knowledge and certification define exclusive relationships;
3. Intergovernmental networks, typically clusters of local or state government authorities which provide similar services;

4. Producer networks, economic interest groups such as unions and business organisations; and
5. Issue networks involving large numbers of participants who may have little else in common.

The virtue of this classification system is its breadth. The old categories of interest group, network and social movement are removed, and we can see in one place the many types of association likely to occur in political life. The attempt to distinguish between groups on the basis of the membership attributes of their chief participants, however, is prone to make these categories problematic. What distinguishes a professional network from a producer one? Further, the categories do not describe separate phenomena. Could not an issue network, a policy community and a producer network involve many of the same people?

A similar problem with conventional policy network analysis is its static quality. Networks are classified but not always explained. But why do they arise in the first place? What factors cause them to develop or die? How are their dynamics related to the actions of governments and other key participants? The standard assumption that networks are composed of those with the same jobs or the same outlooks begs the question. Why are these actors linked when many others are not?

The concept of the actor network is based on the assumption that there may be only very general characteristics binding it together. Common occupation and similar sources of dependency may create opportunities for network formation—and yet something else is still needed. One important part of the answer lies in the fact that the activity being undertaken represents a new or pressing idea for those willing to contribute. Even when the reasons for valuing the action differ, the source of network solidarity remains.

A useful example is provided by the many networks currently being established within recreation policy systems. Older people's recreation networks link professionals, actual and potential funding agencies, program managers, volunteers and people participating in older people's leisure activities. These networks cannot be explained away as interest groups designed to lobby governments for funds, although this is certainly a task they undertake. Nor can they be reduced to some notion of service delivery in which network participants get benefits commensurate with their contributions, although practical outputs are certainly important ingredients.

These networks undertake actions which express new ideas

about the way older people wish to be treated by others and revised conceptions of how they see themselves. The networks are thus self-producing systems of identification and recognition, as well as being instrumental agencies for getting this or that service delivered. A major part of their role is to provide a model and an advocacy function for those who previously saw themselves as unable to undertake sport or other active pursuits. By drawing these people into a network in which alternative role models are provided, this form of organisation creates a new set of ideas about old age. This creative, educational purpose distinguishes the network from the more traditional interest group where some rational common interest is taken to be the entry point for members, not the outcome of membership.

Actor networks therefore operate at both levels of the policy system. They represent the interests which are involved in service development and delivery. Depending upon how these major political and economic relations are arranged, this will result in pluralist, corporatist or monopoly patterns of interest group organisation. Additionally, actor networks will express old and new ideas about what is to be valued in the policy system. These may be utopian notions of fraternity, equality or freedom, and they may also be reactionary ideals of racial superiority, exclusive rights or élite dominance. All actor networks seek to articulate some view about why things are as they are, or about the way things ought to be.

In practice actors form networks in order to learn about, and respond to social or political facts which they consider important. Their communication is therefore purposeful. The type of issue which brings them together will therefore tend to be both material and ideological.

Interest Groups

The standard works in the policy analysis area describe the associations which attempt to influence policy as interest groups. Before proceeding further with a discussion of networks and their different characteristics and effects, it is worth looking at some of the strengths and weaknesses of interest group accounts of the policy process.

Interest group theories operate in three domains. They wish to explain why people join groups, how power is distributed within the group, and what groups can achieve in their relations with governments. Not all interest group theorists are equally interested in each of these three levels. Taken as a whole, however, the approach does present coherent claims about the individual, group and political levels of policy making.

Olson (1965) presents the most comprehensive account of the interest group school. His classic study may be formulated as six key propositions:

1. The primary function of groups is to advance the common interests of individuals;
2. Groups seek to provide collective goods, which are benefits all those in the field, group members or not, will enjoy;
3. It will often not be rational for self-interested individuals to contribute to the groups which deliver benefits to them;
4. Groups will often have to provide extra incentives or sanctions to get potential members to join;
5. The larger the group, the smaller the value of participation by rational individuals;
6. Non-economic or social incentives are mainly important only in the small group.

Before discussing the detail of Olson's case, it is perhaps useful to see where he differs from traditional theories of group association. In the writings of earlier political scientists and sociologists such as Mosca (1939) and Simmel (1950), groups were viewed as natural engagements which individuals sought because of 'herd instinct', sociability or other natural propensities. Olson (1965: 20) rejects this view on the basis of evidence which shows that 'the average person does *not* in fact typically belong to large voluntary associations'. It is worth noting in passing that Olson may be right about large voluntary associations, but wrong about group affiliation if one admits family, clan, church and club to this category.

The second more traditional account which Olson wishes to attack is the one which holds that group interests rather than individual ones are those which dominate politics (Truman 1958, Verba 1961, Galbraith 1952). Bentley (1949: 220) is perhaps the best known advocate of this position. He argued that pressure between groups was the main force in politics and that the 'balance of group pressures *is* the existing state of society'. The democratic character of the political system was only preserved in these traditional group accounts by the fact that there were many groups available to represent the individual; the groups were in tension or direct conflict, thus keeping the political system open; and the groups exercised influence which was roughly approximate to their numerical strength. Moreover, writers such as Galbraith and Truman argued that as one interest group grew and became influential there would be a tendency for others to enter the fray and counter this power, thereby producing a form of equilibrium among interests.

Olson's decisive critique of these pluralist accounts is based upon two central aspects of his own theory. Groups only exist to the extent that individuals within them find it rational to contribute. But only some types of groups will be able to induce people to join. Large groups which are based on economic interests will find it more difficult than small ones. Olson uses this distinction to explain why business associations fare better than farmers' organisations and trade unions. Most industry groups are composed of a hundred or so firms. Anthing larger than this and the organisational costs, plus a tendency for individuals to take a 'free ride' at the expense of the larger membership, will make it difficult to mobilise the potential group into an actual one:

> Since relatively small groups will frequently be able voluntarily to organise and act in support of their common interests, and since large groups normally will not be able to do so, the outcome of the political struggle among the various groups in society will not be symmetrical.
> (Olson 1965: 127)

The account given by Olson is consistent with, and to some extent drawn from the economic theories of politics which are today known as Public Choice and agency theory. Popular terminology lumps these together into all-purpose categories such as 'the New Right' or 'economic rationalism'. The common link in Olson's work and that of Public Choice theorists such as Buchanan and Tullock (1962) is the belief that individual rationality is the driving force of group and organisational action. Closely related to this idea is the belief that individual rationality is primarily economic in character—that is, is based on measureable comparisons of cost and benefit.

This summary account provides an insight into the strength and limitation of the interest group school, whether they be old fashioned pluralists or born-again economic rationalists. In the first place the notion of 'interest' is allowed to remain static. Either for the individual or the group, the interest being represented is fixed and quantifiable. This is a rather limited view. Individuals and groups may in fact discover or develop their interests as they go along. Their separate or combined interest may be one of the achievements of the action being undertaken. Whatever it was that drove them into collaboration may be quite remote from the ultimate activity which the group produces.

This is a problem for many economic accounts of politics. The consumer going into the marketplace in search of the best apples is quite unlike the local resident arriving at a town meeting to discuss the new traffic plan. Both require rational deliberation but in each the conditions are significantly different. In the competitive food market it can be assumed for the moment that the individual has authority over his or her own resources, can obtain necessary information quickly and reliably, and can expect neither reprisals nor secondary benefits from the choice finally made. Purchasing apples, in other words, is a single transaction by a sovereign individual.

The town meeting sees no such independence. Here it is values that are being determined, and these only exist in and through the formation of groups. To be successful, the individual will need to join with others, to negotiate and to compromise. In so doing he or she will require trust, shared sympathy and perhaps a willingness on some occasions to put the interest of others first. Rationalists may protest that *in the end* the choice is the same as the one found in the single, individual transaction, but in practice there is no end, no day of reckoning. Individuals persist in patterns of co-operative behaviour in which they cannot be expected to keep tally of their economic gains and losses. Instead they develop rules, routines and cultures to guide them through complex choices.

The Olson model may suggest what the rational individual *should* do while being unsuccessful in showing what they often *will* do. There would be little point, on economic rationalist grounds, in attending a street demonstration, for example. No single individual could hope to influence an outcome by their attendance. Yet such demonstrations have become a regular part of political life. In such cases it is obvious that something other than an individual calculation of probable success and likely cost is at work.

To summarise, then, interest group theory displays two contradictory tendencies. Traditional accounts assume a balance or equilibrium which is based on dubious claims concerning the systemic logic of group behaviour. Rationalist accounts seek an explanatory order in the economic calculations of the rational individual. This fails to consider the group origin of preferences and their modification, the fact that individuals usually cannot act alone in policy systems, and that belief and culture may provide short-cuts in cases where time and information costs prevent economic calculation.

Network Creativity

In employing the idea of actor networks we are seeking a more interactive, dynamic approach to the formulation of interests in policy making. Rather than viewing power as an all-or-nothing struggle between a regular cast of interest group élites, the network approach seeks to identify sources of creativity and change. In policy systems we find a wide variety of actors who are capable of this kind of creativity. Experts, professions, social movements, entrepreneurs, technicians and citizen groups seize upon social and political opportunities in order to express new ideas concerning what is feasible and desirable. Why do policy systems respond to such pressures? The standard literature represents interest groups as inherently resistant to change. It is also generally true that systems employ institutions as a means to impose stability and order in the face of pressures, but the power of this routine and regulation is limited.

Demographic change, new technologies, altered economic conditions and other shifts in the environment in which policy systems operate all conspire to render institutional power incomplete (March and Olsen 1989). Moreover, persistent conflicts between different classes of actor generate a permanent potential for agitators to exploit. The very reason that institutions are needed in the first place is that these conflicts are endemic, widespread and persistent. Actor networks may be either the termites chewing at the base of existing institutions, or the worker bees earnestly fashioning the new.

Groups and the networks which link them are therefore formed around two sets of problems: development and regulation. Writers and observers disagree about which of the two is the most important factor in any explanation of policy strategies. For those more interested in social regulation, groups are viewed as forms of social closure and monopoly. Weber, for example, argues that any exclusive group attribute such as religion or occupation can become the basis of collective action aimed at the gaining of social or economic advantage and the exclusion of others from that field. He suggests that 'this monopolisation is directed against competitors who share some positive or negative characteristic; its purpose is always the closure of social and economic opportunities to *outsiders*'. At its strongest, he points out, this form of interest association establishes itself as 'a legal order that limits competition through formal monopolies'. Kelley (1989) follows the line developed by Olson in pointing out that regulation usually means coercion:

> In the 1700s if a silversmith in Boston began to practise without serving the normal seven years apprenticeship, already practicing smiths would simply ransack the shop.

The debate between developmental and regulatory theories of actor networks help isolate the main questions which we would like answered in our analysis of policy making. It directs attention to the need to identify and penetrate the overall system of interactions within the policy field being explored. How are the links between individuals and groups characterised? What cleavages exist between major interests? What ideas and priorities predominate? What are the regular (if informal) links between groups? What mechanisms or circumstances hold interests together or pull them apart? Where are the boundaries between them? How are these boundaries maintained? In what ways do groups infringe on each other's territory, or engage in other forms of conflict and negotiation?

Network Structure

Actor networks include a wide variety of individuals and groups. This openness is their strength, making them more available to novelty and change than are formal organisations with settled purposes. Networks come into being according to several general kinds of stimuli. Some appear to be demand-led; others are more likely supply-driven. In other words, some result from initiatives taken by groups themselves, but others are stimulated by actions which governments or third parties take to which others then respond. The nature of the network's purpose or joint project will vary according to the character of this 'push-pull' relationship with other actors. It will also vary in response to the degree of value consensus among participants. Low consensus networks are based on information sharing, while high consensus networks seek to articulate a common interest. These two factors provide an approximate scale running from strong to weak which in effect registers the extent to which participants are tightly integrated or are merely loosely allied.

1. Supply Driven Information Networks

At the most general or loose level an actor network may be built around actors who have a common interest only in sharing information in a policy issue or program which did not result from any action or initive of their own. So, for example, the consumers of a government sponsored health program may form themselves into a network to share information about funding, new initiatives and future policy. They may not have any common objectives and few independently shared resources. This kind of loosely federated, supply driven network may be capable of action designed to maintain government funding, but is unlikely to achieve larger impacts on policy development.

2. Supply Driven Interest Networks

Those groups which develop as a response to an existing program, but which also achieve some form of value consensus regarding the present and future needs of consumers or service providers, are capable of applying strong pressure for either the maintenance or extension of existing services. They are, however, vulnerable to any move to close down this area of service, since they lack their own, independent reasons for collective behaviour. Neighbourhood houses and employment creation projects provide good examples of this type. They often achieve a strong consensus regarding policy values but are prone to collapse when governments lose interest in their service. Moreover, their organised pressure may itself provoke such a loss of support where authorities come to believe that a cut in the program will serve to silence a critical source of pressure.

3. Demand Driven Information Networks

Networks which arise from a shared social condition or common need, but which lack a strong value consensus regarding appropriate solutions do not owe their identity to anyone else and are therefore better placed to survive changes in government policy. Their lack of attachment to an existing program has its costs, however. It may be difficult for them to develop an organised identity. They must operate as outsiders so far as the policy making process is concerned. This may limit the information they get, as well as reducing their credibility in wider public debates over what needs doing. Their pluralistic value system also limits their input into the maintenance or extension of existing conditions.

As far as policy change is concerned, they can do little more than publicise needs, pressure others to take action and act as watchdogs as far as new initiatives are concerned. Professional associations often fit this category. They prove far better at protecting existing interests than at initiating reform.

4. Demand Driven Interest Networks

Undoubtedly the most potent networks are those which are both self-developing and consensual. At their strongest these may often become social movements. Environmental groups and women's networks often fit this type. They nurture their membership on the basis of strong values or significant personal experience, and they are largely immune to gestures by government aimed at demobilising them. Indeed such responses by antagonistic interests or unsympathetic officials may help galvanise support and clarify new strategic objectives.

These networks may also operate across several policy issues and more than one policy system. For example, the Australian networks established to help nursing mothers in the 1960s had an initial purpose of providing practical self-help. This soon developed into a critique of orthodox medical practice, and a means for revaluing the role of mothers and midwives. Feminist ideas influenced these networks in the 1970s, stimulating their involvement in related activities concerning infant health, child care and community medicine.

This brief sketch is sufficient to highlight the variety of forms of non-formal organisation or association in most policy systems. In most cases, however, to make meaningful judgements about these networks requires two types of information about them. What is the functional, social or ideological appeal from which groups or networks emerge? This can be called the social base of the groups in the network. Second, how is the network organised? What is the system of communication and decision making which draws people and groups together? How are the necessary resources for this organisation obtained? Is there some characteristic division of labour or allocation of roles?

The Network Support Base

To sketch these patterns of affiliations, it is useful to begin by identifying the number of groups and the types of factors which lead to network formation, leaving to one side for the moment the important question of why some forms of network organisation appear to be favoured in certain environments. Functional, social and ideological ties are the most common groupings.

1. Functional Affiliations

As the term suggests, functional groups are those which form around a task or transaction. For the most part, such functions have a material orientation and may be divided into corporate and occupational types, each of which has a somewhat different style of formation. Business organisations typify corporate networks which come together in a rich variety of formal and semi-structured associations. At the tightest level, share ownership patterns link large sectors of the economy together in a web of financial interdependence. Memberships of boards of directors provides a further layer of bonding between certain firms and key individuals. Conglomerate companies and multinationals are another potentially important link. Patterns of interconnection brought about by regular purchasing and supply of raw materials or support services are also sources of linkage.

In addition to these semi-formal commercial relationships, corporate interests are also often drawn together through a variety of trade federations, peak groups and sector lobby associations. These are the strongest networks, in that they have a visible structure. Some are highly specific, such as the local chambers of commerce in each town and city. Some are all-embracing, such as the Business Council of Australia. They fit the definition of a network in so far as they link organisations which retain their independence and can choose to act differently from others in the network. In a formal organisation this independence is not available.

Further, corporate interests are linked and nourished by the many training institutions which provide management with both a skill base and a long-term school or class solidarity. In some cases these ties are strengthened by leadership programs which aim to bind executives into alumni and similar forms of mutual aid. At this point the functional tie becomes a social bond, supported by clubs and private school reunions, reminding the observer that these categories possess the capacity to become duplicated and reinforced.

Occupational linkages operate at a large number of levels. Formal associations such as trades unions act as representatives, leaders and educators of large groups of workers in common employment. Depending on whether they are craft unions or general unions of the semi-skilled, these groups also seek to promote standards of conduct, skill and training among their members. Within the workplace the union also acts as an organising point, social link and political force. Connections between unions and between them and other political and social organisations provide further avenues for action.

The other important occupational group is the professional association. The stronger types include medical associations, law societies and guilds of engineers and architects. They touch the centre of the policy maker's world. So vocal are these interests in the health sector that one reformer has described the policy process as 'planning by decibels' (Sax 1984: xi).

Professional groups act as organised interests by working through their representative organisations such as the AMA or the Society of Engineers. They also create an imposing force through the conventions and practices which they observe and enforce within the health system, where they are linked to nurses' groups and health administrator associations, forming a potentially powerful alliance of professions.

Finally, there are a large number of non-professional associations devised to promote and protect everyone from undertakers to national park rangers. These groups conduct meetings, conferences and organise industrial action. They also inform, educate and entertain their members. Like the other two types, non-professional organisations have significance beyond their own members. They set standards and help establish routines to which many other groups must then respond.

Frequently, the 'map' of the networks which traverse a given policy sector will include rival occupational and interest groups. The most obvious division in the occupational category is the division between professions, managers and consumers. Alford describes the first two as professional monopolisers and corporate rationalisers (Alford 1975), and Duckett (1984) describes the third as equal health advocates. For Illich (1973) these conflicts are best seen as part of a long-term process of 'occupational imperialism', in which groups fight hard to gain and hold control over key resources and opportunities.

Even in those sectors which lack strong professional monopolies or powerful unions, occupational associations may be found just beneath the surface. In the Australian rehabilitation field, for example, there are several loose associations of safety officers, occupational health nurses and welfare advisers. None of these fit easily into the larger, more institutionalised groups such as the Nurses Federation or the Association of Social Workers. So they have carved out their own small space in which they run workshops, exchange information about government policy, and press for better working conditions. However altruistic, these associations always own a strongly political role, not in the sense of governmental politics, but of the power play within the organisations which constitute the policy sector;

> Individuals and groups are engaged in a continuous process of conspiracy, evasion, negotiation, and conflict in the course of coping with the varying circumstances and situations of their work, in some sense shaping the terms, conditions and content of their work no matter what the formal mode of organisation being used. (Friedson 1976)

2. *Social Bonds*

Race, gender and class lead the list of social affiliations which may facilitate network formation. Other sources include regional, age group and ethnic identities, each of which may be the basis both of collective interest and trust. It is frequently the common experiences which these groups have in their delaings with social institutions which give them their shared identity. Education through the school system, for example, may reinforce the norms and expectations of a particular class or sex, granting them access to different forms of status. For instance, the way the family and the school system treats girls in their early years may shape their view of themselves as different and unequal.

What is clear is that social origins, social experience and the shared identity of being one of a group arise as part of a learned process. Whether or not a social characteristic emerges as a source of some wider solidarity will depend very largely upon how the social institutions and dominant network practices of a given community will interpret those features.

One of the important things which actor networks may do in any policy system is to help define and explain the common conditions and experiences to their members. In other words, a membership does not arrive at the front door of the Brighton Women's Collective ready to take action on abortion or equal pay. Rather, groups seek supporters among those they believe to have had a shared experience. They then educate and direct attention to particular issues. Analysis begins with an assumption that it is possible to recognise the basis of group mobilisation through an understanding of various forms of common experience, but there are limits to this. The way groups interpret and understand their shared histories is variable. It is essential to look both at the basis of social similarity, and at the sets of ideas through which those experiences are understood.

3. *Ideological Affiliations*

All forms of network association are ideological, making a necessary nonsense of our attempt to carve off one single category. Business groups share norms about the importance of private enterprise; women's organisations adopt views about patriarchy and gender difference; neighbourhood networks promote characteristic values concerning the qualities of their suburb or town and elevate the qualities of those they view as 'people like us'. All these things create and convey norms and values which are highly political, even if unconsciously so.

For many forms of association, however, ideas perform a dual role. They not only act as an expression of some core characteristic such as a common class origin or culture, but also work as the prime means to create identity. The most obvious case of this is religion. Here a set of complex beliefs binds part of, or a whole community, crossing class, gender and ethnic lines. Although Weber may be correct to associate certain religious movements such as Protestantism with the emergence of new social formations (in this case early capitalism), it is also clear that the ideals themselves are somewhat free-forming.

Durkheim (1965: 47) provides the sociological definition of religion when he distinguishes it as 'a unified system of beliefs and practices relative to sacred things, that is to say things set apart and forbidden—beliefs and practices which unite into a single moral community called a church by all those who adhere to them'. Immediately it is clear that the basis of organisation is belief or ideology and that such beliefs are capable of exerting tremendous power.

Other systems of thought also motivate actors within groups. Indeed, almost any set of claims about the world and the causes of its problems can become a magnet for those seeking explanations, revelations or saviours. Polanyi (1958) argues that there is a common structure to all sets of ideas about society and the natural world. His often critical view draws upon the fact that all comprehensive belief systems tend to be somewhat circular: that is, they contain assumptions which enable certain difficult problems to be ignored, or dismissed as unworthy of explanation. A corollary to this characteristic is that alternative beliefs, new ideas and rival points of view can be dismissed by a refusal to grant legitimacy to the basic values upon which they rest.

It is not necessary, however, to identify fully developed ideologies in order to recognise that ideas form the primary link inside many actor networks. Broad commitment to a certain understanding of human life and the role of the traditional family may bind the members of an anti-abortion group. An elementary notion that nature holds a source of well-being and authenticity may motivate environmentalists. Further towards the fringe one may find smaller groups held together by conspiracy theories and suspicion. Davies (1973) quotes a Tasmanian judge who had held a Royal Commission into the fluoridation of water, and had been pressured by groups with all kinds of fears and phobias:

> He had been told that fluoride caused the first World War and the Russian Revolution; that fluoride was a Zionist plot or the nefarious design of some group of international financiers to dominate the world; that water with fluoride in it smelled foul because it was decomposed; that taking fluoride had the effect of a 'chemical lobotomy' producing a lackadaisical attitude with over indulgence in sex, sleep, food and spending money; that it was responsible for an increase in gross indecency and child molestation cases; that it caused an increase in juvenile delinquency, the failure of elementary school children to pass examinations and that it was an organised attempt to undermine Christian standards. . .from dandruff to tinea, acne to abortion, cancer to haemophilia, blindness to bed-wetting, sterility to stammering—most known ills to which the flesh is heir have been laid at its door.

It is helpful to summarise the character of these group affiliations based upon ideology in the following way; a broad set of beliefs and priorities is a part of every network's explanation of itself to itself; it seeks to explain current social and political problems in terms of larger dynamics and issues; and it distinguishes its own approach from those of other actors.

Social conflicts or tensions concerning the future are a powerful source of ideological affiliation. Individuals need not be actually experiencing these events in order to be motivated by them; they need only regard them as widespread and significant. Technological changes produce a wide range of such affiliations. Ecology groups, Greenhouse action networks, health associations and peace movements all respond to fears about actual or potential damage arising from new technologies. Although some patterns of affilitation based on social group membership inform these actor networks, many join who have no material or sociological connection to others in the group.

Network Organisation

Organisation involves several dimensions. The first is the level of institutional development. Plainly a field, such as health, which is populated by large hospitals and universities, has a strong profession at its core and is supported by a large bureaucracy. It has quite different capacities to create association from another field, such as conservation, where there are many small or medium sized community groups and a few government organisations.

Institutional development refers to the extent to which a policy system is regulated by authoritative organisations. Systems where there is a high degree of regulation will usually provide incentives and opportunities for dense networking. Time, staff, and information will be more readily available than in sparse, poorly regulated systems.

Organisation is also influenced by the relative size and affluence of the groups which make up the network. Where the average size of groups is large, links between groups are more likely to be strong. Larger average size will frequently mean greater circulation of staff between groups and increased probability of these associations taking joint action. Even where some of the groups are antagonistic, or have diverse ideological positions, the greater the average size of groups, the more likely it is that stabilising or mediating mechanisms will have developed.

The larger the average size of the group, the greater the opportunity for each or all to obtain publicity and gain the attention of policy makers. If all the chief executives of a city's major teaching hospital issue a press statement announcing that health care standards are falling because of government inaction, they may expect to make front page news. If a dozen community health centres issue the same kind of statement they may not attract any media interest.

After average size of the groups in the network, the next dimension to consider is the number of associations which make up the total population. Are there a few small groups or many? A large number of medium sized groups or a handful? Obviously the communications problems and scope for diversity will increase according to the total number of associations present. In the education field one may distinguish between high schools where a very large number of organisations exist, and the tertiary sector where a comparatively few large universities dominate. High school Principals might be expected to find it more difficult than university Vice-Chancellors to create strong links.

The other dimension of size which matters is the degree of concentration among groups in the network. This is a difficult aspect of size to estimate, since groups often do not share a market or own similar forms of property which could be aggregated and proportioned. Alternative ways to estimate the relative strength of the bigger organisations or more powerful actors is to include the number of committee positions they occupy in representative associations, the proportion of the budget they contribute to joint actions, and the share of total members enrolled in the top groups, as compared to the total enrolment in all groups in the field. Concentration refers to the amount of action conducted by the leaders or top groups. In highly concentrated fields a small number of actors may be seen to control the majority of the resources needed for articulating goals, pressuring governments, preparing submissions or organising demonstrations.

In action and policy formulation, concentrated networks are among the most potent. If they also happen to be from large policy systems such as health or transportation, then the concentrated network will be capable of the most effective forms of participation in policy making. Not everything works to the advantage of the concentrated network, however. Smaller animals are frequently annoyed by the insensitive movements of elephants, and may be tempted to break ranks if alliances with other groups offer advantages. Those outside the network may regard highly concentrated associations as undemocratic or unrepresentative, causing these groups to lose legitimacy among other policy making interests.

Conclusions

Networks may be defined as non-formal methods of system wide learning and regulation. They are based on the shared need to trade information, to create agreed values and to ward off threats. Networks include interest groups and other formal participants and their associations, but extend beyond their ranks and functions. They may be thought of as 'interest group mediation' (Schmitter 1970, Marsh and Rhodes 1992), and as the sociological subsystem which governs a policy sector (Ripley and Franklin 1980).

There is significant debate concerning the exact character of such networks and their likely policy impact. These issues cannot be settled by definitional fiat or normative assertion. They are empirical matters. The analysis presented here has attempted to provide a recognised framework for such an investigation by showing the factors most likely to influence formation and participation. Networks are, therefore, before anything else a system of interacting actors. They are not individuals or formal groups, and nor are they institutions. They are continuing relationships formed to enable private and public actors to influence policy in a particular field or sector.

Actor networks may be composed of participants who share a common status as professionals, clients, employees, traders, service providers, true believers or neighbours. Government action may propel them into co-operation or they may have a social origin which predates the programs they jointly seek to alter or defend. Above all, networks are non-formal mechanisms of communication and action and as such are both powerful and brittle. Understanding policy requires some appreciation of the patterns of network formation and the conditions under which a particular set of such relations may decline and change. This in turn requires an appreciation of the social conflicts and sources of tension which encourage actors to seek allies and supporters.

References

Benson, J. K. (1982) 'A Framework for Policy Analysis' in D. Rogers, D. Witten and Associates, *Interorganisational Coordination*. Ames: Iowa State University Press

Buchanan, James M., and Tullock, Gordon (1962) *The Calculus of Consent: Logical Foundations of Constitutional Democracy*. Ann Arbor: University of Michigan Press

Carney, Shaun (1988) *Australia in Accord*. South Melbourne: Sun Books

Crisp, Mr Justice (1973) *the Melbourne Herald*, 18 March 1969, quoted in A. F. Davies, *Politics as Work*. Melbourne Politics Monographs, May

Davies, A. F. (1973) 'Politics as War', University of Melbourne Monograph

Dluhy, Milan J. (1981) *Changing the System:Political Advocacy for Disadvantaged groups*. Beverly Hills: Sage

Duckett, S. J. (1984) 'Structural Interests and Australian Health Policy', *Social Science and Medicine*. 18 (11): 959–66

Durkheim, Emile (1984) [1893] translated by W. D. Halls, *The Division of Labour in Society*. London

— (1965) [1912] *The Elementary Forms of the Religious Life*. New York: Free Press

Emery, F. E., and Trist, E. L. (1965) 'The Causal Texture of Organisational Environments', *Human Relations* 18(1): 21–31

Friedson, Eliot (1976) 'The Division of Labour as Social Interaction', *Social Problems* February: 304–13, 310

Galbraith, J. K. (1952) *American Capitalism: The Concept of Countervailing Power*. London: Hamish Hamilton

Giddens, Anthony (1979) *Central Problems in Social Theory*. London: Macmillan

Ham, Christopher, and Hill, Michael (1984) *The Policy Making Process in the Modern Capitalist State*. Brighton, Sussex: Wheatsheaf Books

Illich, Ivan (1973) 'The Professions as a Form of Imperialism', *New Society*, 13 September: 633–35

Kelley, E. W. (1989) 'The Evolution of Intermediary Association', Paper delivered to International Political Science Association, Regional Conference, Melbourne, January, p 4

Mcintyre, Stuart, and Mitchell, Richard (eds) (1989) *Foundations of Arbitration*. Melbourne: Oxford University Press

Melucci, Alberto (1980) 'The New Social Movements: A Theoretical Approach', *Theory and Methods* 19: 199–226

— (1985) 'The Symbolic Challenge of Contemporary Movements', *Social Research* 52: 789–816

Mosca, Gaetano (1939) *The Ruling Class*. New York: McGraw Hill

Parsons, Talcott, and Smelser, Neil J. (1956) *Economy and Society: A Study in the Integration of Economic and Social Theory*. London: RKP

Peters, Guy (1986) *American Public Policy*. Basingstoke: Macmillan

Rattigan, A. (1986) *Industry Assistance: The Inside Story*. Melbourne: Melbourne University Press

Sax, Sidney (1984) *A Strife of Interests*. Sydney: Allen and Unwin

Sennett, Richard (1970) *The Uses of Disorder: Personal Identity and City Life*. New York: Vintage Books

Simmel, Georg (1950) *Conflict and the Web of Group Affiliations*. Glencoe: Green Press

Strauss, A. (1978) *Negotiations, Values, Contexts, Processes and Social Order*. London: Jossey Bass

Touraine, Alain (1981) *The Voice and the Eye: An Analysis of Social Movements*. London: Cambridge University Press

— *The Self-Production of Society* (1977) Chicago: University of Chicago Press

Truman, David B. (1958) *The Governmental Process*. New York: Alfred A. Knopf

Verba, Sidney (1961) *Small Groups and Political Behaviour*. Princton, NJ: Princeton University Press

Weber, Max, G. Roth and C. Wittich (eds) (1968) *Economy and Society*. New York: Bedminster Press

6

Participation

Policy systems are built, layer upon layer, circuit after circuit from the contributions of different kinds of actors. The purpose and effect of these contributions is not always the same, however. Policy always involves a dual structure. It has an instrumental dimension in that it produces decisions, programs and other outcomes which actors value. It also has a set of developmental relationships in the way it allows for the communication of moral and ethical norms, and the building of trust and solidarity between actors. Conversely, policy has the potential to produce outcomes which produce anti-values such as dominance, or non-developmental processes which are divisive (Barber 1984, Putnam 1971).

Many academic treatments of participation in policy making unfortunately undervalue the developmental aspect of individual and group action. They tend either to embrace a simple rationalism which assumes that it is only products which count (Elster 1989), or they adopt an élitist political realism which views participation by non-government actors as a source of chaos and overload (Crozier, Huntington and Watanuk 1975).

In this treatment, however, participation is viewed as a primary structure within all policy development and implementation episodes. The central propositions of this framework are that participation describes three types of action: it facilitates rational deliberation; it creates and communicates moral principles, and it expresses personal and group affects and needs. When all three forms of action are available, then participation provides a means for the creation of the social capital from which all central democratic objectives spring, including legitimacy, co-operation and innovation (Bernardy, Boisgoutier and Goyet 1993).

It is because of its role in generating solidarity and the continuous reconciliation of competing values inside the policy system that it is possible to argue as a first principle that all policy making must be based on the widest possible level of participation, consistent with an effective process of decision making. Participation is therefore viewed both as an instrumental and a developmental value. It is judged as a means to improve decision making or implementation, and as a process for binding, improving and securing the group or system. The instrumental value of participation is the observable effect it has upon the improvement of any single decision or plan. The developmental value of participation is the effect it has upon persistent capacities within a system or community. Developmental values include increased knowledge, greater understanding, increased solidarity, trust and sympathy. These two dimensions of participation can perhaps be grasped most effectively through a simple illustration.

Traffic Problems

Suppose the people living in a local neighbourhood experience problems of severe traffic congestion. This brings with it noise, pollution and dangerous accidents. As a result of complaints or their own observations, city officials recognise that action needs to be taken. If the policy task is defined as reducing the number of cars on designated streets in the neighbourhood, an obvious set of solutions will emerge. City engineers will be asked to measure the volume and flow of cars and trucks, and will then prepare options for government decision makers. A choice will then be made based upon the cheapest method for inducing the largest traffic reduction, subject to any other policy goals which decision makers might have. Residents may be invited to comment on the available options and a decision will be made. Some time later the engineers may check the new pattern of traffic flow to make certain that the new policy is working in the manner planned. In this case policy is a question of choosing the right instrument and the choice process itself is based on the selection from known traffic measures—in this case, civil engineering techniques.

An alternative approach might view the issue as part of a continuing set of problems which residents have with their local environment. The invasion of cars and trucks then appears as a problem of domination and the goals of residents are viewed as only partly to do with the measured flow of traffic. If their protests are seen as complaints about lack of control and autonomy to live as they wish, policy making becomes an effort to restore their potency. To achieve this, city officials will wish to engage in continuous communication with residents to find a forum through which they can discuss the permanent problem of establishing boundaries between their local interests and the ever-persistent needs of other external interests. The process of meaningful involvement in policy making will almost certainly change attitudes and demands by residents, officials and other groups. Decisions will not complete this learning process so much as punctuate it with a series of agreements which are open to further amendment.

In the first scenario, policy seeks to limit and complete action and participation is primarily a means to gain clearance for an efficient official decision. In the second scenario the policy making process is a valued transaction in its own right. Whether or not the participation of groups in making policy transforms the process from an instrumental exchange to a developmental relationship will depend upon the way the already established mechanisms for involvement are structured.

Overload

The major objection to developmental participation is its cost. It is argued that any form of participation will increase the demands which individuals and groups make. These excessive demands are then identified as the prime cause of 'overload', a condition in which governments are thought to become exhausted by the many programs they are required to run (Birch 1984, Murray 1984). A related criticism is the one raised by Stigler (1949, 1982), who claims that the involvement of interest groups in policy making results in the 'capture' of government regulatory institutions by the major interests they are established to control. Producer interests such as manufacturers and professions are Stigler's primary target. Although they pretend to oppose government regulatory policy, he says, they actually become its main beneficiaries, through restrictive rules which prevent competition and consumer choice.

Paradoxically we find one important refutation for this argument in the work of Olson (1965) whose masterwork, *The Logic of Collective Action*, is very much an economic view of political participation. Olson's work, however, provides an important distinction between different kinds of benefits available to people in groups. The main economic benefits, or collective goods, are supplemented in the case of large groups with non-economic benefits. Olson uses the case of large trade unions to illustrate the point. If they relied on their ability to secure wage improvements alone, large unions might find it difficult to attract members. So they provide insurance, welfare services and superannuation benefits as a supplement.

One need not accept Olson's exclusive focus on economic priorities in order to see that he is accepting different sources of benefit in participation of this kind. Similarly, one might view the state as facing equally complex problems of gaining the support and participation of their citizens. Simple rules of cost-benefit might suggest that no citizen ought to participate in anything. Indeed, the most rational course of action, following Olson, would be for individual citizens to sell their right to vote to entrepreneurs capable of collecting sufficient support to enact policies. If voting is taken as a developmental activity as well as an instrumental one, however, the benefit derived will include a sense of belonging, fostering of civic responsibility and increased knowledge on the part of ordinary citizens (Putnam 1993).

Whether or not these forms of participation lead to increased demand, overload or capture will surely depend upon the institutions used to facilitate such participation. Rules and rituals establish the expectations which participants have, the range of issues that can legitimately be discussed, and the kinds of bids which will be viewed as possible. Since all systems require some form or participation (at least by élites), the question is not so much one of whether to foster participation, but what kind is appropriate to different public policy issues.

Within each policy system there will tend to be certain basic forms of variation in the opportunities which different types of actors have to participate in policy. These include, among other things, the extent to which policy making is segmented and hierarchical, and the degree to which it is subject to significant time and resource constraints.

Segmented Policy Making

The policy process is always segmented in some manner. Such divisions entail practical distinctions grounded on principles of efficient, timely implementation. They also enact historical patterns of inclusion and exclusion based on class, gender, race and ideology.

In order to make them manageable, or through historical enactment, issues are routinely broken down into smaller fields and these are colonised by particular groups or élites. For instance, most political systems divide the education field into specific institutions for kindergarten, primary, secondary and tertiary teaching. In addition, separate responsibility is allocated for the running of trade and technical training, or for specific occupations such as nurses and apprentices.

This segmentation limits the role which any particular policy actor can have by creating multiple arenas of power and influence. Some influential actors may be able to cross boundaries and give effect to preferences in a number of areas, but this will be difficult for a number of reasons. In some cases rules exist to contain public officials to a specific field. The legislation which establishes their bureau or the ministerial direction setting up their unit may explicitly limit their field of action. Those not formally bound may be informally restricted by the sheer impossibility of following the debates, complexities and rapid value shifts in more than one or two fields. These distinctions support social arrangements such as professionalisation in which teachers and administrators obtain control over certain kinds of decisions and activities.

Some policy systems or issue areas within them are more segmented than others, and the greater the degree of segmentation the more likely it is that decision making will be concentrated among specialists. Highly segmented fields also display a tendency towards interest group dominance. Where a bureaucracy is responsible for a fixed and defined aspect of policy or program delivery dominant interests will find it both possible and economic to form close links and to develop supportive structures of consultation and mediation.

A second important source of variation in the policy process is the degree to which issues and debates are managed hierarchically. Hierarchy refers to the extent and manner of élite control inside and between organisations. In the more severe cases of hierarchical policy making only a handful of Cabinet ministers and public servants have access to information, and authoritative judgements are made without consultation with clients, citizenry and the staff responsible for implementation.

In cases of national security or commercial sensitivity governments may justify this hierarchical control by pointing to the risks of subversion or corruption which premature discovery might entail. The risks of failure in hierarchical processes are, however, also high. They include:

- Overlooking of important alternative strategies;
- Failure to anticipate opposition;
- Inability to generate support;
- Premature sacrifice of policy priorities.

Within this general universe of variables or common elements there are important sub-categories. Not all policy making regimes are the same, but their variations show some common types. A frequent source of distinction is the type of coercion which the form of policy making employs. Another way to view this is to recognise that quite different forms of action are implied and anticipated in policy making. Some aim to alter the individual behaviours of key players, such as citizens, consumers and firms. Others attempt to change the underlying environment in which individuals move. Lowi (1970, 1972) distinguishes these two and sets them alongside the degree or likelihood of coercion. He produces four types of policy leading to four forms of political exchange.

Example: Industry Policy

A useful illustration of the effects of these two dimensions—individual/group and coercive/non-coercive—is industry policy. When Prime Minister Deakin and his supporters introduced New Protectionism in Australia in the early part of this century, they saw themselves as granting benefits to individual firms and to citizens able to enjoy the proceeds of a more sophisticated industrial society.

Since New Protectionism required firms to pass on their good fortune in the form of better wages, employees also gained from this distribution. According to Lowi (1970: 300) this combination of remote forms of coercion and policies designed to alter individual conduct produces a characteristic politics—'strong partisan politics. . .dominated by localised log rolling, non-ideological parties'. A further characteristic of this distributive type is its reliance upon, and encouragement of an institutional process of committee deliberation and parliamentary involvement in the cutting up of cakes and the passing out of privileges. The costs associated with the distributive system are manifold. They are often at the opposite pole from citizen empowerment:

> If we want an open and public politics, we are limited to certain kinds of politics—regardless of whether the manifest goals of these policies

> are fulfilled. Again we would try to avoid distributive policies, because nothing open and democratic can come of them. (Lowi 1972: 308)

The second important industry policy regime is the regulative type. It, too, aims to change individual conduct but the form of intervention by government is now that of immediate coercion. Consumer protection legislation provides a good example: firms must conform to government authorised standards or face the immediate prospect of fines or other penalties. Regulatory politics tend to create common cause among interest groups who then come to dominate policy making. In order to get regulatory measures enacted as legislation, policy makers must build coalitions among these powerful groups. The institutional process, therefore, is marked by devices and arrangements to enable brokering, dealing and trading. At its strongest this process reaches into the realm of corporatist policy making styles (Streeck and Schmitter 1985).

Also characterised as involving direct forms of coercion is Lowi's redistributive regime. Unlike the regulative type, this is aimed not at the individual actor but at the total environment or political economy. Company taxation is a prime case. It is coercive to the extent and degree that it is a precise and inclusive system of rules which will tax contributors and give deductions to beneficiaries. But the focus is upon the whole matrix of relations between all taxpayers and all beneficiaries.

The policy regime in this case is also marked by interest group brokering. Here the government's need is to establish a centralised program which encourages very regular, organised relations with interest groups. These policies also demand strong leadership and determined effort, so it is no surprise to learn that policy making in this quarter is usually driven by the executive branch, by Presidents, Prime Ministers or strong senior ministers.

Lowi's fourth type is called constituent policy and refers to institution building, and activities designed to engender support and commitment. Although less empirically compelling than the other three, it captures those measures which have a 'system maintenance' quality about them. They are certainly non-coercive in the sense that their effect on citizens is highly attenuated, although presumably the stronger forms of propaganda and political 'hard sell' might be considered to be mildly invasive, if not actually coercive.

Constituent policies are associated most obviously with party politics, and include various forms of executive or leadership competition. A good example of this type is electoral reform. The terms under which citizens contest elections or vote for others will tend to create strong party activity. The more use that is made of this type, the more Lowi expects parties themselves to grow in importance (Lowi 1972: 309).

Constraints on Participation

Very few policy development processes are fully resourced, and only a very few employ sufficient time to investigate and present different options. Most emerge as program commitments which command funds insufficient to meet demand. These limits encourage a resort to existing and well-known strategies, and an unwillingness to experiment. They also create incentives for policy makers to promote solutions which have already been tried in other systems. These not only deliver 'short cuts' in the policy development process, but give decision makers useful feedback regarding the policy impacts in 'real world' situations. Seldom is there an opportunity to run trials or pilot programs to compare alternative solutions.

A number of pressures restrict the time likely to be available to those wishing to initiate policy. First, all governments, departments and agencies are subject to the institutional time restrictions imposed by elections, budget cycles and annual reporting and auditing requirements. These generate a number of dynamic effects which may prove very influential. For example, pressures may exist to generate 'shopping lists' of new initiatives in the few months immediately preceding an election or immediately after the appointment of a new Minister or Chief Executive Officer. Second, as we have noted above, Budget preparation, together with the form of budgeting used, will restrict the times at which new initiatives are considered.

Within the agency or group attempting change, time will also be constrained according to work load and priority. Being granted twelve months to draft a new policy on consumer complaints will have considerably less effect if the officers given the job already have charge of a full list of demanding roles. In situations of overload, officials will either not produce at all or, more likely, will limit their proposals to ideas already circulating among dominant policy networks.

Internal government priorities are reflected in such things as the amount of time allocated to tasks, but are not limited to them. The lack of a clear statement by leaders that the policy being developed is of high priority will usually condemn it to oblivion. Indicators of priority include: advance announcement of the intention to develop new policy; allocation of senior staff to the task; commitment of funds, and willingness to link successful outcomes to internal incentive system such as pay, promotion, status, publicity and career development.

Each of these pressures acts as a specific constraint upon the types of actor who may participate in any given process. The further one moves from the élite core of ministers, senior bureaucrats and party leaders towards interest groups and citizen activists, the greater are demands for time and resources to nourish effective participation. Quick decisions generally mean ones based upon very limited consultation, narrow opportunities for the consideration of alternatives, and highly constrained opportunities for developmental action.

Agenda Setting

Because of these kinds of constraints, very few episodes of policy making occur in a climate of calm contemplation. A great deal of the policy developed by governments emerges as a response or reaction to issues over which they have limited control. Little is known of the way the policy agenda is formed, how items come to find their priority listing, nor why some things appear to move rapidly up the agenda and into action, while others languish at the edge of attention.

Kingdon's (1984) study provides one of the few insights into this process. Using a methodology involving élite interviews at regular time intervals, he identified a three-part sequence. In order to progress onto the agenda of government officials, an issue needed to be recognised by key interest groups, to arrive or arise at an opportune time, and to find political support among bureaucrats and politicians. Kingdon viewed this as a rather incoherent process in which circumstance and chance played a major part. Nevertheless, among policy makers and political scientists, there is wide support for the idea that issues do suddenly become 'hot' and that at certain moments a package of ideas and proposals will achieve such wide attention as to become virtually irresistible to decision makers.

Behind this notion lies another, more fundamental conviction: that through the selection of agenda items, élites control the policy making process in modern societies. Sometimes termed the second face of power, the private setting of public agendas is thought to occur when vested interests act positively to have their concerns addressed by public officials, and act negatively (or have others act on their behalf) to have dangerous or potentially subversive issues kept off agendas. Schattschnender's (1960: 68) well-travelled quote captures this point well: 'The definition of the [policy] alternatives is the supreme instrument of power.' But it is Bachrach and Baratz (1963) who developed the theory to its current level of sophistication. In their view the policy agenda became narrow as a result of élite manipulation and socialisation. Key actors such as business leaders were seen to have sufficient influence to keep threatening issues such as the redistribution of wealth off political agendas. In many other cases this was thought not to be necessary, because dominant values would provide an effective filter.

Elite Power

The background to this problem is an important debate among sociologists and political scientists of the 1950s and 60s regarding the definition and measurement of power. Some believed that it was possible to identify power holders by defining the *positions* in society which were likely to grant access and authority over political decisions. Predictably, they chose to identify leaders of organisations which they *presumed* were in some way significant—large corporations, trade unions, civic groups and churches. For sociologists such as Mills (1956), there was no doubt that these people constituted a power élite.

While this view of power had a certain logic, it failed to produce a compelling explanation of the way élites participated in the actual process of policy making. In too many cases a number of the proposed power brokers were absent altogether, or did not get what they wanted.

A second approach, pioneered by Hunter (1953), attempted to locate power holders through a process of nomination. In essence, Hunter was attempting to get the élite to signal its own membership. Again, the approach made good sense. Those close to the action would surely be able to distinguish others who had been decisive or whose interests were regularly taken into account.

This reputational approach came closest to providing a firm foundation for the linking of power and policy problems. It too foundered, however, in the face of some important methodological objections. Hunter's approach might easily be corrupted, it was argued, if those providing the initial nominations were not themselves a central part of the power élite. There were also doubts that élite nominators would understand the difference between the exercise of power and the capacity to express strong opinion. As a result, many of those nominated might be little more than the noisy celebrities and commentators who surround most policy systems.

Dahl's (1961) attempt to rectify this problem succeeded only in creating another, far deeper trap. In developing the 'event analysis' approach, it broke from the 'power-élite' prescription of many positional studies. Instead, it argued that the influence of key individuals in a community tends to be localised to one general issue or area of concern. Political office holders are often excluded from this because their functional roles force them to act across a range of fields. Dahl's methodology was based upon a review of actual decision making in three local government fields: urban redevelopment, education and the selection of political office holders.

Obviously this event analysis had the great virtue of being soundly grounded in empirical work which showed exactly who did what to whom. At some point in their quest all theories of participation in policy making need to establish themselves as credible methods for describing actual decision making episodes. But Dahl's preference for a purely behavioural account (that is, one which relies primarily on the review of events and current tactics of actual participants), has severe limits.

A theory of power and participation which relies so heavily upon an account of the way issues are resolved by formal institutions of government is inadequate on several counts. First, not all issues are contentious. Some may pass through the decision making process without attracting the kind of contest which reveals the relative strengths of combatants. Lack of knowledge, time pressures or want of any real hope of change may lead potential contestants to be absent. Second, the arena of power may not be the political process but the administrative domain. Key issues may be subject to pre-decision bias if those in charge of financial and other bureaucratic support services fail to bring a full and fair set of options forward for political contestants to consider.

Third, groups or interests may be protected if issues likely to threaten their prerogatives are kept off the agendas of decision makers. This second face of power was identified by Bachrach and Baratz (1963) who argued that non-decisions might well reveal power holders mobilising bias through strategies to prevent certain grievances from becoming subjects of policy debate. This suggests that the structuring of the 'rules of the game' may be more important than the actual contest if the rules include devices to weed out issues considered to be too contentious, too radical or too difficult to resolve.

A fourth problem with taking policy contests as primary evidence of the structure of the policy process is that it may omit important historical and contextual influences. The culture and climate of expectations which participants experience and which helps determine the efforts they will make, the choices they will face and the options they will exclude, come from concrete historical understanding. Too simple a reliance upon the current facts of the matter, the body count of policy wins and losses, may obscure from view the effect of changing perspectives borne of previous encounters; stories of such encounters; local information regarding the successes and failures of the past; and eccentric perceptions only explicable in the context of a specific history. The examination of policy episodes must test itself against this tendency to accept the world views and commonsense expectations of both participants, and knowledgeable observers.

Citizen Politics

In all policy systems based on democratic norms the citizen remains the primary source of sovereignty. In practice, citizens adopt different roles and live within distinct, diverse relationships. Each has its own dynamic and is capable of influencing the policy development process in characteristic ways. For example, citizens act as voters, political party members, community activists, advocates of special rights, protesters, campaign workers, work place opinion leaders, professional association members and as members of political audiences at rallies, meetings and for the mass media.

Until recently, the prevailing view of the citizen so far as social science was concerned was that he or she was a case of ignorance and apathy punctuated by occasional outbursts of active prejudice. Rarely did the ordinary citizen meet liberal intellectual standards of civility or rational deliberation. As survey techniques caught on as a prime method in the 1950s, disillusionment grew. Berelson *et al.* (1954) summed up the post-war consensus:

> Our data reveal that certain requirements commonly assumed for the successful operation of democracy are not met by the behavior of the 'average' citizen. . .Many vote without real involvement in the election. . . The citizen is not highly informed on the details of the campaign. . .In any rigorous or narrow sense the voters are not highly rational.

The highly acclaimed study of public involvement in politics produced by Almond and Verba (1963) generalised these findings though a five nation comparison of Britain, Italy, West Germany, Mexico and the United States. Most citizens were not involved in parties, and nor were they active in political associations. Only a minority said they discussed politics frequently, and most agreed that they did not pay attention to media reports of government actions on a regular basis. Clearly this expression of disappointment displays as much about the social scientists' preconceptions as it does about citizen politics. What is defined as a political act or political involvement? Many of those found outside the membership of the major parties may have been active in other ways. Membership of local clubs and cultural groups might have been considered as a means for the creation of important social values. Family, clan and neighbourhood politics might have served as a base from which other politically relevant values and action strategies could develop. And participation could have been understood as a changing historical process, rather than a single census based on conventional measures.

Dalton (1988: 65), for example, shows that protest activities increased in most Western countries during the 1970s and early 80s. Involvement in demonstrations grew to 10 per cent or more in these countries and reached 26 per cent in France during this same time period. In 1974, some 58 per cent of American citizens signed petitions, and by 1981, this had grown to 61 per cent. In Britain, the growth was from 22 to 63 per cent, and in West Germany from 30 up to 46 per cent.

The Dalton study (1988: 71) showed that the form of participation had been changing in most Western societies: 'Participation in citizen-initiated and policy-oriented forms of political activity is increasing. . .Political input is not limited to the issues and institutionalised channels determined by élites.' The increased use being made of direct forms of democracy, protest and community-based action by citizens provides new forms of policy influence, different in scope and method from more traditional channels provided through parties, elections and interest groups.

The state has responded to these changes not by altering its own concepts of sovereignty, or by granting more authority to citizens, but by various strategies of mediation and incorporation. While autocratic governments in some areas persist in trying to restrict the right to demonstrate, in most Western countries it is now accepted that demonstrators may block traffic, take over streets and public parks, conduct debates and blockade buildings without fear of summary arrest or élite retaliation. New codes of conduct for police and city officials guide protagonists towards acceptable forms of protest, and laws are routinely bent and broken so that the higher value of political expression is protected.

Equally, state organisations engage in a wide range of micro-consultations with citizens, each of which may strengthen the link between the public arena and the policy process. Arnstein's (1969) eight level model captures the conditional character of many of these forms of citizen involvement. Although it employs a rather simplistic set of graduations, it alerts analysts of policy making to the fact that the most critical issue in all cases is the extent to which citizen involvement involves some real form of power sharing. Is there some guarantee that participation will influence the outcome of policy making? Does the process give confidence that citizens have the real potential to make a difference?

Figure 6.1 Sherry Arnstein's (1969) Ladder of Citizen Participation

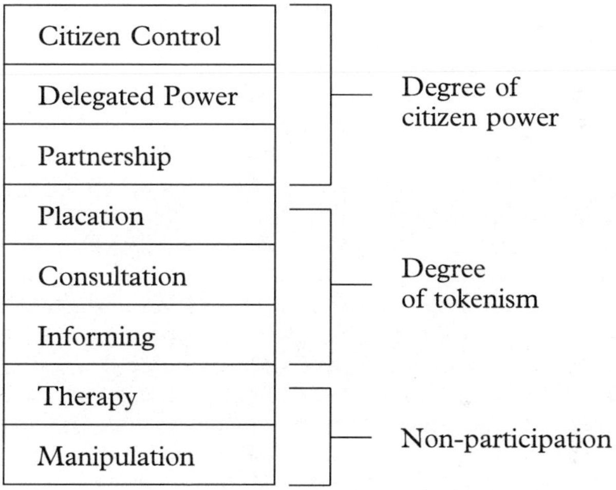

This categorisation was heavily influenced by both the optimism and the frustrations of the 1960 programs of urban renewal and poverty relief in the United States. It provides a clear definition of citizen involvement which puts its emphasis on the re-distribution of political power:

> It is the strategy by which the have-nots join in determining how information is shared, goals and policies are set, tax resources are allocated, programs are operated, and benefits like contracts and patronage are parcelled out. (Arnstein 1969: 216)

Perhaps the most provocative aspect of Arnstein's model is its explicit recognition that public institutions will frequently oppose and subvert participatory systems. The first two rungs on her ladder suggest tokenistic relationships in which citizens are included in policy making only so that the agency can educate them about management goals or pacify them when complaints emerge. Typical examples of this form of participation include one-off public meetings called by officials to explain their goals and objectives, suggestion box strategies for gathering client feedback, and program consultations which do no more to create involvement than placing advertisements in newspapers inviting submissions from the interested public. Arnstein includes in this category the various rubber stamp advisory committees which politicians establish in order to include citizen interests while limiting their real influence. While she may be correct in her assessment of the results achieved by such committees, there is no automatic means to exclude these devices from a review of the potential for involvement in policy making.

The likelihood that officials, élites and other participants may wish to use any form of involvement by citizens as an opportunity to advance their own interests should not cause surprise or disillusionment. This kind of chicanery exists in all policy making, and the higher the stakes, the more incentive there will be for individuals and groups to subvert, derail or dominate avenues of participation. The analyst's task is to identify strengths and weaknesses in alternative strategies of involvement, and then to show how the citizen role might be expanded. Any serious strategy is likely to provoke some form of conflict or dissent—both among citizens and between them and the various agencies of government. The overall objective to increase the relative power of citizens must therefore accept as a first premiss that this process will involve considerable struggle and real costs to élite actors. It is possible to distinguish alternative assumptions about the role of participation by seeing the way the participant is defined in five common typologies used by contemporary policy makers.

1. The Shareholder

In this perspective participation is intended to protect certain residual rights. Shareholders are entitled to accurate reports concerning their property, and they are entitled to know what plans the corporation has for the use of resources in which they have an interest. Participation is designed to give *protection* to the shareholder, but only with respect to certain primary economic rights based on his or role as a contributor, investor or taxpayer. The shareholder might expect to participate through the election of the board of directors, through the attendance at an annual meeting and through the receipt of standard reports and plans. These protective relationships may also include legal rights to claim damages if property rights are ignored. But this is as far as it goes. There is no place for direct involvement in decision making.

2. The Consumer

Consumer participation in policy making is defined by recognition of the rights of the consumer and the incorporation of these into a set of rules designed to both increase knowledge of consumers' needs and provide compensation when these are ignored or undermined.

In the public sector the consumer is defined as the purchaser or user of commodities. He or she is found using hospital services, receiving social service benefits or driving on public highways. The consumer's participation is specific to the service already defined and operated, but unlike the shareholder, consumers' actual needs for service outcomes are considered important, at least within this limited context. Great effort may be expended to study the consumers' attitudes. In the weakest form this may occur through surveys and consumer satisfaction reports which keep consumer opinion confined to individual-by-individual communications. In stronger forms it may include elaborate processes using focus groups, local meetings, neighbourhood consultations and consumer choice experiments. In these latter cases consumers are permitted to work together, to have some influence on the definition of the task being undertaken, and are given assistance to increase their knowledge of the problems and options in their product or service area.

A key determinant of the scope of consumer involvement is the uncertainty or vulnerability of the producer. If those responsible for providing the service already have ample demand and do not lack external credibility, their interest in consumers' preferences will be low. Other pressures may force providers to grant redress to dissatisfied consumers, and the regulatory arm of government may succeed in forcing such service providers to adopt measures to enhance safety and the quality of services. Beyond this, however, the actual participation of the consumer will remain weak. Consumers will be more powerful where providers need detailed knowledge of their preferences in order to win contracts or satisfy those in authority.

3. The Stakeholder

Those individuals or groups who contribute important services essential to producing a program, will often participate in the policy process as quasi-proprietors. Although formally external or subordinate to management, they are so necessary to the success of the policy that they are permitted to join an inner circle who plan and execute public policy. Their status, however, is quite different from that of the ordinary citizen. Their relationship to the state has little to do with shared visions, mutual aid or a generalised system of rights and obligations. The stakeholder has a status which is entirely fixed through strategic exchange.

In the contemporary setting, stakeholders are often business leaders, top professionals and representatives of trade unions. Their veto power grants them opportunities to participate which may be out of proportion to the roles of other groups for whom policy is created.

4. The Community Actor

Participation which takes the form of community action widens the scope and intensity of citizen involvement and is therefore regarded by some observers as the premier type. Through active organisation, the development of group solidarity and the popular expression of preferences, community actors achieve much greater opportunity to understand their own needs and to pressure policy makers to respond. Acting through groups maximises the actor's capacity to gain an audience at court, increases the legitimacy of claims, and yields benefits of its own in the form of recognition, common regard and a sense of belonging.

This form of participation may also be able to range across several issues and is not confined to a reactive posture of protest. Community actors are distinguished from sectional interests to the extent that they allow involvement to be somewhat self-defining, and are not limited by a specific status controlled by others—such as that of consumer, employee or shareholder.

Participation which stems from community activism also has its limits, however. Being largely self-selected, community actors may be unrestrained by rules and unencumbered by the need to be accountable. In the broadest categories of action, such as public demonstrations organised by social movements, key actors may be non-elected, semi-charasmatic figures whose role as interpreters of public opinion can be quite eccentric. A policy making process governed by this form of citizen involvement might well be among the most innovative and adaptive—but it would also be risk-prone and subject to manipulation.

5. The Citizen

In the classical definitions of citizenship, involvement in policy making is viewed as being direct, frequent and decisive. Republican models grant more autonomy to the citizen. The expectation is of variation, difference and a degree of dissent. Next to the community actors' legitimate claim for equal treatment, the citizenship model demands equal autonomy, the right to formulate its own projects—as well as the right to shape the agenda of rulers who regulate the system as a whole.

What is important in this view is the recognition that policy making has severe limits. In addition to creating new obligations and regulations based on majority will or equal representation, policy making must acknowledge the rights of non-participants and those who are under-represented, even in the most exhaustive processes of incorporation.

Citizenship models of participation accept the notion that in most forms of action many individuals will be strangers to each other. This fellowship of strangers requires, therefore, a special mix of tolerance and activism, the boundaries between the two being set by institutions and policy making processes which nourish a flexible form of political learning. For example, the citizenship ideal accepts the need for representation to replace many forms of direct democracy but refuses to allow representatives to break from their obligations to their constituents. In the classical definitions of citizenship, the ordinary citizen is protected from élite dominance by institutions which require accountability, frequent elections, separation of legislative and judicial power, and protection of the living standards of citizens so as to enable effective participation.

Example: Citizen Panels

Enhanced forms of participation which rely upon direct citizen involvement in the policy process are rare. Most forms of involvement require intermediaries such as 'community actors' or 'proprietors' to act on behalf of an undifferentiated public. Governments treat their own forms of citizen involvement with scepticism for precisely this reason—they are a poor indicator of public values and needs. The consumer satisfaction approach, however, is also extremely limited: people have strong tendencies to express acceptance of the status quo in opinion polls. They rightly treat imaginary alternatives as hypothetical and risky. For example, before extensive privatisation of public utilities in Britain in the 1980s, opinion polls showed most people favouring public ownership. Afterwards many were more favourably disposed to private ownership. If successfully implemented they might also favour re-socialisation, even though polls cannot predict this. So consumer satisfaction studies and most opinion polling only measures the services and relationships currently directly experienced.

Citizen panels, policy juries and planning panels are a significant advance on both the actor/proprietor approach and the shareholder/consumer models of participation. Policy juries are modelled on the judicial jury system. They retain the roles of expert advice and impartial adjudication, but focus their effort, not on questions of guilt and innocence, but on a choice of acceptable solutions to community problems. For instance, selected from the electoral roll, jury participants represent others by acting and speaking for themselves—not by attempting to become delegates or stand-ins for others. Participants are paid to attend a series of meetings where they are given information about policy problems, listen to argument from contending interests, and then deliberate. The recommendation of the panel is published and delivered to government decision makers, who must then either act on the proposal or justify ignoring it.

Panels have two practical applications. In a field where attitudes and commitments are not fully or firmly set, citizen panels may be used to develop options which are consistent with the needs and perceptions of ordinary people. Unlike opinion polls, they allow people to become fully informed of technical and ethical issues and they facilitate both learning and compromise. A related but different application is their use in the resolution of conflict. The Jefferson Centre, which has developed the panel technique in the United States, suggests that their approach works well in situations where controversy dogs an issue to the point where an agency feels that to move in one direction or another will bring charges of high-handed, autocratic intervention. Sensitive issues such as sex education in schools, AIDS prevention, abortion, and parole for serious offenders provide scope to use this approach. The methodology of a citizen panel is straightforward:

1. An issue or problem is defined by a public agency, and terms of reference for a panel are prepared;
2. A random sample survey of citizens is conducted to identify current preferences regarding the policy problem. The aim is to discover a 'pool' of potential panel members who are balanced so far as their views are concerned and who 'represent' existing distinctions such as sex, class, race and age;
3. A panel of twelve to twenty members is selected according to the principle that within their number there should be the same balance of views as are currently found in the community;
4. The agency sponsors experts to present background information and to put options before the panel;
5. Preferences and the interests of individuals and groups are acknowledged;
6. Depending on how complicated the problem is, panels meet over a period of weeks, organising themselves around weekends and evening times to maximise participation;
7. Panel members are paid for their time and the sponsoring agency provides child care, translation, literacy and transport support where this is required;
8. A small staff is appointed by the agency and they work through an outside professional facilitator who chairs and manages the panel hearings;
9. By eliminating least favoured options, the panel works towards a final recommendation which all feel able to accept;
10. The final outcome is publicised and the agency is encouraged to provide a timely response.

There are many other possible methods for combining different forms of participation, varying amounts of agency control, and diverse types of interest group involvement. The main elements of this approach can be defined as:

- *Commitment:* Individuals, leaders and groups are educated to support the policies and programs being developed;
- *Resources:* Money, staff and organisation are provided to enable effective involvement;
- *Expertise:* Technically feasible options are widely discussed,

new technologies fully understood, and participants have the means to obtain the facts they require;

- *Strategy:* Participation is part of a larger strategy which aims to act on serious, long-term issues, not just on current crises.

It is possible to see these factors at work in two different case examples. The first is typical of what might be termed prescriptive policy making, where participation is minimal, actors are forced to react defensively, and decisions produce highly antagonistic outcomes. The second shows participation as an integral part of policy and program development. Actors involve themselves in a wide range of initiatives, and policy making authority is shared more generously than in the defensive approach.

Case Study 1: Poor Participation Strategy: National Investment Fund

The Whitlam Labor government's decision in 1973 to establish a National Investment Fund (NIF) provides an instructive example of the risks of attempting to make important policy without involving key actors. The National Investment Fund (NIF) proposal was part of an interventionist strategy adopted by this government. It was in fact a policy which was introduced in tandem with another, the proposal to reform the Australian Industry Development Corporation (AIDC). In essence the AIDC was derived from of capital-welfare measure implemented by the Liberal-Country Party Coalition in 1970. It was a device designed principally to fill finance gaps for Australian firms wanting to expand, but unable to find support in the existing local capital market.

In August 1973, Labor's Overseas Trade Minister, Dr Jim Cairns, introduced into Parliament a Bill to expand the role of the AIDC by lifting the constraints on its borrowing powers, and enabling it to raise funds both locally and overseas. The new Bill was also a measure aimed at widening the scope of the AIDC by permitting it to assist a wider variety of firms. It would be able to buy equity in firms which it proposed to assist, and actively to seek investment opportunities, rather than continuing to wait upon applications from companies in difficulty.

To finance these expanded operations, Cairns proposed to establish the National Investment Fund. The debates which followed tended to regard the two Bills as one, although as it turned out their fates were different. Nor was there any necessary link between them. While short-term considerations encouraged the view that the NIF was to be a finance arm for an expanded AIDC, it could equally have been used for direct government investment in a variety of other public and private sector schemes.

The NIF proposal rested squarely on a view among some Labor leaders and advisers that the resources of large superannuation and endowment insurance offices ought not to remain outside public control. This was thought to be particularly so given the fact that these financial organisations enjoyed substantial government protection through tax and regulatory measures at the federal level. The proposal was that the federal government should require them to contribute to a national fund, which it would administer and from which the insurers and other institutional investors would derive an interest dividend. In addition, Labor argued, there needed to be a means for 'the ordinary Australian to participate in his [sic] country's development'. So the NIF would take individual deposits as well.

> Labor's interest in the investment role of insurance offices was informed by widespread criticism within the labour movement of the prevailing pattern in such investments. In particular, Labor MPs attacked the increasing tendency for such investments to be concentrated in speculative, quick-profit property developments in the commercial districts of capital cities. These ventures were regarded by Labor as 'hedges against inflation by people who have not used the criterion of the Australian national interest when making their investment decisions'. (*CPD* 1974: 1,770)

The NIF would obtain the participation of insurance companies and financial institutions by requiring them to increase their investments in Commonwealth Securities by 10 per cent. It would also seek individual contributions. Cairns argued that the 'purpose of the NIF [was] to provide for the ordinary Australian a readily available chance to invest his [sic] savings into the ownership and development of Australia' (*CPD* 1974: 1,170). Labor advocates of these reforms were happy to consider them in the context of the party's socialist objective, even if the logic was somewhat strained:

> We are not at all reluctant to use the word 'socialism'. The word 'social' is good; so is the word 'socialism'. Indeed, it means that the community itself is involved in these projects. (*CPD* 1974: 1,170)

The immediate response of the business sector was strongly negative. It launched a public campaign against the NIF and AIDC policies. It was far from being a unified or overwhelming attack on Labor's Bills, however. There were differences amongst business leaders and opposition parties.

In the Senate, where the Labor government lacked a majority, the Bills attracted a tepid reaction. The DLP was attracted by the social democratic intent of the measures, but was unable to set aside its distrust of the ALP Left. This resulted in an initiative to refer the two Bills to committee. Almost immediately the façade of a united business condemnation of the policies crumbled. In an attempt to quell rumours that the AIDC was itself opposed to the direction of the reforms, AIDC Director and leading businessman, Sir John Dunlop, went before the Senate committee to make a supportive submission. He argued that he was 'quite simply, not worried at all about backdoor or any other socialisation'. He stated that he believed what Dr Cairns and other members of the government had said, and that socialisation was 'no part of the AIDC's function' (*Sydney Morning Herald*, 2 February 1974).

Dunlop's endorsement brought a strong reaction from his fellow members of the Board of the Bank of New South Wales. They immediately asked him to withdraw his statement of support or resign his place on their board. He resigned. This provided the government with some useful debating points, but it cost them a valuable ally (Indyk 1976).

There were also differences inside the Labor Caucus. These came to light in arguments concerning the work of the Senate select committee. The committee could not, or would not, present a written report on the Bills. This failure reflected the difficulty which it faced in dealing with the issues associated with these Bills. Without a favourable report, the government had little change of securing Senate support. The Committee experienced both ideological and procedural problems. The first were to be expected; the second were unnecessary.

The original membership of the Committee heard a wide variety of submissions, including the one from Dunlop referred to earlier. It developed a sympathy for the government's proposals, but had many reservations. In February 1974, however, the Parliament was prorogued and the Bills lapsed, as did the membership of committees. The two proposals were included in the ALP's election policy speech and were reintroduced into Parliament, in modified form, on 16 July 1974. The government took this opportunity to castigate the Senate for its 'remarkable record of delay' in considering the original proposals.

Labor's own representatives on the committee took exception to these remarks, pointing out that the government had itself contributed substantially to the committee's problems and to its inability to reach agreement. Apparently undeterred, the government pushed ahead with the Bills, and the Senate lived up to its expectation by rejecting the NIF legislation in its entirety.

The NIF proposal was both novel and radical. It aimed to equip the Australian government to become an equity investor in a potentially wide range of private sector ventures, and at the same time to become an influential actor in the capital market. Although reference was made during the debates on these Bills to the possibility that their implementation would mean a decrease in foreign control of the economy, no detailed argument was ever presented concerning the impact of the measures. Without specified benefits it was difficult to identify beneficiaries. This in turn limited the potential for support.

Meanwhile, the method that the government adopted to get its reforms through Parliament again did nothing to generate support, to improve the proposals, or to shield them from attack. There was no public inquiry, so the advantage of a favourable expert report was absent. Also missing was the substantial publicity which an inquiry attracts and which can provide the basis for governments to educate public opinion. Instead, the fate of the reform was allowed to rest with the Senate and its Select Committee. This process favoured those most able to veto proposals. The Senate committee had no brief and no resources to explore the issue of increased public investment in detail. What expertise it managed to develop was allowed to be dissipated by the proroguing of Parliament in February 1974. These conditions favoured well-organised and articulate actors such as banks, insurance companies and other business groups, who could most easily approach committee members with detailed information and argument.

In both these cases, Labor did not provide a means of dealing with its antagonists. It made no effort either to negotiate with them, or to reduce their unity and public credibility. Yet there was evidence at the time that these interests were far from impregnable and were capable of being placated. Had Labor chosen to include interest group participation in some part of the policy formulation process, it might well have found a formula for gaining the active support of at least some key groups.

Further, had it been conscious of its needs, Labor might have done more to generate support among those not already represented in these policy struggles. These, after all, were the groups which these policies were intended to assist.

Case Study 2: Effective Participation: LandCare

One of the most serious environmental problems in all agricultural societies is land degradation. Australia has a major crisis in this area which emerges in the form of salination of agricultural land, soil erosion, depletion of fertility and loss of vegetation. Indicators of the problems are well documented. In Western Australia, for example, it is estimated that 250 square kilometres of agricultural land is being lost annually; in parts of the Murray-Darling Basin groundwater levels are rising by more than 25 centimetres per year, and in the Darling Downs in southern Queensland it is expected that much of the rich topsoil of the upper slopes will have been totally eroded in the next 30 to 50 years (Eckersley 1989: 2, Kellow 1992).

The policy response to this problem has been highly innovative. In essence the federal and state governments have developed participatory programs to involve land users, local community groups, schools and interest groups in a wide range of educational, remedial and strategy development activities. As a result, there are now more than 1,400 LandCare groups in rural and urban Australia. Linking them together is an impressive network of regional, state and national conferences, newsletters, training systems and decision making bodies.

The structure of the LandCare policy originated with the various state and federal government authorities responsible for soil conservation, erosion control and rabbit and noxious weed erradication. Since formal authority for agriculture and land use resides with the states, and since property rights protect individual landholders from strong action by governments, this policy has had to be developed through negotiation, consultation and agreement.

The Commonwealth government became directly involved in 1983 under pressure from the rural lobby, including the National Farmer's Federation (NFF), and from the environmental movement, particularly the Australian Conservation Foundation (ACF). In that year a National Soil Conservation Program was established with the aim of providing support systems to assist other governments and community groups in taking action. Federal funds for this program flowed into these groups to support the development of local strategies for tree planting, erosion control and education. By 1988 this program was distributing $200 to $300 million nationally.

Central to the political success of the federal program was the joint support of the NFF and ACF, who together pressured the government to expand the program and adopt the participatory structure which now characterises it. Phillip Toyne from the ACF and Rick Farley from the NFF made joint submissions to the government in 1988 to secure the extension of the program and to gain special support for a National Landcare Facilitator's project to co-ordinate the state-based efforts of Landcare groups. Both organisations were clearly committed to finding common ground in the otherwise conflictual terrain of environmental politics. LandCare thus provided a welcome opportunity for common action at the policy level. This also provided both groups with an opportunity to improve their public image at a time when vested interests were being accused of undermining the national economic recovery (Kelly 1992).

At the local level LandCare quickly developed a reputation for flexible and effective treatment of land degradation problems. By the end of 1991 there were large numbers of groups in all states and territories and a wide variety of projects were being completed. Government funds were used to part-pay salaries for local organisers, and to supply information and communications needs. Most of the other resources were obtained through state agriculture or conservation departments, from private benefactors or through local fund raising.

Groups developed their own local strategy in response to particular district needs and were aided by expertise provided through government agencies. They engaged in such things as property management, training sessions for farmers, soil monitoring projects, demonstration projects and community programs for revegetation and reclamation. Most of the energy for these activities flowed from volunteer labour secured through LandCare group membership and local community working bees.

The federal program and its state government equivalents also provided funds to train group leaders, to facilitate strategy development by local groups, and to resource the many educational programs being mounted in primary and secondary schools. This resulted in the production of an extensive range of manuals, how-to guides and information packages for local groups. It also supported regional and national meetings and technical sessions at which expert assistance was provided to increase local knowledge of the various soil and vegetation sciences.

In 1991, the federal government revised its program and developed the *Decade of Landcare Plan*, which proposed a further ten years of funding and institutional support for this policy, with the ultimate aim of creating a land use regime which was ecologically sustainable. Accordingly, a new Natural Resources Management

(Financial Assistance) Act was passed in 1992 with significant support from all political parties. Once again the government made clear that it would fund the establishment and support of LandCare groups, but not itself undertake reclamation programs, except on government land.

Undoubtedly the success of the LandCare program has been its strong participatory structure. Local groups made up of farmers, local government officials and other community leaders have been able to harness rural values of self-reliance and independence and to prevent land users recoiling from environmental pressures initiated in the city. Indeed, LandCare has been able to provide a means for farmers to resist criticism that they are responsible for many of the nation's worst environmental problems.

These groups have also succeeded in mobilising other key actors in the rural community, whose participation has legitimised the program in the eyes of both local and national policy makers. Women form a key part of the LandCare movement, as they do in participatory afforestation programs around the world (Cernea 1989). Their traditional strength as community builders in rural Australia, their experience in domestic horticulture, and their extensive familiarity with the working of schools and local government make them key actors in this realm. Similarly, LandCare has been able to bridge the gap between farmers and other local interests such as teachers, health workers and professionals, drawing them into a common concern with local environmental problems. With government funds to help facilitate group formation and to fund the development of local change strategies, the LandCare policy has drawn its strengths from both the policy centre and the periphery.

Criticisms of the program are plentiful, but thus far are rarely deep-rooted. Increased awareness of environmental problems at the local level inevitably leads to greater demands for assistance from government. It has also led to greater pressure on governments to behave as responsible land-users on their own extensive holdings of public land. This increase in demand, however, does not appear to have undermined confidence in the scheme because government funds have been distributed through local groups where the criteria for allocation and the nature of fiscal restraints are well understood. In other words, the program educates potential claimants about the nature of resource constraints and provides them with a means to shape local priorities for spending.

Other criticisms of the program relate to the role of experts and other government officials. In evaluations of the program participants often report frustrations with the overlapping roles of different agencies and delays and bottlenecks in getting officials to play their part (Wegman 1989). The long timelines required by bureaucracies often led to discontent, as did the paperwork needed to secure funding. Campbell (1991: 8) reports that there was often a clash of cultures between the participatory style of local groups and the hierarchical systems employed by bureaucracies. He claims, however, that there has been increased recognition on the part of communities that 'the overwhelming majority of state agency staff working with groups, and those on co-ordination roles in head offices, work extremely long hours in trying circumstances and are completely committed to LandCare'.

Conclusions

Policy making necessarily involves some process of participation in which different interests share in the determination of an outcome. In most cases, however, these actors are already involved in a pre-existing policy system which shapes the values and resources available for negotiation. Participants bring these existing roles and expectations with them to any fresh encounter. The enacting of participatory processes should therefore be seen as a recurrent historical activity rather than a spasmodic or episodic one. Even when the specific action or form of participation is new, the participants bring with them experiences of previous cases, or start from expectations schooled by stories handed down from parents, neighbours and workmates.

Participatory structures therefore rest on their credentials as a practical source of relief or improvement in regard to a given problem. They also depend on the creation of a climate or culture of recognition which grants participants various kinds of non-instrumental benefit. These two issues are present whether actors are conscious of them or not.

Since there is a strong likelihood that each new episode of policy making will contain aspects of previous entanglements, and that decisions made or positions taken will be conditional rather than absolute, some general principles or prudential rules of participation can be described. These cover four major dimensions of policy participation:

- types of negotiation
- nature of conflicts

- knowledge issues
- participatory institutions.

The effectiveness of programs can only be guaranteed by giving all actors an appropriate stake in the continuing work of defining and redefining both the means and the ends of programs. This creates legitimacy and improves knowledge, and thus effectiveness. There are two kinds of risks, however. Wide participation may generate an increased opportunity for vested interests to veto good proposals or to overload governments with increased demands. The costs of participation may also weaken the efficiency of programs by slowing down implementation, causing large numbers of modifications and adjustments, or by delaying decisions for long periods. While some policy systems are prone to participation failure because conflicts are deep and previous encounters have led to deep suspicion and antagonism, most perform well in at least some of the key forms of participation.

Negotiation

Explaining the difference between success and failure therefore begins with the degree of commitment to negotiation. Negotiation is the willingness to trade and compromise some of one's objectives or preferred strategies in order to secure some other valued outcome. Locating the issues which can be negotiated at any one time is therefore a first step to explaining outcomes.

In the first case discussed, the Whitlam government was seen to have an interesting proposal to treat an important problem. It had, however, no strategy of negotiation to manage the inclusion of Senate committee members, interest groups, citizens or consumers. As a result the agenda became dominated by banks, insurance companies and other élites. This loss of control was terminal, because the government had no means of winning back support from key interests because it had presented them with a fixed position, had failed to create a common understanding of the problems being addressed, and had chosen adversarial approaches from the very beginning of the policy process. In a sense the government helped create the form of participation most likely to undermine its own position.

In the second case, the government aimed to draw key actors into the development and implementation stages of policy. Its dependence on community support for the running of the LandCare program meant it could not afford to fail in its bid to win active support. This fact, rather than any special commitment by the sponsoring agency, helps explain the success of the program. When policy makers recognise the functional value of participatory approaches, they quickly find the support structures to make them feasible.

Conflicts

Actors vary in the intensity of their commitment to policy outcomes. This may reflect the nature of their material dependency on others in the policy system, or it may be the result of value or cultural differences. Government policy makers are reluctant to engage in extensive consultation with deeply antagonistic interests for fear that this will give their opponents ammunition. As a general rule, however, the deeper the conflict the more elaborate and extensive the participatory structure needed to harness it. Different forms of conflict imply alternate arrangements for actor participation. Conflict over primary objectives, for example, suggests a need to have all key actors participate in the early stages of research and priority setting. Differences over the means to be used to implement an agreed priority suggest the need for involvement in planning actual programs.

Not all actors will wish to be actively involved. This does not mean that serious conflict does not exist, or that a policy system has achieved high levels of legitimacy in the eyes of key groups such as consumers, suppliers and regulators. Previous encounters may have dissuaded actors from making strong commitment to joint action. Resources may be lacking to mobilise actors. The variety of values and preferences present in the system may not have been subject to the kind of education and consciousness raising which clarifies the possibilities of action.

In the NIF case the potential for conflict was high. This was not because this policy initiative promised severe intrusions into major rights and entitlements, but because previous experiences with this government had led insurers, employers and unions to distrust the value of negotiation. The government felt the same way. Trench warfare therefore became an accepted first response.

In the LandCare case it was certain that environmental conflicts would create a climate of suspicion and hostility between farmers, bureaucrats and ecologists. By focusing attention on their one area of shared concern—degraded farm land—policy makers forced key actors to acknowledge a common problem. State and federal government leaders were quick to create a regime of values which emphasised shared social responsibility for these problems, and this helped prevent a struggle over which group was to be blamed. Co-responsibility was institutionalised in a policy development system which required each group of actors to contribute to fact finding, strategy development and to the provision of resources. This did not remove conflict. Farmers continued to express their antagonism to city-based environmentalists and bureaucrats. Ecologists maintained their criticism of traditional farming techniques. Officials retained their scepticism in regard to volunteer programs. But conflicts were contained and harnessed by a participatory strategy which gave each group of actors a role which was consistent with their primary interest. Farmers kept control over their farming decisions. Environmentalists were given the capacity to shape policy and to recruit volunteer forces in the countryside. Officials retained the key functions of research and dispensing funds.

Knowledge

LandCare also demonstrates how participation may be achieved in a climate of serious conflict, without there having to be an explosion in demand for government funds. Far from becoming budget maximisers, participants appear to adopt the goals and constraints of the policy system they have helped create. The knowledge base of this system was shared in a way which forced each group to focus upon a set of facts which each had helped validate. Participation may actually have helped restrain demand by giving each group of actors a realistic understanding of the resources available for implementing programs.

In the NIF case knowledge was controlled by a few officials who alone determined the definition of the problem and the criteria for selecting solutions. When forced to confront the Senate committee, the government found it difficult even to win the support of its own members because none had been directly involved in studying the problems to which this policy was responding.

Participatory Institutions

Through active design or by neglect, policy makers choose from a wide range of institutional devices allowing participation. They consult advisers, involve party committees, refer issues to parliamentary committees, commission expert studies, set up inquiries, establish bureaucratic committees, create corporatist authorities, conduct opinion surveys or invite community submissions. Each of these institutions grants access to certain kinds of actors.

Advisers generally hold opinions close to those of the officials who employ them and are able to present only a limited range of outside opinions. If they have been recruited from sympathetic constituency groups, they may be able to facilitate informal consultation between governments and these particular interests. The careers and biographies of such people therefore become important in cases where participation is limited to this inner circle.

Party committees create a wider net, but one which is still limited to those with similar backgrounds and outlooks. Parliamentary committees widen the potential for diverse opinion and this generally forces policy makers to answer informed criticism. But such groups rarely have incentives to create new ideas, or to help foster innovation. Participation at this level runs the serious risk of veto and bad publicity. Expert studies and commissions of inquiry are less likely to foster blatant opposition. Experts can be chosen for their known views. This increases the inside credibility of what is decided. It also allows for various other views to be submitted and acknowledged. Policy makers lose a certain amount of control under such circumstances, however. Experts and official inquirers might agree with the general priorities of the government and yet may promote options which governments dislike. This gives them strong incentives to distance themselves from inquiry recommendations and to seek to grant limited authority to such bodies. Inquirers also lack the means to involve actors who are outside the ranks of articulate and well-resourced interest groups. Since the inquiry recommendations will bear their name and be backed by their expertise, strong incentives exist for them to impose their own preferred views and count submissions as no more than useful evidence. Bureaucratic committees display similar strengths and weaknesses. If their advice is to be tendered confidentially they may be more open in their criticism of government policy, but at the cost of providing no outside source of legitimacy for new proposals.

Corporatist structures serve to share power with recognised interest groups such as business, trade unions and the professions. This has major advantages. Policy will then be accepted by these constituencies and there will be strong incentives for powerful groups to reach innovative solutions which reflect the needs of those able to secure the success of the policy. When these interests have a wide base of support in the policy system, this form of participation offers the prospect of real power sharing in the community and may harness a valuable source of new ideas and novel solutions to difficult problems. Such arrangements rarely extend beyond the one or two dominant interests in a policy system, however, and as a result may tend to consolidate existing power blocs and prevailing ideas. Emerging interests are often excluded. Smaller interests frequently lack the status to gain a seat at the table of consultation. Once empowered, these bodies may challenge government authority by building their own public profiles and preferred priorities.

Community-based consultations require elaborate and careful planning in order to reach a wide audience in a meaningful way. Opinion polls are a reliable guide to what the public already knows, but fail to measure the potential for change. Focus groups, citizen panels and other local consultations require higher levels of commitment from government, and may reveal an unwelcome range of views. Bureaucracies typically lack the expertise to run such consultations effectively, and must often be re-organised in advance of any such initiative in order to become competent and open to their benefits. When properly organised, such approaches offer the prospect of far better policy, particularly in regard to implementation issues and emerging problems in the policy system.

The most structured forms of participation are those in which both corporatist and wider community interests are combined with bureaucratic involvement. Several successful cases have been identified, in which policy makers have included key non-government actors in the research stages of policy development (Considine 1992). Using project teams which are resourced by the responsible government agency, representatives of key actor groups are brought together to discuss with government experts the parameters for study.

In the Land Conservation Council (LCC) case in Victoria, the key task of deciding policies for the use of public land have been devolved through a multi-level structure of participatory commitment. The minister shares his or her authority with the Council which is established by Parliament and contains key bureau heads and representatives of landowners and conservationists. The Council employs scientists and policy advisers who study state forests and other public lands in order to assess their best use. This study process involves the establishment of project teams which contain representatives of other government departments, landholder groups and environmentalists. Over a period of months this scientific study proceeds to identify key issues and solutions. Recommendations then pass to the Council which undertakes further public consultation through special meetings, visits to local areas and mass media campaigns. Finally, the minister is presented with a set of recommendations which the government may accept or reject. Because of the extensive process of consultation and mediation of different interests, governments of both political persuasions have adopted the majority of key recommendations even though many have been highly controversial.

In this final case it is possible to see each of the key elements of participation at work: negotiation, conflict, knowledge and institutional structure. Not all cases are as comprehensive for the reasons already suggested. But where actors invest time and commitment to the longer-term objectives of creating knowledgeable and negotiable systems, specific conflicts show a greater inclination towards resolution.

References

Arnstein, Sherry R. (1969) 'A Ladder of Citizen Participation', *AIP Journal*, July: 216–24

Barber, Benjamin (1984) *Strong Democracy: Participatory Politics for a New Age*. Berkeley: University of California Press

Berelson, Bernard, Lazarsfeld, Paul and McPhee, William (1954) *Voting*. Chicago: University of Chicago Press

Bernardy de, Michel, Boisgontier, Pierre and Goyet, Georges (1993) 'The Ecology of Innovation: The Cultural Substratum and Sustainable Development', *International Social Science Journal*. 135, February: 55–66

Birch, Anthony (1989) 'Overload, Ungovernability and Delegitimation: The Theories and the British Case', *British Journal of Political Science* 14: 135–60

Cernea, Michael M. (1989) *User Groups as Producers in Participatory Afforestation Strategies*, World Bank Discussion Paper 70, Washington, DC

Commonwealth Parliamentary Debates (House of Representatives), 8 April 1974: 1,170

Considine, Mark (1992) 'Alternatives to Hierarchy: The Role and Performance of Lateral Structures in Bureaucracies', *Australian Journal of Public Administration*. 51 (3), September: 309–20

Crozier, M., Huntington, S. P. and Watanuk, J. (1975) *The Crisis of Democracy*. New York: New York University Press

Dalton, Russell J. (1988) *Citizen Politics in Western Democracies*. New Jersey: Chatham House

Eckersley, R. (1989) 'Regreening Australia', CSIRO, Occasional Paper 3, June

Elster, Jon (1989) *Nuts and Bolts for the Social Sciences.* Cambridge: Cambridge University Press

Hurford, C.J. (1974) *Commonwealth Parliamentary Debates* (House of Representatives) 8 April: 1,177

Indyk, Martin (1976) 'Establishment and Nouveau Capitalists: Power and Conflict in Big Business', *Australian and New Zealand Journal of Sociology.* 10 (2)

Kellow, Aynsley (1992) *Saline Solution: Policy Dynamics in the Murray-Darling Basin.* Geelong: Deakin University Press

Kelly, Paul (1992) *The End of Certainty.* Sydney: Allen and Unwin

Lowi, Theodore J. (1970) 'Decision-making vs Policy-making: Toward and Antidote for Technocracy', *Public Administration Review* 39, May-June

— 1972 'Four Systems of Policy, Politics and Choice', *Public Administration Review* 32

Murray, Charles (1984) *Losing Ground: American Social Policy 1950–1980.* New York: Basic Books

Offe, Claus (1984) *Contradictions of the Welfare State.* London: Hutchinson

Olson, Mancur (1965) *The Logic of Collective Action.* Cambridge, MA: Harvard University Press

Putnam, Robert D. (1971) 'Studying Elite Political Culture: The Case of Ideology', *American Political Science Review* 65, September: 651–81

— (1993) *Making Democracy Work: Civic Traditions in Modern Italy.* Princeton, New Jersey: Princeton University Press

Stigler, George (1949) *Five Lectures on Economic Problems.* London: Longmans

— (1982) *The Pleasures and Pains of Modern Capitalism,* Occasional Paper 64, London: ILEA

Streeck, W. and Schmitter, P. C. (eds) (1985) *Private Interest Government: Beyond Market and State.* London: Sage

Wegman, J. (1989) 'An Evaluation of Rural Community Participation in the LandCare Program', The Research Network Pty Ltd, Land Protection Division, Department of Conservation and Environment, Victoria

7

Organisation

> The large corporation. . .seems to be a uniquely powerful instrument for carrying on economic activity. This organisational construct has come to embody collective rationality for all industrial and post-industrial societies.
>
> Michael Crozier

Policy actors are organisers. They argue, insist and cajole others in a relentless effort to make their particular worlds different, and to protect their interests. Among the many obstacles they confront along the way are the ingrained resistance of formal organisations and the habituated preferences of official procedure. Understanding organisations and the role of organisational skill is therefore central to explaining resistance and change in policy making.

Effective policy actors are those who read organisational life thoughtfully, and shift attention to places where movement and novelty are most likely to be welcome. How do actors achieve this understanding? What are the dynamics of organisation which inform and support transformation? In this chapter we consider the basic traditions of organisational analysis as they impact upon the policy system. Much of what we observe will be familiar, since policy analysis is a hybrid science based in part on studies of organisational dynamics. Our purpose is to identify certain key problems and strategies within the organisation, and to investigate how these are resolved through an understanding of the architecture of policy systems.

Background: Beyond Stable Systems

As has been demonstrated in earlier chapters, most of the research in the organisation studies field employs metaphors which liken organisations to mechanical or organic systems. The corporation and the local health centre are seen to share a common character. They import energy from their environment, transform it into goods and services, and then export these products to outsiders.

Starting from this simple model analysts then begin to identify different influences upon the system. What shows through is a common set of structural characteristics: the nature of the control system, the type of service, the technology used, the legal framework, and the labour market. Each of these is seen to be capable of shaping the organisation and forcing it to adapt in a characteristic way.

Working from the inside, researchers find ample evidence that the ability of the system to successfully transform energy into products is governed by a set of specific problems such as scale of operation, span of control, communication and performance evaluation. Theorists like Fayol (1925), Gulick (1937) and Urwick (1937) have developed recommendations for owners and managers which express great optimism in regard to the manipulation of these organisational activities.

The traditional Systems approach has provoked several lines of research, and produced different recipes for improvement. In its strictest applications the structure of the organisation is framed in quite rigid, mechanistic terms, and theorists struggle to reduce important relationships to measurable, scientific variables. The organisations most likely to benefit from the findings of this type of research are those which operate under conditions of great regularity and stability. So, for instance, an industrial firm producing a simple product, using a known technology for a defined market, would display many of the features of a fixed, mechanical system. Improvements are therefore associated with energy saving inside the organisation through better supervision, reduced waste and the more timely importation of raw materials and labour. In other words, change becomes a matter of better system engineering inside the organisation. By achieving greater, more exact definition of objectives, and by careful measurement of performance, this stable system is pushed to its most efficient level of achievement.

The principles of organisation which these early systems theorists developed include recommendations that work be divided by function (sales, engineering, accounts etc.), and that tasks be simplified and routinised. Each worker was to be given a specific, measurable task which he or she would then be able to perform with maximum efficiency.

Co-ordination is not seen as a political problem in this case. Instead it is viewed as a technical matter. Each part of the organisation has its allotted goals, and provided tasks are rationally allocated to advance these, each sub-unit plays its part in final success. Management's role is therefore to set goals and allocate tasks. The hierarchical authority of management is universally accepted as the main generalised co-ordination technique required. Managers use a combination of accounting and command to assure that this hierarchical division of tasks functions smoothly.

A summary of the claims of this Classical Management school goes like this: authority is centralised in a hierarchical chain of command. Each level is subordinate to the one above, allowing purpose to be established at the top, and communicated effectively to the bottom. Each supervisor must have a span of control over his or her subordinates which is adequate to fix this communication of purpose, without being so limited as to raise costs. Staff are given stability of employment and a renumeration and promotion system which is governed by clear rules and methods of appeal. The reward system and the actions of supervisors are seen as critical in encouraging compliance and commitment among lower-level employees.

The military served as a model for these early theories, and as the modern standing army developed its elaborate division of labour in the nineteenth century, industrialists took careful note. Here was a system in which a complex mix of staff and machinery could be welded into a purposeful unit, while apparently retaining the flexibility to tackle different kinds of strategic problems on land, sea and in the air.

F. W. Taylor developed this Classical Management theory to its highest levels. The key to his approach was the determination to remove knowledge and discretion from the individual's hands and embed it within the management techniques of the organisation. Using precise measurements of the worker's actions, Taylor's work-study teams identified the least wasteful and most exact work methods. Training and monitoring of the workflow were then directed to ensure that employees and supervisors followed these practices. This relentless pursuit of routine and measurement distinguished Taylorist approaches to organisation and helped institutionalise the idea that owners and senior managers were responsible for the intellectual side of work, while those on the production line were employed as instruments of the organisation, their independent capacity to think and act explicitly repressed. In policy making terms this cut the senior levels of the organisation off from much of the learning which might have occurred at the workface among employees, and between them and the public.

Ford (1924) was one of the most spectacular converts to Taylor's Scientific Management school. The success of his Model-T factories owed much to this form of organisation. He went out of his way to try and legitimise the routine and repetition which Taylorism championed:

> Repetitive labour—the doing of one thing over and over again and always in the same way—is a terrifying prospect to a certain kind of mind. It is terrifying to me. I could not possibly do the same thing day in day out, but to other minds, perhaps I might say to the majority of minds, repetitive operations hold no terrors...To them the ideal job is one where the creative instinct need not be expressed.

Many of these ideas found their way into the public sector, where Weber's (1968) ideal of hierarchy and strict subordination appeared to coincide with the management principles emerging from the industrial sector. The neat division of functions between policy at the top and execution within a subordinated organisation also found favour with politicians and senior bureaucrats wishing to reassure the public that an enlarged bureaucracy held no threat to democracy. In fact, as Perrow (1970) and others have pointed out, the adoption of these ideas often resulted more from ideology than from concern about good practice. Where Taylor's scientific management worked best, which is to say where it increased efficiency without major breakdowns in industrial relations, was in those organisations with simple products and compliant workers. Bureaucratic factories of clerks checking forms and processing standard payments yielded to this approach—but not for long.

Many organisations faced greater complexity and change than this classical organisation theory could manage. Routine was of no value wherever pressures demanded 'one-off' solutions to client problems. Moreover, machine technology quickly replaced much of the manual labour which Taylorism had worked to regularise. Finally, the dramatic rise in the use of technical and professional workers meant that lock-step compliance was no longer likely to be functional. These officials were trained to exercise professional judgement and were employed to do just this whenever complexity required it.

Open Systems Theory

This approach modified the more rigid aspects of Scientific Management without abandoning its top-down approach. From the internally directed efforts of the classical systems tradition came a focus upon work procedure and internal hierarchy. These more sophisticated systems theories saw the organisation as akin to a living organism attempting to adapt to the environment from which it required sustenance. In other words, the external world was at last acknowledged as a critical determinant of the organisation's effectiveness.

In its simple form this 'open system' was described as a circuit of transactions which were not necessarily goal-oriented. More exactly, the main goal was seen in Darwinian terms—good organisations survived, while bad ones did not. The key was found in the movement of energy. Organisations gathered resources (inputs), transformed them using routines and decisions (throughput), and then into products and services (outputs), which attracted support in the form of further resources and legitimacy (feedback). The organisation and its environment were wedded in a process of interdependence.

According to this cybernetic theory, systems of this type would expect to seek equilibrium or stability. They did this by achieving standard or regular relations with their environments, through such devices as joint goal setting, privileged rights for regular clients or customers, vertical and horizontal integration, and dominance or monopoly practices. As Steinbrunner (1974) notes, policy making in these systems was concerned with small behavioural adjustments designed to return the relations with the environment to stability. He quotes the famous example of Ashby's cat, which sits at a distance from the fire which is maximal for warmth and comfort. Should the fire grow too hot or too cool, the cat will make a series of small moves until it has regained the desired balance of warmth and comfort. By keeping its moves small and sequential the cat avoids making matters worse, while giving itself the best possible chance to absorb information regarding the temperature of each new position.

As the environment becomes more complex, Open Systems theory predicts that organisations will undergo greater focus of internal specialisation and differentiation—that is, their internal structure will reflect the external world in its complexity. Simple stable organisations will not survive in complex, turbulent environments. Overly complex organisations will be too expensive and troublesome in straightforward areas which demand simple, regular activities.

One important consequence of this shift to viewing the organisation as a kind of living organism was that some of the simple certainties about the role of the employee were exposed to criticism. Although the head could still be said to rule over the body, none of the organs could be regarded as dispensable. So, without changing the hierarchy of importance, Open Systems theory promoted a reappraisal of the contributions which all subsystems made to the whole's survival. Two consequences followed. First, greater attention was given to incentives aimed at compensating workers for the ill-effects of rountinised labour. The costs of high turnover rates, absenteeism, rule breaking and variable work quality of the more rigid organisation helped justify the new concept of interdependence of management and workforce.

The second change was a shift towards designing the workplace with employee 'needs' in mind. The Human Relations school, initiated by Elton Mayo and first tested at the Hawthorne plant of the American company Western Electric, argued that organisational performance was only partly determined by formal organisational structures. The other determinant was the human side of work. The sub-group of employees working on a specific set of tasks were now viewed as a sub-system in their own right and questions were asked about the conditions under which this organism would function best. Surely their needs and those of the wider organisational environment must also be in equilibrium? For this to be so, greater attention to individual needs would be required. In the 1930s, the expanding field of psychology rose to meet this challenge. Mayo, following Barnard and others developed a new, more complex account of the conditions under which individuals would become committed to contribute to an organisation. Their emphasis was on shifting attention away from management's power to compel, and towards its responsibility to motivate.

Here again the search for equilibrium or system balance was clear. Simon (1947) in his path breaking *Administrative Behaviour* viewed those in control as having a rational inclination to find out what employees wanted, attempting to give as many incentives as might be required to gain employee commitment:

> No matter what the personal objectives of the control group, their decisions will be heavily influenced by the fact that they can attain their objectives through the organisation only if they maintain a positive balance of contributions over inducements, or at least an equilibrium between the two. (Simon 1947)

In its most sympathetic form, this Human Relations tradition was expressed by Herzberg (1966), McGregor (1960) and others as a determination to take account of the individual's full range of needs and desires. Work was viewed as a site for human development, not just a place to earn a living. Theoretically this shift widened the responsibility and the surveillance of management, an increase in effort they were often not equipped to make. Job rotation, job enhancement, reskilling and team-centred control were all strategies which hoped to take account of the individual's hopes for a more interesting work life. Of course, as Morgan (1986) notes, there was also the expectation that happy workers would become more productive employees, and that the extra costs associated with humanising the organisation would be more than rewarded by improved productivity and better quality:

> the much-publicised idea that Volvo workers are happy in their jobs [led to] the idea that perhaps therefore they made better quality cars.
> (Morgan 1986: 42).

The liberation from stultifying bureaucratic work would now involve management intervention to control and organise the personal side of organisational life. Team building, the use of softer control skills by supervisors, improved physical environments and the expectation of greater team spirit embodied a new theory of psychological control.

The Tavistock Institute's attempt to combine elements of the more traditional mechanistic aspects of control with a theory of group psychology produced the Socio-technical Systems school. The key to this account was a new understanding of how change occurred. The established beliefs of people like Lewin (1947) had claimed that systems achieved a steady state, hit periods of upheaval during which this was 'unfrozen' to allow adaptation, then became refrozen at a higher, more sophisticated level. In place of this, Emery and Trist (1965) proposed a model of continuous change. They identified the 'causal texture of the environment' and its interrelation with the internal life of people working in organisations. The Tavistock group studied the reactions of employees to different technical and environmental pressures and employed psychological and psychoanalytic theory to identify points of resistance, repression and the transference of affects such as aggression, envy and greed. The respect given to feelings and relationships took the study of the small group to far greater heights than had been achieved by the earlier psychologists with their transparent interest in pushing motivation buttons. But the extremely local character of much of the socio-technical research left the clear impression that this school saw most of the interesting structural questions as embedded in the psyche, rather than in the sociology of the organisation.

Resource Dependency

The approach which provided the best corrective to both the overly-individualised strategies of the Human Relations group and the excessive functionalism of the classic Systems theories is the Resource Dependence school. For this group the key to understanding organisations was power. Organisational systems were viewed as elaborate mechanisms for creating, converting and sharing power. Organisations provided different conditions under which individuals or groups used power. The key variable was interdependence—that is, where units needed one another for the achievement of some task or outcome, a power relation would inevitably develop. In other words, power is the action or capacity which enabled co-ordinated effort. This is what Lukes (1977) had in mind when he distinguished power from structure. To say a situation is highly structured is to say that the outcome is fixed, set in concrete. Power, on the other hand, comes into play precisely because various outcomes will be impossible unless someone or some group intervenes to prod the organisation in the desired direction.

According to the Resource Dependence perspective, the chief source of vulnerability which caused the members of the organisation to yield to the power of others was their dependence upon the flow of resources from elsewhere. Whenever one unit required information, money or authority from another, it was subject to influence. The pattern of transactions which then took place would establish a power relation which would shape outcomes. Like many of those who work in this field, Pfeffer and Salancik (1978) did much of their theorising in regard to politics between organisations. When organisations interacted there was seldom a clear line of command to decide contentious issues. Suppliers were required to negotiate with customer organisations, and health and education ministries had to be cajoled into co-operating in a joint service. The thing which would always bind them was their common need to acquire and protect their resource base. Only when official goals coincided with this reality would activity match the expectations of dominant policy makers.

This approach offers a politically sensitive analysis inside and between organisations. From dependence grows dominance. As Hawley (1950) notes: 'Dominance attaches to the unit that controls the conditions necessary to the functioning of other units.' Pfeffer and Salancik (1978: 44) give a list of conditions under which an organisation will comply with attempts made to control it. These include: awareness of the demand being made; the importance of resources; lack of an easy alternative source of these resources; lack of a retaliatory resource move available to the organisation; capacity to observe whether compliance has occurred; and the technical and legal possibility that the organisation can comply. Other assumptions are made regarding the consistency of the demands made by different actors wishing to control the organisation, but these are of less importance than the central dynamic of dependence. The key to this relation is that the organisation will be controlled to the degree that others are able to make offers which cannot be refused.

Benson (1977) distinguishes the explicitly political consequences of the Resource Dependence group's strategy by setting it alongside the Classical and Human Relations approaches. These two are viewed as being concerned with goal achievement and need fulfilment, the first referring to the mental/manual distinction discussed above, and the second pertaining to the incorporation of individual needs into corporate strategy, as part of the work humanisation strategies.

According to this, much of what occurs in the organisation can be understood as a result of goal pursuit and/or need fulfilment. This view has been coupled with a methodological stance which accepts the conventionally understood components of the organisation as scientific categories. The combination has uncritically accepted existing organisational arrangements and adapted itself to the interests of administrative élites.

The recognition that organisations contain diverse interests does not in itself threaten earlier approaches. After all, much of the purpose of Classical and revised approaches to Systems theory was to find strategies to bind the whole together, a project which would neither be intellectually interesting nor functionally necessary if the whole were more or less compliant. The great problem of these theories, however, was their failure to examine the social basis of conflicts, and to recognise an abiding tension between them and any top-down view of organisational methods. This was especially true in the public sector, where democratic norms provide the justification of the ultimate purpose of organisations.

Example: Gender

Feminists have been among the first to see how much work must go into sustaining the organisation's ordering systems, and how great the tension must be between these objectives and the wider social aspirations and rights of citizens. Women employees, including women managers, cannot abandon their difference, and as a result find themselves excluded by the normal incentive systems used to structure the organisation. For instance, Game and Pringle (1983) studied six work processes and identified characteristic gender 'rules'. For example, they noticed that when women worked on machines they were far more likely to involve stationary, repetitive tasks which created few opportunities for status or influence. Male workers were more likely to be found operating larger, more flexible machines and were 'able to represent the power of the machine as theirs and experience themselves as having "technical" expertise'.

Once raised in the open, this question of difference changed the ground rules for organisation theory. As Silverman argued, 'it would be more fruitful to analyse organisations in terms of the different ends of their members and of their capacity to impose these ends on others—it suggests an analysis in terms of power and authority'. But difference in itself is not enough to challenge the traditional perspectives for difference, which may simply be cast as the pluralism which allows there to be alternative methods for achieving a single goal. The resource dependence perspective claims more than difference. It identities a key role for wider social conflicts. In other words it cannot be assumed that all those involved in the organisation will want the same things; nor will they have similar capacities to achieve full participation. The same policy or program may be driven by people with opposing values. These contests will then become decisive in struggles over scarce resources.

Power

The resources which are important in providing opportunities for power and dependence will vary from place to place, and may change over time. Analysis therefore needs to be specific to the actors under examination. Nevertheless, Pfeffer (1992: 29) and others have identified some common sites. The ability to influence the setting of objectives is critical. It is not for nothing that the management literature is emphatic in its attention to 'the importance of consistency in purpose: having the calendars, the language, what gets measured, and what gets talked about—all focus on what the organisation is trying to achieve'. Power is seen to accrue to those in authority who also have accurate information, access to networks which bind them to other key players, and those able to demand consultation before decisions are taken.

The actions and manoeuvres which Pfeffer and others recommend suggest that power is nevertheless available for use by all those in the organisation, even though they do not have the same resources. It is possible to construct a scenario in which an organisation or sub-unit is totally dependent and therefore without power—but this cannot define most reality. Even the most autocratic managers or leaders require co-operation from their subordinates and become vulnerable if quality falls or external criteria are not met.

Giddens (1979) describes this condition as one whereby 'all power relations, or relations of autonomy and dependence, are reciprocal: however wide the asymmetrical distribution of resources involved, all power relations manifest autonomy and dependence "in both directions"'.

This corrective to the view of organisational power which sees those at the top as the only potent players considerably complicates the analytical task. Each individual and each sub-unit are seen to experience at least three kinds of conditions: those where they are dependent, those where they are autonomous, and those where they exercise control. But these are not found only in separate transactions: 'X is dependent upon A, autonomous in relation to B, and exercises control over C.' Instead, all three conditions are possible and likely in regard to all X's relations with A, B and C.

This integration of each organisational actor, whether an individual or group, to identify the web of dependence and control, will produce situations in which the balance of relations does not predict a certain outcome. Control then will be worked out in the cut and thrust of battle, however brutal or genteel its manifestation. The only other clues which theorists provide is that the strategies available to players will result both from their own quota of strengths and weaknesses, and from their present position on the playing field.

Positional analysis suggests that the particular configuration of other actors will often change the relative power of a single player. Indeed, it will most likely change everyone's options. In his discussion of Foucault's work, Hoy (1986) points out that this view of power looks to the 'field of possible actions in which the action occurs. . .Power is not, Foucault says, like two adversaries confronting each other; it is comparable to "government" in a broad sense, where to govern means "to structure the field of the eventual actions of others".' This might be compared to a game of chess. It is important to understand the individual authority of each piece and the ranking of each in regard to the others. But this is not enough to explain an actual game and its outcome. For that, one has to see how particular clusters of pieces enhance or diminish the powers of one another, and of their whole colour.

The Class and Control school informs this analysis by keeping the emphasis upon difference and conflict, but extending the organisational boundary. Many of the theorists who work within the Resource-dependency school also accept assumptions from this tradition. Often the differences are more in relation to the focus of research rather than in underlying approach. Benson, for example, is primarily interested in the way organisations are linked together, and he recognises 'powerful forces which tend to occasion the reproduction of existing social structure'. He defines the dynamic of this process, however, in a characteristic way, as 'a cluster of complex organisations connected to each other by resource dependencies and distinguished from other clusters or complexes by breaks in the structure of resource dependencies'.

Habermas (1976) and Offe (1985) extend this argument into a dual linkage. Functional ties between the organisation and the society around it are recognised, but so too are certain value-based connections. The functional issues are relatively straightforward: organisations insist upon class divisions in the workplace between managers and line staff, blue and white collar jobs, male and female work, and so on. This set of distinctions both reflects and reproduces society's overall system of stratification.

But beyond this, Habermas (1976) claims that the organisation is a key site for society to express the legitimising values which will motivate people to contribute, or at least to comply. Capitalist society's development of the achievement drive is seen to be at the heart of this motive. Learning to achieve according to the rules of organisational progress amounts to learning society's definition of itself. Organisational norms or rules stand in for general or moral standards of achievement and the 'ladder of success' can then be generalised as a means for placing everyone. The status of the manager is not determined by what he or she is known to be able to do, but by where these people are in a large organisation's authoritative chain-of-being. Life inside society's large institutions therefore carries the bulk of the load so far as the creation of social peace is concerned. According to Offe (1985), this is because the organisation employs labour, and is thus a key player in modern society's most important institution— the labour market.

In capitalist societies, this market is the main institutional solution to a dual allocative problem that must be solved in all societies. On the one hand, the production system must be supplied with the labour inputs it requires. On the other, labour power must be provided with monetary (income) and social (status) means of subsistence.

The organisation, through the agency of the employer, faces certain rational alternatives when entering the labour market in search of employees. Within the options available they will tend to favour some workers over others and in so doing will contribute to structured inequality. For instance, hiring involves certain fixed costs and 'investments' in selection, induction, training, and so on. Employees will be seen as more or less 'available' according to how many of these investment costs they generate and how long they will be willing to stay, thus enabling the organisation to recoup its investment and avoid the need for new recrutiment. In this way, Offe (1985: 39) argues, the organisation ranks employees and fits them to jobs: 'the young, those just commencing an occupation, (younger) women, foreigners, immigrant labour and older employees are treated preferentially as "candidates" for those jobs for which the recruiting enterprise is not dependent on the hired labour power completing costly processes of familiarisation and qualification'.

Just as important is the boundary between those in work and those outside this labour market. Here again the capacity of organisations to replace labour with machines, to move out of labour-intensive work, and to cast off whole parts of their former profile, sends shock waves through the whole society. This threat to the organising power of the labour market is viewed by many within this perspective as being the portent of an entirely new social structure, the form of which they do not yet identify. The sociology of this new form is closely interwoven, however, with the formative role of organisations, in particular their changed attitudes to labour, new hiring and contract arrangements, decoupling their own internal sub-systems to form semi-privatised units, and new forms of management. All these are implicated in changing social relations.

Hirschhorn (1974) sees the change in work as precipitating an entirely new life process. The industrial model is one based on the male breadwinner entering the workforce through employment at the lower rungs of a large organisation, working and training his way into the middle layers, marrying and buying a house, then raising a family and working to retirement. This linear life course was made possible by labour market and employment patterns which are disappearing. The junior message boy or mail clerk who had hopes of working his way up has been replaced by a kid on a bike carrying messages on a fee-for-service basis, with no expectation of the entitlements of organisational membership.

With this decline of career paths and the breakup of traditional job categories, two new forms of diversity dominate the organisation's horizon. First, the increased traffic between work and non-work categories changes expectations about tenure, promotion, willingness to train etc. Second, without predictable, ingrained rules about work paths, without visible production lines and outputs, management problems intensify. Management and managerialism then become the preoccupation of the organisation and of the network or sector to which it belongs.

Organisation and Policy Making

The important differences between these organisational perspectives or schools of thought have dramatic consequences for policy development in the public sector. First, they suggest radical differences regarding the definition of the actors to be included in policy analysis. For instance, in the Classical Systems writers' view the organisation is an instrument, not a thinking device. Owners or senior managers do the brain work and have all legitimate authority over goal setting. In public models, the minister has been substituted for the owner, and managers have often been viewed as being equivalent to senior public servants. Second, these frameworks each have their own views of why it is that the organisation engages in policy making. For some it is an adaption of management goals. For others it is a coalition of group and personal needs, and for still others, policy expresses a power relation based upon the control of resources. Third, the strategies for change which flow from each school are quite different. Classical theory is preoccupied with clear purpose and straight lines of control. Human Relations seeks greater personal investment in work as a means to raise productivity. The power theories aim at negotiated systems of resource control.

The great temptation in classifications of this kind is to fail to see organisation theory as an unfolding discourse, and instead make each theory a separate box or category. Apart from missing the point about the dialogue and contest between the perspectives, the real problem with such boxes is that they promote isolation and amnesia. Having seen the differences in their assumptions and interests, it is also necessary to view the practical achievements of these researchers. This may now be achieved by analysing the common problems facing the program delivery agency and its clients. We will see the same tensions evident at this level as were obvious in the comparisons of different analytical traditions. Now, however, we may see the direct policy consequences of problems to do with control, goals, conflicting interests and motivation.

Organisation Structure

How many people does it take to run an effective public employment agency? How should the flow of work be organised? What kind of specialisation works best? If there are large numbers of employees in the agency, how are they to be supervised? What support services will they require?

It is a long-standing contradiction in organisational design that in order to improve effectiveness, tasks are divided, and immediately this happens must then be re-united, or grouped. A constant struggle to divide and join characterises all attempts at adaptation to new issues. And however they are divided and joined, each part of the organisation must be co-ordinated and steered.

Modern organisations tend to divide their tasks into three broad types: management, line and support. Mintzberg's model described in Figure 7.1 defines these roles. Management is located in the core, implementation is found in the line, and other services are defined as support and technostructure. As the preceding discussion has indicated, there is much controversy surrounding the placement of people and jobs into each of these three categories, and the degree of flexibility between them depends upon the nature of the work, the ideology of those in control and the composition and bargaining power of the labour force.

Management is the group of authority holders whose official job it is to direct the organisation and make sure that it functions effectively. This might involve setting goals or interpreting those set by others such as governments, owners or shareholders. Whether reasonable or not, management is held responsible for the knitting together of the efforts of others to ensure a satisfactory outcome. The metaphor of the ship's captain is often invoked in these situations. Others run the engines, operate the navigation gear or gather information about weather and winds, but it is the captain's job to fit this into a strategy for reaching port. More will be said about this issue in Chapter 9. For now it is necessary only to acknowledge that all organisations, even highly democratic ones, require a strategy setting system.

The 'line' is the main operational arm of an organisation. In

Figure 7.1 Mintzberg's Five Basic Parts of the Organisation

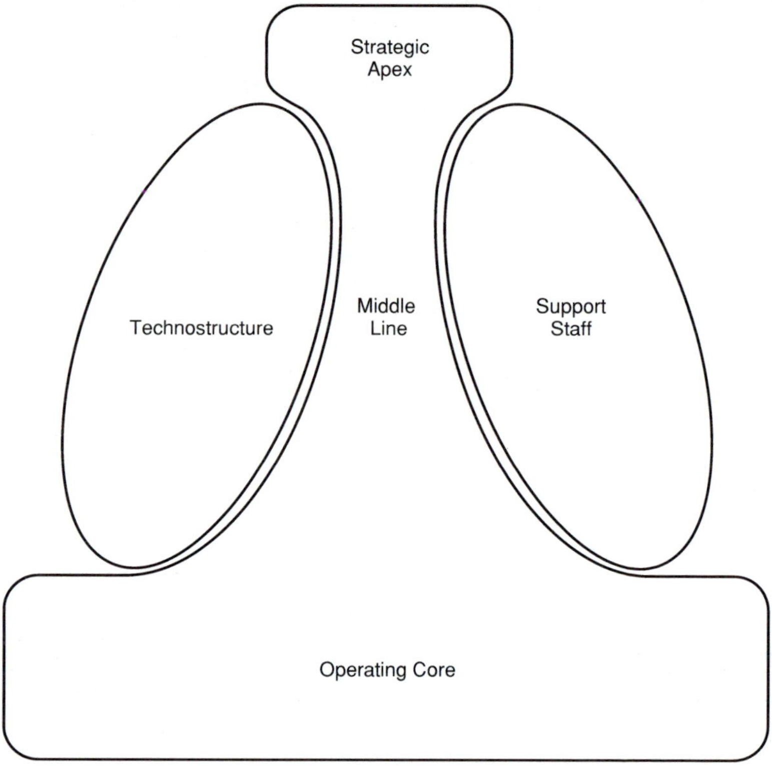

Source: Henry Mintzberg (1983) *Structure in Fives: Designing Effective Organisations*. Englewood Cliffs, NJ: Prentice-Hall

factories the line is an automated platform along which semi-completed products flow. In non-industrial organisations such as those commonly found in the public sector, it may be more difficult to identify the main line of work. In most cases the easiest way to visualise it is to draw a line backwards from the client or customer to head office. Those at the front office give direct service. Next to them stand co-workers who add extra services as required. These may include librarians, counsellors or sports instructors in the case of a school. Of course there may be many layers of staff involved in the line, not all of them having direct contact with the client. Some supply the paperwork or bring equipment. A simple definition of the line is one which describes it as the place where raw materials are turned into services.

The support function includes all those tasks which assist, but do not define, the main work of the organisation. In a hospital, for instance, the accounts office and the cafeteria help staff care for patients, but do not have a say in whether or not Mr Jones is given treatment for his heart or his haemorrhoids. In some accounts the support function is defined as 'staff' and is distinguished from the 'line' in class terms, with the former being seen as a superior group in terms of education, pay and status. This is clearly a direct result of the time when all these divisions (and indeed the language itself) were based upon factory demarcations.

Minzberg (1983) suggests that support tasks need to be further divided into what he calls support and technostructure. In the latter case he argues that there is a basic difference between the work of the accounts branch and, say, the computer office. In the technostructure, he says, will be found specialists who measure, design and plan the work of the line. This certainly appears to distinguish them from groups such as kitchen staff or cleaners. The form of support, however, will vary in different places, and will undoubtedly change over time.

The proximity of the support roles to the main line will generally be determined by the strategy being used to deal with external pressures. The same cleaning and maintenance unit may be peripheral one year and vital the next if, for example, it becomes part of a plan to raise revenue or assist patients cope with life back home.

The different types of support role need to be identified in each case. This can be summarised by the question asked of those in the line: whose assistance will they need in order to get the job done? A series of concentric circles then appear. Close to the workface are the immediately necessary staff who introduce new employees, put them on the payroll and secure the buildings and offices where work goes on. Next come technical people who provide telephones, computers, filing systems and the means to measure and plan the work. Finally, the analysis reaches the planners and system designers who, from time to time, assist in the transformation of the work process into a new stage. There is no way in which occupations can be clearly divided between these three fields, despite the hangover from the days of line/staff, or blue collar/white collar distinctions. An engineer might be either manager, line or support, and the same is true of clerks, cleaners and computer operators.

These three types nevertheless constitute the first part of the division of labour. Within each field there will invariably be a wide range of further specialisations which, like these three, are an attempt to put into practice Adam Smith's famous parable of the pins:

> One man draws the wire, another straightens it, a third cuts it, a fourth points it, a fifth grinds it at the top for receiving the head; to make the head requires two or three distinct operations; to put it on is a particular business, to whiten the pins is another; it is even a trade by itself to put them into the papers...(by this method ten men are able to produce 4800 pins per day)...But if they had all wrought separately and independently, and without any of them having been educated to this particular business, they certainly could not each of them have made twenty, perhaps not one pin in a day.

Although this parable suggests unlimited efficiency gains to be had from specialisation, it should again be noted that the dominant image is that of the factory where a production line orders and controls the flow of work. In addition to the human costs of this kind of repetitious work, the organisation faces strict limits on the extent to which it employs these kinds of divisions.

Woodward (1965) showed that a combination of task and technology usually set the pattern for particular forms of specialisation. 'Process' production is exemplified by a pin factory or a car assembly plant. Many copies of a single type are produced, and thus a standard work system is employed. The existence of a special tool required for a task being done at a given stage of the job often suggests the means for specialisation. 'Batch' production describes the activities of a workshop or training centre. Here, the work system is developed for a limited number of cases, has to be put in place quickly, then disassembled in readiness for the next contract. Staff need to be skilled at a greater number of tasks, although a standard repertoire will often tend to emerge. 'Unit' production is described as hand-made or one-off jobs such as might be done by a tailor making individual suits.

There are two important dimensions of Woodward's types. Task specialisation is easily recognised. The nature of the product drives the internal economy of effort, and leads to an elaborate division of labour. There is another level implied in the typology, however—a form of problem solving. In the process system most decisions are built into the production technology. Support staff and managers have already made all the key decisions. This is an effective arrangement as long as the organisation does not need to learn anything new from the line staff. The moment the environment demands new kinds of pins, or pins which are tailor-made, this approach becomes rigid and error-prone.

Batch production is more flexible but is apt to be frantic and stressful. A great deal depends upon there being well trained staff who can cope with change. Effective relations within the work group are critical, and this form is more sensitive to tensions between managers and staff. Unit production is capable of extremely high levels of performance and the rapid implementation of new information, since each case is treated as special. Every patient receiving surgery receives their own unique application of the skills of the team. By definition, there are few economies of scale and less room for the dividing up of tasks. Workers require extensive autonomy, and other strategies for co-ordination (such as training) are required.

The explanation of organisational divisions therefore requires critical analysis of: the nature of the product or program being produced; the technology or methods available for producing it; the sequence of possible steps; the knowledge needed at each stage; and the learning and problem solving requirements of each individual involved. For the policy maker these distinctions represent opportunities to order the organisation around program goals, and to create information and expertise on ways to improve services.

Grouping Tasks into Divisions

Having in mind that the organisation is divided by management, line and staff, it is now possible to attend to the other key device for structuring work—the grouping of tasks. Three main forms of grouping are seen in modern organisations: function, program and location.

A fourth type, the matrix design, combines elements from the others. Functional divisions were typical of most large organisations until the 1970s. The definition of functions varied widely, but the intention was the same: collect together all those responsible for tasks of a similar type. Thus all bookkeeping was done by the accounts branch, research had its own unit, marketing stood separately, and the line tasks were run by a division often called operations. The strength of this design was that by putting specialists together, the organisation maximised their support system, their opportunities for specialist promotion, and their technical performance. The downside was that they might develop their own interests and standards of performance which could fail to mesh with those of other divisions. Co-ordination then required elaborate and expensive extra effort.

The program grouping is often also referred to in the management literature as the product form and the activity centre model. A wide variety of designs are found in both private and public sector organisations. Here the emphasis is upon common outputs. In other words, the structure divides the organisation according to its relations with the outside world.

As Lorsch (1970) argues: 'different environments require varying degrees of differentiation among organisational units. Basically, the extent of organisational differentiation depends upon the certainty or uncertainty of the environment and its diversity or homogeneity.'

All those involved in a major hospital's geriatric care service, for example, might be grouped under a single division including surgeons, physicians, physiotherapists, nurses, social workers and administrators. They will be exclusively dedicated to a unique set of services for older patients, and will have minimal contact with other workers of the same type dedicated to other activities.

This design will maximise specialist knowledge of a class of services, and lift performance in these areas. Programs will also be more visible, both inside and outside the organisation. This model will also facilitate clear recording, pricing and accounting for each program or service—a very popular goal among senior managers and funding agencies. The problems with the program grouping are of two main types. First, taking specialists away from their own group and locating them with multi-disciplinary, multi-task groups will lower their technical performance in the medium and long term. Second, there will be less flexibility when pressure of work requires extra effort or when slow periods release potential effort. Separate program divisions, each employing their own social worker, will find it difficult to share these welfare resources under such circumstances—a facility made much easier by the functional design.

The locational grouping is almost self-explanatory. In order to deliver services to a widely dispersed population or take advantage of local resource supplies, most large organisations will have several dispersed offices. A state Department of Conservation will typically have a head office in the capital and regional offices at strategic intervals across the state. Within each regional office will be found a scaled-down version of the whole organisation. Each program area will be represented and each specialisation, and a local management hierarchy will take change of control and co-ordination functions.

Varying degrees of autonomy are found in these locational divisions. No fixed formula exists to predict why this might be so. Management ideology, tradition and local conditions influence the amount of discretion available. Generally speaking, each program delivered by the local office has a standard form which has been designed or sanctioned at head office. Resources are also likely to have been allocated to the local unit on the basis of either a fixed budget or a per-client-per-service formula. However, since the major resource of most organisations is their staff, local managers generally retain some scope to use any slack staff time to emphasise local issues, and even run local projects.

The matrix design combines aspects of the functional and program model and, in some cases, can also accommodate regional divisions. In essence the matrix is a dual management structure devised to keep the advantages of functional specialisation and maximise the virtues of interdisciplinary teams. Typically, the organisation will have a normal functional structure running from senior management through to line operators. Cutting across this will be a series of cross-divisional work groups which have their own managers who answer to a senior project executive. At the workface this will mean that employees have two kinds of work to do in a normal week. They will perform the tasks assigned by their functional manager and will also participate in work required for their joint project.

Increased flexibility results from this arrangement, with staff being able to maintain a supportive functional base, yet travel out to commitments elsewhere in the organisation. The parochialism of the functional design is partly overcome by the existence of a separate management system with the authority needed to keep attention focused on the project work. Clearly this structure is best suited to organisations with both operational and policy development obligations. It is therefore the design which is favoured for highly turbulent environments.

The problems encountered by matrix structures relate to the costs of duplicating the management structure. A special internal value system is needed to make this work, since many issues will have to be solved by negotiation rather than the simple issuing of instructions. Establishing this culture will require extra training and support, particularly for employees habituated to more traditional systems.

Co-ordinating the Effort

In a small democratic group, co-ordination is achieved through face-to-face communication at a daily or weekly meeting. Plans are made, decisions taken and roles allocated. In larger, more traditional organisations, co-ordinated effort requires a six-fold system of carrots and sticks. These are hierarchy, technology, training, planning, budgeting and rewarding.

Hierarchy is the most common device for co-ordination. Management is charged with the job of pooling every effort and making sure that waste is minimised. This is achieved through special meetings, memos and direct instructions. How many staff can a manager co-ordinate in this way? This question appears and reappears in every text and in virtually every consultancy report commissioned to improve efficiency. In the language of organisational analysis this is the problem of 'span of control'.

Two types of organisation emerge in studies of the manager's span of control—the long/tall and the short/fat. When managers have ten or more people reporting directly to them, the organisation will require fewer layers of supervision and the distance from top to bottom will be short. Much recent debate in the public sector has argued that this structure is 'flatter' in two respects. First, with fewer managers, there will be less costly intervention in the work process. Second, operators will have better jobs with more responsibility for their work. This suggests greater democracy and increased efficiency, all in one structure.

The research on so-called flatter structures, however, indicates that they often involve greater direct supervision, more routine tasks and less autonomy. These organisations are generally more centralised. In the tall structure the manager is responsible for four to six staff, and it is generally thought that this increases decentralisation by making local managers responsible for more of the work.

In fact, as Perrow (1986) has argued, the span of control issue cannot be dealt with independently of the other forms of co-ordination. If employees follow strict codes of practice covering most tasks, spans of control can be very wide, yet employees will have little autonomy. In units with only three or four staff, there many be great autonomy if the staff are professionals with a well-developed understanding of their work.

The form of hierarchy must therefore be considered alongside training and technology—where technology refers to standard methods, not just machines. Training builds a form of standardisation into employees' intellectual standards, and this allows the manager to stand back from the line, intervening only to check quality and resolve problems. A technology such as a filing system does much the same job. Computer systems may ask standard questions of employees, require completion of a fixed repertoire of tasks, and measure the time and resources spent on each client or transaction. This greatly reduces the need for manager involvement.

The organisation's planning procedures also assist with co-ordination by providing a means for diverse functions to express and negotiate the terms of future co-operation. The need for planning is driven by the form of structural division used, which in turn expresses the relationship between the organisation and its environment. Functional structures trying to cope with turbulent environments often engage in exhaustive planning procedures. Frequently these become the responsibility of a special planning branch, which gathers submissions, writes scenarios and publishes plans and planning updates on a near-continuous basis. Matrix structures, on the other hand, incorporate planning into the work of every division. All that is required is a means to set project priorities from time to time. In between these limiting cases are numerous variations, all driven by the demands of structure and the nature of the environment.

The budget system of the organisation is critical to the co-ordination of effort. The flow of required resources acts as a powerful incentive system inside and between organisations. Although recent program budget models suggest that budget issues can and should be subsumed under the planning system, in most organisations budgeting stands above all these other processes. Most budgets are run on an annual cycle and have critical paths which determine bids and outcomes. Organisations co-ordinate effort by establishing budget priorities, by creating special categories for the allocation of funds, and by signalling their intentions through the choices they make about what is to be measured. A typical example is the attitude of the budget to local savings. Each organisation has its own rules and conventions regarding what should happen if a sub-unit's annual allocation is underspent. Some encourage this form of saving by allowing the unit to carry over the savings into the following year, Others pull back unspent funds at the end of each year. In each case a different rationality emerges. In the first a perverse incentive may be created for managers to strangle programs of much-needed funding so as to 'save' resources in anticipation of demands in the new year. In the second scenario, managers will engage in willful spending in the last few weeks of the year in order to avoid losing funds back to the centre.

The organisation's reward system completes the battery of tools available for the co-ordination of effort. In addition to general incentives such as those embedded in the budget and planning processes, organisations reward and punish staff for their contributions. By linking the pay and promotion systems to operational objectives and targets, many organisations steer the effort of employees without the need for detailed daily direction. In the most extreme cases of this type employees act as virtual sub-contractors within the organisation. They set their own hours, bargain for their materials and authority, and are paid on a per unit basis—so many clients per dollar, so many products per contract.

Use of monetary incentives will be limited to those aspects of the job which can be individually measured. If inappropriate measures are used, it will become rational for staff to redefine and dilute their work objectives. For example, in a government-owned rehabilitation clinic in Sydney the management recently decided to measure employee performance by registering the number of cases being processed. This required data on both the total and the average time spent on each client. Staff complained that the system took no account of the degree of difficulty of each case, but managers feared that if they included this in the reward system it would be easily distorted. Every form of low performance would be rationalised as a hard case. Besides, they told staff, over a monthly period the hard cases would balance out against the easy and no one work group would be disadvantaged. When the system was implemented staff reacted by unofficially altering the organisation's selection rules. Clients exhibiting signs of difficult rehabilitation problems were informally 'bumped' to other agencies.

In addition to pay and monetary bonuses, organisations direct effort through granting status, better jobs, extra leave and special benefits to those who maximise their effort in the desired direction. Similarly, they punish inappropriate behaviour by denying access to these benefits and by terminating the employment contracts of those viewed as highly problematic. A distinction can be made between intrinsic and extrinsic rewards (Herzberg 1966) and between immediate and long-term benefits. Intrinsic advantages are those which come from the pleasure of the task itself, including the satisfaction of group solidarity. The organisation alters these by changing task allocation, using job rotation, and altering responsibility. Extrinsic rewards include such things as pay, performance bonuses and holidays. Immediate benefits are contrasted with those such as superannuation and external status, which take a longer time to be realised. Organisations use each of these four types, although managers often pay far less attention to intrinsic pay-offs than to the pressing financial concerns of salary and conditions. Benveniste (1987) provides cases where the emphasis upon short-run quantitative performance missed opportunities to motivate professional staff through their interest in peer status, further education and reputation. The latter incentives, he argues, work far better, and are no more expensive that the more controlling strategies popularised in business schools.

Conclusions

Policy making involves much more than creating new ideas and promoting solutions to occasional problems. Much of what occurs within policy systems is continuous work on persistent issues. The models of organisation which have been examined here are centrally important to the development of an understanding of these regular processes. Our approach has been to regard policy as being an organisational achievement, even where non-formal organisations are involved alongside formal ones.

Policy analysis is therefore always vitally concerned with the internal political economy of these organisations and with the relationships between them, and the external dictates of the policy system. The different assumptions we have examined point to alternate propositions and claims. How are these important to policy making? Policy is concerned with a wide range of organisational processes and mechanisms. These include:

- decision making
- planning
- resource allocation
- negotiation
- motivation.

Each policy episode takes place in a context which is shaped, in part, by these organisational processes. The models we have examined provide a series of frameworks for considering different organisational elements. In some cases the structure of the organisation responsible for a program will be the key determinant of outcomes. In other cases, the ablilty or inability to clarify goals will be a central concern. Elsewhere the policy will depend for its success upon the motivation and commitment of key staff.

It is not possible to detail each and every organisational process which may influence policy development and implementation. However, using the frameworks provided here, it should be possible to locate the major insights and expectations which researchers bring to problems. The next step is to explore the two other sets of actors who regularly influence policy systems—experts and managers. The understanding of their contributions rests, in part, upon the organisational factors previously discussed. Managers, in particular, are an organisational creation. The view one takes of their role, and the strategies seen as useful for improving their contributions, will be informed by the assumptions and frameworks identified here. Experts, as we will see, span organisational, network and intellectual fields. This makes them a difficult group to manage, and an important group to understand. Next to community interest groups of various kinds, experts provide the greatest potential challenge to organisational control of policy systems. Their unwillingness to bend completely to either market or bureaucracy sets them apart. Organisations, meanwhile, remain central.

References

Ashby, W. R. (1960) *Design for a Brain.* London: Chapman and Hall

Benson, J. K. (1982) 'A Framework For Policy Analysis', in D. Rogers, D. Whitten and Associates, *Interorganisational Coordination*, Ames, Iowa: Iowa State University Press

Benson, Kenneth J. (1977) 'Organisations: A Dialectical View', *Administrative Science Quarterly* 22: 2

Benvenists, Guy (1987) *Professionalising The Organisations: Reducing Bureaucracy to Enhance Effectiveness.* San Francisco: Jossey-Bass

Blau, Peter (1968) 'The Hierarchy of Authority in Organisations', *American Journal of Sociology* 73, January: 453–57

Crozier, Michael (1978) in K. Kumar, *Prophecy and Progress: the Sociology of Industrial and Post-Industrial Societies.* Harmondsworth: Penguin

Ewan, Stuart (1976) *Captains of Consciousness.* New York: McGraw-Hill

Fayol, Henri (1925) *Industrial and General Administration.* Paris: Dunod

Ford, Henry (1924) *My Life and Work.* Sydney: Cornstalk Publishing Co.

Game, Ann and Pringle, Rosemary (1983) *Gender at Work.* Sydney: Allen and Unwin

Giddens, Anthony (1979) *Central Problems in Social Theory*, London: Macmillan

Hawley, A. H.(1950) *Human Ecology.* New York: Ronald Pres

Herzberg, Fredrick (1966) *Work and the Nature of Man*. New York: Crowell

Hoy, David Cousins (1986) 'Power, Repression, Progress: Foucault, Lukes, and the Frankfurt School', in David Cousins Hoy (ed.), *Foucault: A Critical Reader*. London: Blackwell

Lorsch, Jay W. (1970) 'Introduction to the Structural Design of Organisations', in G.W. Dalton and Paul R. Lawrence (eds), *Organisational Structure and Design* Homewood, Illinois: The Dorsey Press

Luther Gulick (1937) 'Notes on the Theory of Organisation', in Luther Gulick and Lyndall F. Urwick (eds), *Papers on the Science of Administration*. New York: Institute of Public Administration, Columbia University

MacGregor, Douglas (1960) *The Human Side of Enterprise*. New York: McGraw-Hill

Meyer, Marshall (1968) 'Two Authority Structures of Bureaucratic Organisations', *Administrative Science Quarterly*, September: 211–28

Morgan, Gareth (1986) *Images of Organisation*. Beverly Hills: Sage

Offe, Claus (1985) 'The Political Economy of the Labour Market', in *Disorganised Capitalism*. Cambridge: Polity

Perrow, Charles (1970) *Organisational Analysis*. London: Tavistock

Silverman, David (1970) *The Theory of Organisations*. London: Heinemann

Simon, Herbert (1976), *Administrative Behaviour: A Study of Decision Making Processes in Administrative Organisation*. New York: Free Press

Smith, Adam (1910) *The Wealth of Nations*. London: Dent

Steinbrunner, John (1974) *The Cybernetic Theory of Decision: New Dimensions of Political Analysis*. Princeton, NJ: Princeton University Press

Urwick, Lyndall F. and E. F. L. Brech (1957) *The Making of Scientific Management*. London: Pitman

Woodward, Joan (1965) *Industrial Organisation: Theory and Practice*. London: Oxford University Press

8

Expertise

> Professionals assert secret knowledge about human nature, knowledge which only they have the right to dispense. They claim a monopoly over the definition of deviance and the remedies needed. . .In any area where a human need can be imagined these new professions, dominant, authoritative, monopolistic, legalised—and, at the same time, debilitating and effectively disabling the individual—have become exclusive experts of the public good. (Ivan Illich 1977: 20)

Expert knowledge is essential to policy innovation and it also makes the implementation of complex programs possible. At the same time, other parts of the policy system soon become dependent upon such expertise and this grants to experts the forms of power which are most difficult to identify and control. As a result of these intersecting facts, policy analysis takes a close interest in the forms of knowledge used in policy systems, the way this knowledge is deployed and controlled, and the consequences of these arrangements for other actors in the system, or nearby (Bell 1973, Larson 1977, Golembiewski 1983).

We have seen in previous chapters that in the making of public policy, and in its implementation, there is often a contest over the status of new ideas. Often this struggle lies just beneath the surface of bureaucratic and interest group posturing. But its imprint is not difficult to find. In every policy system we see the decisive role often played by consultants bearing new techniques, new managers with novel objectives, and the hard-bitten certainties of long-standing practitioners. Each of these point to the intensity of the policy battles over what is to be regarded as valuable knowledge.

Because policy making is such a battle over ideas, opportunities for change and attempts to preserve existing arrangements always involve a war of words and techniques, as well as more conventional wars over resources and authority.

Three Levels of Analysis

Our purpose in this chapter is to examine how expertise shapes the policy system and how its knowledge may be restrained and harnessed within the patterns of material dependency and culture which we have already described. To do this, we will examine three different approaches to the understanding of the creation and definition of expertise. These approaches also involve different levels of analysis, starting with the broader social questions, then moving to occupational arrangements, and finally examining organisational levels. At each new level we will also see some of the major weaknesses of the previous approach.

The first level is the most global and embracing. At this social level policy knowledge is seen as the intellectual property of a class of trained experts known as technocrats (Touraine 1981, Yeatman 1990). In examining the idea of technocracy we see how the social construction and protection of particular forms of knowledge may create prevailing frameworks or paradigms within the policy making system as a whole.

The second approach, or level, is more interested in experts as an occupational group. It traces specific groups of experts through the process of professionalisation. This approach peels away the apparent unity of the technocratic framework and inserts important sources of contextual dissent and conflict. Yet this analysis shows a pervasive form of control by experts and an intransigence and unwillingness to negotiate with the citizenry. Conflicts with managers in public organisations reveal the contours of this stalemate without fully showing why it exists.

The third level at which expertise is examined is that of the particular expert inside the organisation. Here the problem is one of control and discretion. How can experts be included in the process of innovation without allowing them to monopolise it? If they are too tightly restrained, how will new ideas and values circulate effectively? If turned loose, what will prevent them subverting public interest objectives?

Technocracy

To be defined as a technocrat is to be pinned within a paradox. Technocracy suggests the sterile world of the unfeeling expert. On the other hand, the deference and status which attend the technician's work and the power and money which emanate from the professional's suite invite social respect, if not reverence. It is clear that technocracy—rule by experts—promises the policy actor both reassurance and fear.

When sociologists and commentators talk of technocracy they mean rule by a class of experts who are trained in the skills of investigation, diagnosis and manipulation, and who offer this expertise impartially to the state and the corporation. Inclusion in this class is usually defined by the level and type of education, and by the nature of the employment undertaken. Senior level technicians are viewed as a different breed from the hundreds of thousands of technically trained workers in fields such as health and education. What sets the technocrat apart? Two characteristics are distinctive. First, at the senior levels of expertise the nature of work itself expands. In place of the specific, procedure-driven world of the junior professional (Edwards 1979) we see a liberation into all fields. At this level technocrats may speak and work across fields in which they have no formal training, and consult on problems concerning which they have little previous experience (Hyman and Streek 1988).

The second feature of the division between the technocracy and the sum total of technically trained workers is that in the case of the former there is an acknowledged group or caste system. This is often enforced through attendance at special schools, possession of special post-degree qualifications, membership of special grades or ranks within the Public Service or the corporation, or acceptance into jobs carrying special rights, such as the right to see classified documents or exercise high levels of discretionary authority. Although a hierarchical continuity connects the technocracy to the lower order bureaucracy, there is in every large organisation a line which insiders recognise as the division between those whose power is largely proscribed by their position, and those who enjoy a latitude across the organisation, and out into its immediate environment.

Why does this technocracy matter? To the extent that officials of this kind adopt common standards and push similar ideas, the existence of such a class is centrally important to understanding policy, and critical to any strategy of change. Technocrats appeal to other decision makers on the basis of their authority as experts. They know things which the general public does not know. They see things which other officials do not see. They offer the possibility that, using special powers of observation and deduction, it will be possible to see part of the future and avoid disasters. Further, when set astride large Public Service organisations and corporations, this group extends its influence through a vast techno-bureaucracy which, in many countries, forms the backbone of the state itself, and in others remains the only credible alternative to the military (Knights and Wilmott 1988).

But this is only one aspect of their influence. More important still is their role as gatekeepers and interpreters of the new technological changes which present policy makers with a constant barrage of challenges and demands. Genetic technology, salinity, ozone depletion, *in vitro*-fertilisation, and foetal experimentation are examples of policy problems created from within a technocratic system which then must be brought into the political arena where these same experts advise on investment strategies, ethical questions and appropriate legislation to contain cruelty and restrict the loss of individual autonomy.

It is this constant and unrelenting process of change which excites and disturbs other actors, and it is this new level of social turbulence which draws the technocrat into the centre of policy disputes. Where sociologists and systems theorists used once to describe change as a transition between one order and another, they increasingly now identify change as a continuous state in its own right (Toffler 1970, Jones 1982.)

Expert Dissent

Much of the understanding of the technocratic imperative fortunately becomes accessible through competition and dissent among experts themselves. It is this which principally prevents a monopoly of information, even though it may not guarantee an openly democratic policy process. In building strategies for change, policy activists frequently depend upon their understanding of the sources of difference among technocrats and upon the opportunities these may create for debate and a search for alternatives.

In most of the critical social problems faced by modern societies there are discontents about expertise and knowledge. Liberal-minded technocrats seek to share their moral responsibilities with parliamentary committees and, in extreme cases, with social movements. This is what helps provoke debate over such complex technical problems as the safety of nuclear fuel and the long-term atmospheric effects of fluoro-carbons.

The impacts of parliaments and movements upon the technocratic path are found in two separate fields. On the one hand, technocratic dissent opens the way for a challenge to be made to the forecasts or predictions of other experts. By this route the polity may take greater control of the risks associated with technological change. This may also permit a wider public to influence the setting of non-scientific parameters to do with the acceptability of certain kinds of accidents or side-effects. While technocrats may dispute the judgements made, they typically show greater willingness to provide alternatives at this stage. Far less flexibility is evident in the determination of the method proposed to realise a solution to any given technical problem.

Scientific methods frequently dictate the production of a single optimum solution and this itself acts as one of the most powerful sources of restraint on other policy makers. Once a single preferred solution has been 'discovered' by expert experimentation or review, it becomes increasingly difficult for other actors either to challenge such a proposal, or to generate alternatives. This closure is made complete when, faced with an expert solution which they find unacceptable, policy makers come to regard the problem itself as intractable and unworthy of further effort. Only by intervening very early in the process of technical investigation can those seeking change hope to generate a wide range of options. This is impossible until the problem itself has been removed from the control of the technocracy and given to a wider audience whose professional obligations and social rivalries guarantee the possibility of debate.

Professions

All talk of the professions is invariably dominated by accepted understanding of the role of the two most powerful professional associations of the modern era—doctors and lawyers. Theories of society are united by few common concerns, but one such consensus is the acknowledgement that this century has seen un unprecedented growth in the role and significance of professional occupations, their values and their monopoly interests (Bell 1973, Boreham 1983, Bauman 1991). Using medicine and the law as leading cases, theorists and commentators have defined the professions as occupations enjoying a special autonomy from both the market economy and the state-dominated public sphere. The consequences of this independence have unfortunately attracted more debate than the organisational means by which it is created. So while theorists as different as Parsons (1951) and Foucault (1986) seem united by the notion that professions wield a special kind of power, and that this power is capable of being positively or negatively deployed, less thought has been given to the particular conditions under which each professional group gains or loses its capacity to shape policy and alter social values (Boreham 1983).

From their observation that doctors and lawyers control entry to their own ranks, enjoy exclusive rights to practice in the whole of their occupational field, manage their own system of ethics and punishments, and dominate public debates about policy reform, observers have often claimed that all professional occupations enjoy a powerful freedom to dominate their clients. This is clearly not the case. Professions are found in quite variable relationships with other key actors such as state agencies and fellow professionals. They may also vary according to the forms of internal and external organisation used to generate and focus their knowledge and power.

Professional Traits

In reality the professions are a complex mix of occupational groupings. Millerson's (1964) standard definition is typical of those attempting to create a generic category. Professions are those whose skills are based on some form of theoretical knowledge which has an institutional base in university research, journals and academic practice. They allow entry only through a recognised and tested system of training and examination and are regulated through a code of ethics and a means for its enforcement. They are self-regulating as far as work practices and ideals are concerned, and they include a commitment to public service and altruism where service delivery is concerned.

An essential difference of views is evident in the research literature on the role of professions. On the one hand are found explanations of professional authority based largely on the alleged importance of the work they do. To the degree that they perform these roles well, professions may be seen as deserving of the prestige, pay and influence they enjoy. According to this view those who protect our health or safeguard our civil rights deserve high status. Those who design our buildings and teach our children come next in the order of social merit and are followed by the care givers and administrators who maintain the remedial services of the state. This explanation holds less influence now than it has, as a consequence of increasing academic and popular scepticism. Too many important roles are omitted or devalued in such a hierarchy. Investors and entrepreneurs clearly have significant social roles and often derive high incomes, yet their expertise is seldom sanctioned by professional categories. Ministers of religion and academics undergo extensive training and exhaustive selection and recruitment procedures, yet have neither the exclusive status nor the high incomes consistent with their expertise. And in comparisons of the same roles in different societies enough variation is seen to justify rejection of the idea that professional ranks are ordered by the natural importance of each job.

Johnson (1972), Ben-David (1964) and DiMaggio and Powell (1983) have each shown that these inconsistencies point to a fundamental failure in the original idea that professional roles are determined by an objective standard of functional importance. Instead they highlight the organisational strength which some professions enjoy as a result of their combination of expertise and monopoly control. Doctors gain their pre-eminent role through the double advantage of having a secure location atop a highly organised health industry, and through the absence of alternatives to their services. Clients lack other avenues for care and employers lack alternative sources of staff. Although the state may pressure medical schools to train more graduates, or insist upon restrictions on fees and charges, without a viable competitor little can be done to alter the form of medical service provided.

Looking inside the organisation of each professional group it is possible to see more clearly the dynamics which distinguish these from other occupations. Unfortunately the 'trait' theories which provide lists of special attributes, such as possession of a theoretical knowledge base and adherence to a code of ethics, do not distinguish between the profession's own self-promoting ideology and the reality of professional work. In many critical accounts of this problem the disjuncture between ideology and reality is taken to be evidence that the professions cannot successfully be separated from most other skilled jobs. But whether they always follow the code of ethics they advertise, professions differ from most other groups to the extent that they are able to convince their employers, clients and fellow workers that they have the right to specify an independent set of criteria for deciding policy-related questions.

In all cases, even those where the profession is extremely powerful, the legitimacy of this claim to independence remains open to contest (Boreham 1983).

Example: Lawyers

In the case of the law, all the classic elements of the professional 'traits' can be identified. Professional associations of barristers and solicitors regulate the university law schools; establish set standards of conduct, preside over a membership which is frequently self-employed, or is employed in firms established by other lawyers; and provide the nominees for judges and other critical offices. Since no-one may practice law without gaining admission to the associations of barristers and solicitors, and the disciplinary rules of these associations carry the force of law, it may be concluded that this occupation has achieved virtual independence from both of the key regulating institutions of modern society—the state and the market.

Yet even in as strong a case as this there are important pressures which act to create difference and foster change. In the past ten years the law has been subject to a host of pressures which have altered important aspects of professional work. Law schools have been obliged to alter their admission rules to encourage the recruitment of women and ethnic minorities and to teach new courses on environmental law, occupational safety and equal opportunity. The law associations have been obliged by labour market pressures to simplify and improve the apprenticeship systems governing the employment of 'articled clerks'. Governments have begun appointing solicitors as judges where once only senior barristers were employed. State and federal law reform commissions have been empowered to review the law and the work of lawyers, and to compete with professional associations in the tendering of advice to government regarding new legislation. The central role of the Queen's Council or QC has been challenged by politicians, who have grown tired of the high fees and monopoly control exerted by this exclusive caste of senior barristers. And a host of new tribunals, often composed of non-lawyers, has been established in fields such as consumer protection, urban planning, administrative review and labour arbitration. Within large corporations and the Public Service there is also a trend towards employing non-lawyers to managerial and regulatory posts which formerly required a recognised legal qualification.

Most, if not all, of these changes have been opposed by the law associations, though not necessarily by all lawyers. At the very least this suggests that the rights of lawyers to practise their profession are open to considerable contest. Those supporting these kinds of reform make a number of quite different claims about the role of the professions. They argue, for example, that professional monopolies result in high fees and long delays in the administration of justice. This is clearly an economic argument concerning an artificially created scarcity in the supply and price of labour. Critics also point out that access to the ranks of the law has been restricted by expectations and social institutions which restrict the opportunities of women, working class people and those from ethnic groups. Closely coupled to this allegation is the observation that the senior ranks of the law are composed largely of conservative white males whose value systems do not include a full range of social ideals and aspirations. This partiality is seen to create problems for other occupations and interests when the profession's independence is used to protect it from any strong obligation to consult, negotiate and be accountable. This is clearly a political criticism which is hinged upon claims of élitism and bias.

Finally there are several criticisms of the law and other professions which relate to professional knowledge itself. Critics have argued that these associations often create a false aura of complexity and technicality around the work they do. This is demonstrated by resort to unnecessary jargon, and in the widespread tendency to employ systems of classification which shield the practitioner from informed scrutiny by other workers or by consumers. These are obviously cultural facts which are contrived from the particular meaning systems which these occupational groups develop to make sense of their worlds.

It is these challenges to the knowledge base of the professions which strike hardest at their roles since, at their heart, lies a claim that the expertise itself is loaded, partial and inimical to the interests of other groups. Illich took this case to its limits in the 1970s with a series of studies designed to show that the professions created false needs over which they then established an all-powerful control. According to this view, teachers and the school system are seen as rendering students less informed than they might otherwise have been. The law creates a justification for inequality and alienation, rather than liberty and equality. Medicine conspires to make patients dependent and ill, rather than healthy and free.

The effect of this critique on social policy has been profound. When combined with the economic and political complaints identified earlier, this assault acts to undermine an important part of the post-war confidence in policy making, since policy itself had been seen as a culmination of the application of efficient professional techniques to persistent social problems. Without these techniques, where could reformers turn? Professional practitioners now find themselves caught in a paradox: they are widely regarded as responsible for the social institutions established to administer important services such as health, welfare and education, but their learned practices are often rejected as the basis for reform.

It is not too great an exaggeration to view this post-war disillusionment as an emerging crisis of expertise. Once the technical fields of biology, agricultural science, engineering and physics became similarly indicted by the environmental and peace movements of the 1970s and 80s, the predicament of the leading professions of law and medicine had been generalised to other forms of trained knowledge.

Without denying the power of this critique, it is necessary to set some of its more extreme consequences to one side. The critique rejects absolute categories and forms of knowledge, and this provides a salutory lesson. When this knowledge is made relative or conditional to something else, however, it is put back into play as a key element. So to say that policy makers do not trust doctors does not require that patients should therefore suffer injuries and illnesses without scientific treatment. Rather it demands situations in which the form of therapy and its side-effects are fully discussed, and alternative possibilities canvassed with those affected. Although this does not put to rest all the relative knowledge problems revealed by Foucault (1980), Derrida (1976) and others, its does provide a basis for reclaiming the knowledge problem as a matter of practical policy and organisation. That all techniques suffer from the limitations of being particular social creations does not mean that all are equally bad or good. Instead they become such in the hands of actual practitioners acting upon particular problems. It is this element of contingency which challenges us to seek the conditions under which these practices might become more responsive to the needs of others in the policy system, or to those nearby.

Organisations and Networks

One important response to the key issues of actual practice generated by this apparent 'crisis of expertise' is to locate this work within the rules of organisation. Although this appears to avoid the epistemological problems of deciding whether independent knowledge really exists, it succeeds in returning the problem to a terrain on which relative judgements and strategic considerations can be assessed. These are seen through such questions as: Which professions respond best to new pressures? Which professional value systems appear most congenial to other policy values? How are professional power relations different from other power relations in this or that context?

First and foremost, professionals are employed because they solve certain problems for the organisation, and thus for the policy system. Professionals are skilled employees who, above all, are trained to respond to levels of complexity which others would find impossible to manage. Moreover, the professional response to such situations offers the promise of predictable, dependable outcomes.

Because of complexity, policy systems grow to depend upon professions, or at least upon groups of experts who quickly develop incentives to professionalise. Employers may regret that much of the work in their organisations cannot be routinised and made subject to unambiguous systems of measurement and control. This would avoid the need to employ experts. However because many policy organisations lack this machine-like stability, their work takes on a problematic character. Of course some public programs are very routine. Social security and taxation are cases in point. Policy objectives can be structured into the work practices of clerks, counter staff and managers. But many other public agencies lack this routine certainty. Their services have to be hand-made for each person. Doctors, social workers and architects need to gather information in each case and then fashion a particular solution. The official goals and enabling legislation of the agency may specify the broad purpose of the service, and may even identify the kinds of outcomes desired. But they cannot define the exact means, the techniques or the skills likely to be most appropriate. The greater the level of this form of complexity, the more reliant will the organisation and its client base be upon professional practices.

Closely related to this rule of complexity is the fact that professional work is increased whenever the organisation faces uncertainty—that is, when the task to be done today is qualitatively different from that done yesterday, significantly modified solutions will be needed. What program should a youth accommodation service make to rapid changes in family, job and health problems facing young people? What response should a municipal recreation service make to the influx of new immigrant populations? An important part of the answer is to employ staff who have been trained to adapt their practices using widely recognised techniques of diagnosis, research and planning.

Experts are, in this sense, problem-oriented. They possess a trained orientation towards searching for actionable characteristics and they show commitment towards the communication of the results of their efforts to others in the field. Compared with entrepreneurs or artisans, they also show a higher propensity to share and transmit knowledge about new problems and about workable therapies. This makes them a most important link in the organisation's learning chain, and the means by which policy systems develop their capacity to think.

At this point it also needs to be recognised that these qualities do not result from the monopolistic labour market habits of some professions. In fact, many expert groups other than formalised professional groups are capable of this role, provided they possess high level skills and a commitment discussed earlier, to communicate with one another. An interesting example of non-professional expertise is seen in the industrial safety field. Following the introduction of new state and federal legislation in the mid-1980s requiring organisations to improve health and safety at work, many large firms and bureaucracies employed health and safety officers within their personnel departments and required them to develop plans and incentive systems to reduce accidents and other health dangers. Tertiary institutions responded by establishing courses in ergonomics, industrial relations and management skills, and within three years a new occupational group had been formed.

These officials quickly saw merit in forming themselves into a non-exclusive association, and within a short period were found running seminars and conferences to share ideas on how to combat the problems they faced. One of the most significant results of this communication system was that it gave otherwise isolated individual practitioners access to information about successful interventions and problem strategies being employed in other organisations. This was a key ingredient in improving the quality of safety plans and programs. It should be obvious that these forms of professional interaction have more in common with actor network organisation than with the more economic and disciplinary concerns of the major professions.

A useful example of the important role of these relations is given by Von Hippel *et al.* (1988). They found that 'know-how trading' among experts was one of the most important factors in explaining the incidence of innovation in private sector firms in the steel milling, aerospace and waferboard industries in the United States:

> Informal know-how trading is essentially a pattern of informal co-operative R&D. It involves routine and informal trading of proprietary information between engineers working at different firms—sometimes direct rivals. . .The informal proprietary know-how trading behavior I have observed to date can be characterised as an informal trading network that develops between engineers having common professional interests.

The strength of these ties should not be underestimated. In addition to the candid discussion of new techniques at seminars and conferences, von Hippel's engineers went well beyond this arm's length fraternity. In his extensive comparative research cases were discovered of firms training workers from competing firms (without charging them or their employers) and staff were lent to rivals to assist with establishing new equipment or resolving problems with new product lines.

In addition to their willingness to share information, experts offer another important attribute which helps the organisation manage complexity and unpredictability—commitment. One of the reasons they are willing to cross the boundaries of their own organisation in order to exchange information is that the expert has a commitment to his or her career which is larger than the tie which binds them to a particular organisation. To the extent that they have such a vocation, experts are able to offer the organisation a form of independent judgement which often rises above the immediate concerns of local management. In other words, the expert professional derives an important part of his or her identity from membership of the knowledge collective. This energises and protects them from the kind of dependence on the organisation and its incentive system which might otherwise foster narrow vision and sycophancy.

The potential for policy innovation through expert work can now be summarised as:

- formation of congenial networks
- know-how trading across organisations
- commitment to continuous learning
- alternative value systems
- career motivation.

At this point it is important to recall that not all groups of experts obey the same rules or rites. In each group or sub-group there are different views of what constitutes 'good work'; alternative pathways to prestige; and different conceptions of how best to behave as an accomplished professional. Even in the scientific community where tight methodologies and tough-minded standards of performance are often thought to create lock-step uniformity, these group differences are pronounced. Charlesworth *et al.* (1989) spent time with researchers at Melbourne's Walter and Eliza Hall Institute of Medical Research, a world renowned center for the study of biomedical problems. The Charlesworth group had been influenced by Mitroff's (1974) seminal study of the scientists who had worked on the NASA's Apollo moon rock, where Mitroff showed that far from being cool, rational seekers after truth, most researchers turn out to be highly emotional, committed and even ruthless in their desire to prove themselves right. One of Mitroff's scientists observed that:

> If you had scientists who were completely psychologically normal, balanced human beings, they wouldn't be scientists. They would be objective but would there be real progress?. . .The best thing you can do is raise a kid to be deprived, psychologically and materially, so that he has a tremendous drive for success, will trample over people and work like hell.

The recognition of these important sources of drive and of motives for strong commitment showed up in the Australian study as well, although greater emphasis was placed upon the character of the scientific group. The Australians complained that Mitroff's account was far too individualistic, and lacked sensitivity to group norms. As one of the Walter and Eliza Hall scientists: put it: 'Virologists, biochemists, biologists, molecular biologists all have their own "group psychology" and their own ways of doing things', and national differences provide a further influence on such things as the way scientists react to criticism, whether they are competitive and how they respond to leadership.

Among the most powerful factors influencing the way professional skills and values are mixed into a distinctive group character are those directly related to the labour market. A key support for the independence of experts is the flexibility they possess to move from one job to another without losing credibility or seniority. In the most developed cases such as law and medicine, autonomy is guaranteed by widespread use of a system of private practice, or self-employment. At the other end of the spectrum, teachers find themselves dependent upon a single employer and a single career system determined by the state ministry of education. Although tenure entitlements and independent university training may compensate for some of these restrictions, an important source of flexibility is obviously missing.

One effect of these labour market differences is that those in less flexible professional roles are frequently forced to protect their positions by adopting the two strategies employed by other classes of skilled worker—unionisation and bureaucratisation. While they aid in the safeguard of pay and promotional opportunities, these rearguard manoeuvres do not generally increase the capacity of professionals to claim and exercise expert independence. Indeed, in requiring the employer to establish rule-bound entitlements and statutory rights to perform tasks, professional workers are often required to concede the codification of their own skills and standards of performance in a manner which opens them to greater management control. Unless checked, this form of bargaining may ultimately limit the growth of innovation and autonomy, to the cost of both the individual and the organisation.

This tension is most pronounced in public sector organisations and therefore limits the capacity of experts to contribute to public policy. Civil engineers, teachers, nurses and social workers depend heavily on the state to provide employment and promotional opportunities, and even where the state is not a sole employer, it recruits such a large proportion of professionals that its standards become the benchmark for other organisations. In the case of these state-dependent professions, the policy analyst sees in stark clarity the problem organisations face when the claims of professionals clash with political and managerial prerogatives.

When a state welfare agency employs social workers to provide material and psychological support to the homeless or the unemployed, it seeks both adherence to proscribed policy and the capacity to respond flexibly to complex case differences. Managers know that many of the procedures and protocols of the job are too taxing, time-consuming or complex. There are usually an impressive number of reasons, however, why procedure cannot be simplified. In practice, it is left to the professional to modify the rules.

Example: Housing Waiting Lists

In a recent case, in a large state housing department, staff at the regional office were required to keep waiting lists of low income families wanting public housing. Position on the list was determined by a range of objective criteria, including income, number of dependants, and disability. Other than in cases deemed urgent, when a further set of criteria was applied to make special fast-track decisions, all applicants started from the bottom of the waiting list and were offered a house when they reached the top. In most regions this could take two years. In the meantime the applicants' material circumstances might well have changed. They might have found employment, had another child, moved from the area or, in more than a few cases, died! In order to 'clean' their waiting lists, every few months staff would send out questionnaires or telephone applicants to check their status. They were then required to enter any new details into the office computer, and this in turn would alter the waiting list rankings.

When their name had moved into the top twenty, applicants became eligible to be offered accommodation. Staff were required to check their file again, to see what kind of house or flat had been requested, and in which suburb. The departmental rules provided clients with the right to refuse the first two offers made. If they refused a third time they could be deleted from the waiting list.

This was the demand side of the story. On the supply side, each office was responsible for several hundred houses and apartments located in their region. They varied in age, quality and condition. Some were purpose built public housing estates or blocks made from cheaper materials and located in poorer neighbourhoods. Others had started life as private dwellings and been bought at auction by the department. In each regional office there was an unofficial list of 'hard to let' properties which stayed vacant for long periods even during acute housing shortages. Typically they were apartments in semi-industrial neighbourhoods or were in isolated areas. Usually they were built from cheaper concrete and fibro maternals, and looked and felt like institutions rather than homes.

In servicing their clients, housing staff faced many problems. In order to maintain accurate waiting lists they were required to maintain regular contact with applicants and to get from them a true picture of their economic and personal position. But clients resented the long period they had to spend on the list and were often disinclined to volunteer information detrimental to their case. Many also became excited when they received an official letter from the department asking them for an update of their status, thinking this indicated an impending offer. They then became disappointed and angry when it turned out that the organisation was simply cleaning its files.

Staff often responded to these pressures by bending the rules regarding the cleaning out of the lists, with the result that the final allocations became less precise and perhaps less fair in some cases. But relations with clients were less troubled and staff stress was made a little easier to manage.

Corners were also cut on the supply side. Because they knew that 'hard to let' properties would be likely to be refused by clients who had reached the top of the waiting list, officials avoided offering them unless they believed the clients to be troublesome or hard to please. But because the department had a performance system which measured the length of time a house or apartment lay vacant, and counted this against the performance rating of the office responsible for the property, these 'hard to let' cases could not be left empty. A number of local strategies emerged, each designed to ease the unrealistic pressures imposed on the experts responsible for allocations. In some regional offices the housing officers were told by local managers to find worthy community groups who might want low cost offices or meeting rooms. Once found, the group was invited to make a submission to the department asking for assistance, and was given use or one or more of the difficult properties. Even where they received no rent at all and still had to maintain these properties, regional offices were better off than they would have been had the house or flat stayed vacant.

Another innovative approach was simply to ignore the rule which required clients to reach the 'top twenty' before being offered accommodation. One local official described his strategy:

> When a hard-to-let comes up I just take the keys and go out into the waiting room. There's usually half a dozen or more people out there getting information, filling out applications or whatever. I just hold up the keys and say 'Anybody want a three-bed flat in Palmer Street?' I've never had a problem with getting someone.

It would be easy to conclude that in these cases the organisation ought simply to change its rules or procedures to take account of these problems. But the point to note is that the rules remain both rational and necessary if the organisation is going to avoid chaos and systemic corruption of its goals. Expert staff are put in place precisely because they can be expected to take the rules, the clients and the inadequate resources, and bend them into shape.

This exercise of discretion is a characteristic of the expert's service delivery role. Whether at the drawing board or in front of a class, such employees apply the received wisdom of their training and experience to the awkward problems of the present. Striking a balance between too much discretion and too much restriction is difficult. In his study of officials who interact with the public in jobs which have extensive power to influence people's futures, Lipsky (1976) points out that high level stress results from the pressures of inadequate resources, personal threats and conflicting role expectations for groups such as teachers, welfare workers and police. To deal with this stress the 'street level bureaucrat' develops mechanisms which make the tasks easier. They simplify the work. For instance, when workloads become excessive, professionals will rely upon the undigested reports and recommendations of subordinates or other professionals, instead of conducting their own investigations. Further, stress will produce a tendency to lump certain cases together into non-diagnostic categories based on the time or resource demands they make on the officials. Teachers, for instance, will stream all problem cases into a slow learners' program or treat all instances of strong attention seeking as cases of disruption. These stereotypes simplify the work and appear valid to professionals and their superiors. Lipsky points out that this is often because such categories tend to produce self-fulfilling outcomes. Once placed in the slow learners' stream, students will under-perform. If treated as though they are considered incompetent to manage their own welfare, clients may well react in an unco-operative, hostile manner 'confirming' the social workers' diagnosis that they are denying or refusing to manage their problems.

In identifying their capacity to help an organisation manage complexity and turbulence, in pointing to their role in communicating new ideas, and in showing some of the ways in which they manage the stress associated with the discretion they must have to do these jobs, this discussion has concentrated on the expert as an individual worker. While this helps us single out the salient characteristics of the role, it does not tell us all we need to know about the expert role in policy making. For although much policy implementation and service delivery is based in the solo role of the practitioner, policy making is almost always a group process.

The preoccupation with the expert as a solo act reflects the individualist ideology which underpinned the emergence of the professions as a social class in the nineteenth century. It fits these occupations within the dominant value system of Western society by emphasising that they are merit-based, work in private practice, and treat each client as an individual whose rights will be protected through the sanctity of the privileged professional-client relationship. While this may be an accurate picture of the work of some doctors, lawyers and dentists, it does not describe most public sector professional work. Nor does it convey an accurate representation of the underlying group process through which professional knowledge is created.

Here, too, the observer has been systematically misled by the individualistic ideology of innovation. According to this view, most new products, processes or theories result from the occasional genius of an inspired individual. Apples falling on Newton's head create a theory of gravity, and so on. In reality, innovation requires a complex technological system which includes inventor-entrepreneurs, engineers, other scientists, customers and systems designers, who help bring the product or process into use.

For instance, in the 1880s George Eastman and his partner William Hall Walker developed and manufactured machinery for the production of the new photographic instruments they had invented. Eastman worked on a machine which would continuously coat the glass photographic plates with gelatin emulsion, and with Walker's help he then turned this innovation into a system for the production of film to replace the glass plates. Walker concentrated his attention on the development of cameras and machinery for their production. These pursuits were then dovetailed into Kodak's decision to attempt to develop a market for amateur photography (Jenkins 1975).

The important elements of this successful innovation included scientific training and skill, engineering and production expertise, marketing abilities and an imaginative grasp of changing public tastes. The success of Kodak owed just as much to the social and cultural sensitivities of these innovations as to any purely technical quality they may have had.

The social side of innovation has an internal and external dimension as far as the organisation is concerned (Thompson 1973). In both cases experts working in groups provide the linkages which enable change to occur. This is not to say that they alone determine change: they are carriers or conveyors. To the extent that an organisation chooses to design a system in which its experts talk to one another, undertake projects together and share professional responsibility for some aspects of the organisation's future, it designs its own structure for innovation.

These examples suggest that policy innovation is very largely driven by the expert systems which underpin it, and that these are subject to design and direction. This is not to say that all good organisational design will produce workable policy changes, or that poor design will never produce anything worthwhile. But there are two obvious rules which emerge. Team systems are a primary building block. Team involvement needs to reflect task interdependence: that seems clear. The priority is to mobilise the experts who come from the organisations or sections which have knowledge of, and an interest in a policy issue. Second, it is critical to foster a learning culture within the team which will then flow through to the rest of the system's management structure. This is reflected in the support staff are given, the rewards and status which attend team effort, the commitment to training, and the willingness of senior management to personally validate staff seminars and reward excellence.

Innovation

At the wider level this approach also recognises the social construction of innovation through economic, political and cultural change. Serious conflict exists among researchers with regard to the extent to which science is determined by culture. The most determinist sociologists believe that society and its belief systems govern the kind of knowledge that will be permitted. These social constructionists also make the important point that social norms or values shape the definitions of truth and falsehood which are used to evaluate new knowledge and that this may be the strongest device by which innovation is controlled. According to Bloor (1973) and many others, the explanation of the origin, introduction or rejection of new knowledge should be sought in the social rather than the natural world.

It is possible to bring together an interest in the internal political economy of policy innovation and a recognition of the conditional dominance of technocracy through two mechanisms. This can first be achieved by understanding all innovators as social actors—sociologists almost. Second, the whole process of social change can be seen as an elaborated system based on a social struggle over the meaning of, investment in, and use made of technical knowledge.

The easiest place to commence this excursion into social theory is to recall that the framework which unites both the technician and the sociologist is the notion that both the social and natural worlds behave as interdependent systems—that is, they are more or less tangible arrangements of elements which depend upon each other.

In the systems which encourage or discourage innovation there are several key groups, each of which can shift the direction of effort. In the health field for example there are research institutes which conduct pure and applied studies into basic issues such as DNA, and into current problems, such as AIDS. Universities both contribute to this research effort and make decisions about which new techniques will be taught in medical schools. Pharmaceutical companies invest money in this research effort and make decisions about the commercial development of innovations. The legal system and the courts decide ownership through copyright and patent laws which restrict or allow diffusion of new ideas. Public and private hospitals choose new drugs or new technologies and the size and structure of their budgets open or close opportunities for growth. Comparatively small shifts in attention or preferences by any one of these groups is capable of creating major alterations in the opportunities and priorities of the rest of those in the system. This is not a difficult proposition to accept, given that even an abbreviated catalogue like this one reveals enormous diversity and interdependence within the knowledge system. What is more difficult to appreciate is how anything at all gets done when there are so many places for veto, breakdown and dissent.

In attempting to identify and measure the transactions in systems of this kind sociologists such as Hughes (1989) give an account of the dynamic which produces adaptive or innovative behaviour. He points out that in all cases of successful large-scale innovation, system builders were able to 'construct or to force unity from diversity, centralisation from pluralism, and coherence from chaos'.

Although a powerful analytic tool, the system concept proves too limited to embrace the problem of socially constrained innovation, and thus too restricted to help fathom the logic of large-scale policy change. The problem is twofold. Systems theorists strive for an enclosing definition of system components. This assumes that a meaningful distinction can be made between the system and its environment. This works for stable systems such as an organisation and its clients, a firm and its competitors, or a government and its constituents. But in cases of innovation one regularly see actors crossing these boundaries. In fact, one of the primary preconditions for successful change may be the destruction of such existing boundaries. The second problem is the systems theorist's preoccupation with equilibrium. Even the more flexible 'open systems' accounts seek to explain transactions within a field as either balanced and therefore harmonious, or unbalanced and thus in crisis. Ashby's pioneering cybernetics betray this imported logic. For instance, his famous law of requisite variety insists that there be equivalence between the amount and nature of internal complexity, and that which is found in the system's environment. Without this balance of forces the system's model predicts failure and possibly disintegration (Ashby 1960).

Yet in many innovative environments researchers report high levels of disorder, competition and the breakdown of equilibrium, with war or the threat or war being the most graphic example of innovation-inspiring crisis. It is likely that systems accounts distort the extent of negative effects produced by disequilibria. It is also probable that for the same reason they miss the incentives and stimuli which high levels of stress and disorder may create for actors in and around organisations.

Actor Networks

A more promising approach to understanding how expertise may be linked to a variety of other technical, organisational and social processes is to view the relations between these components as forming parts of an actor network in the manner suggested in Chapter 5. This neither assumes systematic integration of experts nor stability in relations between them and other actors. It is, however, an approach which assumes that technical and social questions are tightly interwoven. In other words, physical resources, spaces and computers are active players in the network. Callon (1989) uses this schema in his study of policy development for the electric car project in France in the 1970s. This project, he argues 'conjectured not only that the technoscientific problems could be overcome but also that French social structures would change radically', to allow new forms of transport and communication, and indeed to anticipate the coming of post-industrial society.

The dynamism of the actor network is provided by both human and technical interventions. So, for instance in the French electric car case, optimistic predictions by electrochemists supported forecasts about the availability of cheap fuel cells. This in turn coincided with environmentalist criticism of carbon fuel cars and with the wishes of state authorities trying to revitalise their major cities. In the battle against this apparent tidal wave, engineers at Renault attacked the technical feasibility of the project and were aided by the unreliable performances by zinc/air accumulators and the threatening presence of the major oil companies who could not be relied upon to make their vast system of service stations available for the regular changing of electrolyte.

Actor networks link heterogeneous components such as engineers, protest movements, scientific laboratories, banks and government departments. Frequently the network is powerful enough to re-organise itself and refocus its intentions, making quite complex social and technical judgements. Admittedly these changes occur without collective rational deliberation by all actor-contributors, but through simplification and selectivity issues and problems are nonetheless prioritised or abandoned. Callon points out that in this case actor networks were in reality an intersection point for numerous local networks. The electric car grouping intersected with the high speed train (TGV) network and the Airbus project, to form an emerging sub-system for the formulation of French transport policy.

Another example is provided by the social history of the Greenhouse Effect. Leading scientists had been debating the effect of high atmospheric levels of carbon dioxide since the 1950s. It was not until 1985, however, that scientists from twenty-nine countries attending a United Nations-sponsored conference of the International Confederation of Scientific Unions issued a statement asking politicians to take action. Taplin (1992) shows how an explicitly political process within the scientific community was required in order to move this issue on to centre stage. This involved slowing down some policy work so that developing nations could conduct their own tests, the careful forming and reforming of United Nations working groups which brought scientists and government officials together, and the articulation of strategies for Greenhouse reduction which were politically acceptable and economically feasible. Hass (1990) suggests that in these cases of international environmental policy, success depends upon the creation of 'epistemic communities'. These can be recognised as the political expression of the actor network. Hass (1990) defines the community as groups of officials and scientists who each share a basic set of causal beliefs about a given issue, and also agree on normative preferences about what should be done:

> . . .if epistemic communities exist, and if they can maintain fairly stable access to decision-makers and keep rivals at bay, then international arrangements that closely resemble the community's preferences will develop and endure.

This account probably overstates the importance of consensus, since it is clear from Taplin's account that a great deal of disagreement existed over the causes of Greenhouse and over the apportionment of responsibility. Yet, for their own reasons, nations and their experts found common ground. But even so, both studies agree that an elementary convergence is required, that this usually starts from within scientific and technical communities whose codes and values will often cross national, ethnic and racial borders, but whose networks or project group structures must stretch beyond experts to embrace officials, and in many cases community activists and protest leaders.

The actor network therefore acts as an organising mechanism for both knowledge and techniques. Professions and other expert groups are drawn into relationships with each other, and with others through their day-to-day responsibilities and tasks. From here we find that alliances and common standards often develop. The discussion in Chapter 5 shows how the governmental role may stimulate different kinds of relations among these actors. The distinctive element in this framework is that experts are seen as members of an 'epistemic community' which has an actual, specific content. We can locate like-minded staff, trace those with common qualifications and identify the groups, conferences, journals and other mechanisms used to sustain such a network. How does this account differ from that given by those interested in technocracy or professionalism? In the first case it must be assumed that questions to do with power and control have been answered. Technocracy is a kind of power bloc, and all that needs to be done is to show how it manifests itself. Experts in networks may or may not be powerful. This will depend on alliances, levels of agreement, how far the network's ideas have spread, and so on. In professional models the key difference is self-regulation and separation of the expert from other actors. Professions have power through their autonomy from managerial and market control. Networks are not like this. They link actors with shared experiences; formal qualifications in themselves mean little.

Conclusions

In this shift of analytic focus from technocrat to professional, and to expert within an actor network, two issues have been exposed and recognised. In the first place knowledge itself has been contextualised. Experts bring their own history to the policy world. Sometimes this is a history of professional strength and dominance. At other times it is a history of dependence. Several key aspects of the expert's relationship to the policy systems have been identified:

- The market power of the expert
- The relationship between experts and government departments
- The nature of the bond between experts and the individual service recipient, and
- The relations between expert groups, including patterns of control and exchange.

A further dimension is provided by the social and intellectual linkages between expert groups, entrepreneurs and those groups capable of fostering innovation. This is too particular a matter to be reduced to general principles, but it remains important. Rarely are experts the only source of policy innovation, but they are almost always centrally involved.

The second level of analysis points to certain sources of dynamism and change. These are the places where it might be expected that new policy would emerge or existing policy might suffer a crisis of credibility. The form of value system adopted by experts, the degree of correspondence between this and the dominant values of the state and the economy, and the creative linkages between different sets of experts figure greatly in cases of innovation, breakthrough and crisis. But this is far more than a question of political attitudes. It is more likely to be an interaction between social and technical imperatives in which real world problems and scientific dilemmas interact with a network of other variables, including professional ideologies. Through a process of simplification and juxtaposition, each of these elements is dependent on the other. By understanding the form of dependence and its limits, the analyst may interpret what is occurring. Technical issues feed organisational pressures; these provide opportunities for external groups to make claims; and this encourages the commitment of new resources which, when technical breakthrough occurs, can transform the entire process.

To achieve breakthroughs or transformations it is necessary to examine the resilience within different parts of the actor network and policy system. Which element is undergoing change at any given time: consumers, clients and their preferences? Employers and service providers? Technologies for service development and delivery? Through a close examination of the architecture of particular actor networks, analysts can often explain the technical and social dimensions of change within one account, instead of dealing with the technical and the social as though they were entirely separate parts of the policy world. This is sometimes a problem with other types of analysis.

Theories which look to technocracy as a means to explain the social role of knowledge seek a class status for experts and read back from that into policy making. They often find more variation than they can explain. The emphasis falls too heavily upon ideological issues, suggesting that the technocrat is always and everywhere a dedicated positivist and defender of whatever orthodoxy is ascendent. Technocratic tendencies vie with other values, even in the most recalcitrant of expert castes. There are two parts to this. First is the commitment to continuous education and improvement, which leaves the door open to new knowledge. Even where this is filtered by established traditions, novelty is always possible. Second there are experts who serve defined populations and display a willingness to challenge other power structures and advocate the rights of their clients. This introduces a welcome form of value diversity in most policy systems.

Accounts of the role of the professions may sometimes be reductionist on another front. They find only what they went looking for: that the professionals' independent knowledge base is a defining characteristic. With actor networks the role of expertise is contextualised without necessarily losing the sense of the expert as a special category and, on occasion, a special group. But the impact of expertise must now be explained within a field populated by specific players, and these include non-human elements over which experts have limited control. As experts struggle to impose order and simplicity on these elements they negotiate their authority to act with government agencies and corporations who also try to shape the definition of problems and the selection of solutions.

Expertise within the policy making systems of Western countries cannot be reduced to social structures and categories. By its nature, knowledge and expertise is an element within the policy system which always has the potential to unfold in new directions. Nevertheless the various social arrangements we have examined here act to constrain and direct the pattern of this unfolding. Technocratic ideologies and professional forms of association narrow and focus the forms of knowledge available in the system. Actor networks also have particular styles of communication and operation, although in this case experts are viewed as interdependent actors. Their reliance upon others and upon practical technologies old and new, opens the door to specific forms of variety and change.

References

Bauman, Z. (1991) 'The Social Manipulation of Morality: Moralising Actors and Adiaphorizing Action', *Theory, Culture and Society* 8: 137–51

Bell, Daniel (1973) *The Coming of Post Industrial Society*. New York: Basic Books

Ben-David, J.(1964) 'Professions in the Class System in Present Day Societies', *Current Sociology*

Bloor, D.(1973) 'Wittgenstein and Manheim on the Sociology of Mathematics', *Studies in the History and Philosophy of Science*: 173–91

Boreham, Paul (1983) 'Indetermination: Professional Knowledge, Organisation and Control', *Sociological Review* 31 (4): 693–718

Callon, Michel (1989) 'Society in the Making: The Study of Technology as a Tool for Sociological Analysis', in W. E. Bijker, Thomas P. Hughes, and Trevor Pinch (eds), *The Social Construction of Technological Systems*. Cambridge, Mass.: MIT Press

Charlesworth, Max, Farrall, Lyndsay, Stokes, Terry and Turnbull, David (1989) *Life Among the Scientists: An Anthropological Study of an Australian Scientific Community*. Melbourne: Oxford University Press

Derrida, J. (1976) *Of Grammatology*. Baltimore: Johns Hopkins University Press

DiMaggio, P. and Powell, W.(1983) 'The Iron Cage Revisited: Institutional Isomorphism and Collective Rationality in Organisational Fields', *American Sociological Review* 48 (2): 147–60

Edwards, R. (1979) *Contested Terrain: The Transformation of the Workplace in Twentieth Century*. New York: Basic Books

Emery Fred (1965) 'The Caused Texture of Organisational Environments', *Human Relations* 18: 21–32

Foucault, M. (1980) *Power/Knowledge: Selected Interviews and Other Writings, 1972–1977*, C. Gordon (ed.), Brighton: Harvester Press

— (1986) 'Disciplinary Power and Subjection', in Steven Lukes (ed.), *Power*. Oxford: Blackwell

Golembiewski, Robert (1983) 'Professionalisation, Performance, and Protectionism: A Contingency View', *Public Productivity Review* 3, September: 251–68

Hass, P. M.(1990) 'Obtaining International Environmental Protection Through Epistemic Consensus', *Millenium: Journal of International Studies* 19 (3): 347–63

Hughes, Thomas P. (1989) 'The Evolution of Large Technological Systems', in Bijker, Hughes and Pinch

Hyman, R., and Streek, W. (eds) (1988) *Trade Unions, Technology and Industrial Democracy*. Oxford: Basil Blackwell

Illich, Ivan, Zola, Irving, McKnight, John, Caplan, Jonathan and Shaiken, Harley (1977) *Disabling Professions*. London: Marion Boyars

Jenkins, R. V.(1975) 'Technology and the Market: George Eastman and the Origins of Mass Amateur Photography', *Technology and Culture* 16: 1–19

Johnson, Terence J. (1972) *Professions and Power*. London: Macmillan

Jones, Barry (1982) *Sleepers Wake!* Melbourne: OUP

Knights, D. and Wilmott, H. (eds) (1988) *New Technology and the Labour Process*. London: Macmillan

Larson, Margli S. (1977) *The Rise of Professionalism*. Berkeley, CA: University of California Press

Lipsky, Michael (1976) 'Toward a Theory of Street-Level Bureaucracy' in W. D. Hawley and Michael Lipsky (eds), *Theoretical Perspectives on Urban Politics*. Englewood Cliffs, New Jersey: Prentice-Hall

Lowe, I.(1989) *Living in the Greenhouse*. Newham, Australia: Scribe

Millerson, G. (1964) *The Qualifying Associations*. London: RKP

Mitroff, Ian (1974) *The Subjective Side of Science: A Philosophical Inquiry into the Psychology of the Apollo Moon Scientists*. New York: Elsevier Publishing

Parsons, Talcott (1951) *The Social System*. New York: the Free Press

Taplin, Ros (1992) 'Science and Politics in International Environmental Policy Development: Aspects of the Intergovernmental Panel on Climate Change Process', Paper presented at the New Zealand Political Studies Association Annual Conference, Auckland: 11–13 May

Thompson, Victor A. (1973) 'Bureaucracy and Innovation', in Lloyd Rowe and William Boise (eds), *Organisational and Managerial Innovation: A Reader*. New York: Goodyear Publications

Toffler, Alvin (1971) *Future Shock*. London: Pan Books

Touraine, Alain (1981) *The Voice and the Eye*. Cambridge: Cambridge University Press

von Hippel, Eric *et al.* (1988) *The Sources of Innovation*. New York: Oxford University Press

Yeatman, Anna (1990) *Bureaucrats, Technocrats and Femocrats: Essays on the Comtemporary Australian State*. Sydney: Allen and Unwin

9

Policy Managers

> The last word on how we may live or die
> Rests today with such quiet Men,
> working too hard in rooms that are too big,
> Reducing to figures
> What is the matter, what is to be done.
>
> Auden, *The Managers*

Managers are rationalisers. They exercise organisational power and this is the base from which their influence springs. Of all the actors found in policy systems managers have the most focused responsibilities. In the classic formulation of Public Service responsibilities, the public manager is held to be an implementor, not an initiator. Ministers, ministerial advisers, members of boards of directors, councillors and trustees are held to be the policy makers. Whatever doubtful value this may have had as a description of the past, it is a totally inaccurate view of the contemporary scene. Public managers are at the centre of the modern political system. Not only do they have a substantive role in all aspects of policy making, but also co-ordinate the roles of all other contributors.

The manager's role in public policy is therefore one of the most difficult ones for policy makers to define and control. In private organisations this is also difficult, as we will see from some of the research in this field. In the private field, however, the value questions facing managers are less complex. Price and profit define most problems. Public management requires a far more sophisticated decision making system and incentive structure.

Managers are called upon to understand, respect and even to promote values which extend across the full range of policy issues.

The public manager is accountable to a range of other actors within the policy system and he or she will certainly be dependent on others for resources, authority and support. This pattern of responsibility and dependency constrains the management role in certain ways. But who manages the manager? The practical answer is that other managers do. This poses important challenges to democratic values and to norms of popular participation. There are no simple solutions. For instance, in responding to the need for greater accountability it might be said that public managers should seek a more direct link with clients, service users and citizens. Except in the most modest forms, however, any such initiative might well be seen as the preserve of elected politicians.

In this chapter we seek to understand the complex nature of the public management role and to see how different aspects of the role may impact upon policy making. Research from both the private and public sectors is used in this process, for there can be no doubt that within both types of organisation there are many similarities. In the larger context, however, the gulf between the two is wide.

Background

Co-ordination is the first essential ingredient of any system. In organisations concerned with public policy it is of special importance. The public manager is responsible for the organisation's struggle to survive the extremes of complexity and turbulence which are typical of fields such as health care, conservation and welfare. Why is the manager's role so difficult?

Historically, managers in both the private and public sectors have responded to pressures which are essentially political in character. This is usually done, however, by representing their work as a technical science, based upon skills in accountancy, planning and personnel practice. Nevertheless, the manager's actual success in this field depends upon non-technical skills and purposes, even if these must be concealed. The manager must achieve political control of the organisation and try to regularise its relations with suppliers and clients. These two responsibilities make the manager a key politician within the policy system.

Externally, the public manager's function is to integrate the organisation into a new environment driven by economic restructuring and demands for increased participation. These pressures seek to *socialise* the organisation by giving it direct responsibility for achieving wider goals such as the incorporation of women, ecologically sustainable development, and labour market reform. This tension between the technical and the political role of managers is expressed most dramatically in a changed approach to policy making, with managers challenging experts and interest groups as the dominant influence in policy systems.

The first great revolution in the efficiency of large organisations was achieved through technological breakthrough and cheap labour. The large industrial organisations of the late nineteenth and early twentieth centuries invested heavily in hierarchical systems of control and machine-paced production in order to take full advantage of these factors. This is sometimes called the 'Fordist' model of organisation, following Henry Ford's successful application of these techniques in the United States.

The public sectors of most Western countries followed these private innovations and adapted their bureaucracies to fit industrial production designs. In the Depression of the 1870s, however, the large manufacturers in the United States and Europe experienced serious decreases in demand and rising labour costs. According to the historians of the period, this prompted a shift in attention from technology to organisation. From here there developed new accounting systems, waste management schemes and more elaborate reporting requirements. It was then a short step to Taylor's first incursions and to the particular development of Scientific Management, as well as a more general evolution of a science of management. The public sector took its shape from these developments. The Canadian Civil Service Act of 1918, for instance, incorporated principles of scientific management into public sector job classifications on the advice of the American management consultants, Arthur Young and Company (Tudiver 1982). Australian public sector reformers were similarly impressed (Beilharz, Considine and Watts 1992).

Today managers are one of the fastest-growing occupations in modern society. In Australia the numbers grew by approximately 3 per cent over the recession period of 1990 to 1993, while tradespeople, clerks, machine operators and labourers declined (Table 9.1). Only professions and service workers showed greater increase, with doctors, teachers and social workers all registering up to 8 per cent growth.

The ideas and capacities of managers have thus become more important to those interested in change as the new role of this group propels its contributions into the centre of social decision making. Pusey's (1991) seminal study of the Canberra bureau-

Table 9.1 Australian Workforce Composition 1990–93

	February 1990	February 1993	Change '000	Change %
Managers	842	865	24	2.8
Professional	967	1,043	76	7.9
Para-professionals	458	458	–	–
Trades	1,240	1,140	–100	–8.1
Clerks	1,334	1,270	–64	–4.8
Sales staff	1,130	1,202	72	6.3
Machinists	592	540	–52	–8.8
Labourers	1,222	1,141	–81	–6.7
Men	4,598	4,422	–175	–3.8
Women	3,187	3,235	48	1.5
Total	7,784	7,657	–127	–1.6

Source: Bureau of Statistics, *Labor Force*, April 1993

cracy and the probing work of Bryson (1987), Yeatman (1990), Painter (1988) and others show how management ideologies have come to dominate thinking about the role of public organisations. Paradoxically the ideas which the so-called managerialists have recently championed have been those drawn from dominant economic models of society. One would think this might be the last place public managers would seek inspiration, given the highly critical attitudes of some economic theorists towards the anti-market interests of management. Pro-market ideas have, however, favoured managers over other interests such as staff, professionals and citizens, for a number of reasons.

In the first place when, for one reason or another, the market fails or is not available for use as a universal source of rationality, and when politics has been discredited as pork barrelling and a means for the advantaged to exploit the non-organised, management appears as the only dispassionate means to ensure efficiency. Managers stand in for markets and substitute for politics. They agitate for their roles to be tied to clear economic outputs, limiting the power of other values to intervene. As the value base is narrowed, the power of management increases. This is the process for the organisational construction of the management role and its dynamic is driven by the intersection of ideological and pragmatic considerations, especially, but not exclusively in the public sector.

This way of analysing the new role of managers can be distinguished from the dominant tradition in business education and organisation theory which, like its twin in the studies of professionalism, has been preoccupied with role theory and the analysis of management skills and traits. These functionalist approaches seek to base an explanation of the increasing authority of managers upon objective definitions of the manager's job description. Even a casual examination of the studies undertaken by people working within this tradition shows that managerial tasks are ill-defined and euphemistic. For instance, Mintzberg's (1973, 1975) studies of chief executives in major American companies produces a set of roles termed 'figurehead', 'leader', 'entrepreneur', 'negotiator' and the like. Specific tasks such as communications, liaison and report writing fail to define what goes on beneath these umbrella terms. Stewart's pathbreaking studies of British managers (1967, 1976, 1980) review the work of more than two hundred managers, and she shows that although there are regular activities which involve supervision and maintenance of the work process and the facilitation of new work, much effort is spent on self-definition. In other words, managers are people who spend time working out what it means to be a manager.

The study of management is not simply a question of mapping a set of tasks. In the management science field much effort is expended on a central problem in the day-to-day practice of these jobs. This is the tendency of management to become the repository of all manner of internal disputes and inconsistencies. Studies in the 1960s and 70s devoted considerable space to reactive work. Copeman *et al.* (1963) and Mintzberg (1973) demonstrated that managers spent very little of their time on strategy formulation and planning. Instead their actual work was driven by continual interruption, *ad hoc* meetings and an unsystematic process of responses to other people's agendas.

As the pressures on organisations have changed and new labour market problems, complex environments and political issues have invaded the domains of public and private organisations, management science has attempted to shift attention from operations to strategy. Peters and Waterman's *In Search of Excellence* was the tip of an iceberg of new approaches of this kind. The advice had a consistent pattern: managers should devote themselves to actions likely to put the organisation in a position to exploit changes occurring outside. The means to do so involved revising their own roles towards becoming agents of cultural transformation inside the firm, while acting as entrepreneurs searching for new activities in the wider world.

The ideal manager was no longer viewed as a long-serving senior citizen with intimate knowledge of the products and services of the group. Technical knowledge could be left to one's own experts or imported through consultant contracts. There was little value in having intimate knowledge and experience with a set of products and services which might need to be replaced by new commitments. What counted now was the faculty to search, network and locate new opportunities. For this to be possible the former activities of operational control had to be fixed by other means. A greatly increased investment in financial accounting, planning, budgeting and performance measurement systems made possible by new generation microprocessors helped provide this answer.

In the public sector this change in emphasis was institutionalised in the development of the Senior Executive Service (SES) in the United States and Australia and the rewriting of senior bureaucratic job specifications in most Western countries.

There are four main logics by which this new management role achieves dominance within the organisation: the product format, instrumentalism, integration and purposive action (Considine 1988, 1990, Paterson 1988). The product format is based upon a systematic effort to shift attention within the organisation from an emphasis upon inputs such as resources and values, to an output model based upon cost and efficiency. This alters what is done and the way it is understood. Organisations come to be regarded as tools (hence instrumentalism), through which shareholders or taxpayers obtain an appropriate return on their investments. Predictably, such a framework operates best wherever a clear, measurable output is involved. Organisations become more attentive to the price of their goods and services and to the relative performance of the assets used to produce them. Values which cannot be quantified in this fashion no longer attract positive attention and are either eliminated or consigned to a secondary status.

Once defined as a tool operated by senior managers in the interests of shareholders, organisations shed their commitment to employees and clients except in so far as they conform to goals set at the top. This has two major impacts. The organisation seeks to exploit whatever labour market pressures it can to reduce the power of internal interests such as professions and line workers, demolishing previous career advantages such as tenure, special access to promotions and the value of long service. Furthermore, the role of internal groups in helping set goals and identifying new values declines. This has special significance for experts who formerly acted as a source of divergent, competing advice and initiative. Learning and innovation now become senior management prerogatives, and consequently the organisation gives its attention to refining what it already does, rather than searching for change opportunities. When this occurs at the same time as increased scarcity, the management slogan 'do more with less' is transformed into doing more *of* less.

The success of the new expanded role of managers depends upon their ability to homogenise the organisation and its sub-units through an application of standardised budget, planning and training systems. This may also spill over into the neighbouring territory of dependent organisations which contract for the supply of services. This greater emphasis upon regulation through integration helps management to increase its control during times of uncertainty occasioned by scarcity and political change. In other words it 'circles the wagons', reduces diversity and narrows the band of action to those things best able to be controlled.

This form of rationalisation is a talent in demand in all policy environments which display great diversity of interests and service types. The main agencies of the state operating in fields such as health, welfare and conservation face this kind of problem. A single state welfare bureaucracy might run up to two hundred separate programs, co-ordinate voluntary sector projects, participate in federal government schemes and engage in partnerships with a hundred or more local government agencies. Improved management technique under these conditions offers the seductive hope of greater control and increased focus.

The social construction of the management role is driven by new sources of complexity and turbulence within modern societies which are external to the organisation. The decline in the old industrial sectors and the breakup of the traditional lifestyles which attended them have caused major changes in the class relations of modern societies. No longer are organisations primarily driven by conflict between owners and employees. As Bell (1976) and Touraine (1974) have argued, from radically different perspectives, this change propels technical knowledge into the centre of the system. This new configuration disturbs the old certainties of the industrial organisation where continuous production of goods for the mass market employed subordinate labour in an autocratic system of internal governance.

It would be easy to imagine technical knowledge being easily absorbed into a neo-industrial organisation if these were the only changes being wrought by society at large. But research indicates that a variety of other values also change when these transformations occur. As Schon (1971) has argued: 'Throughout our society we are experiencing the actual or threatened dissolution of stable organisations and institutions, anchors for personal identity and systems of values. Most important, the stable state itself is becoming less real.' What are the value changes and how do they contribute to the emergence of management as a primary problem? Schon lists the main items as: dissatisfaction with consumer-oriented production which leaves other goods such as housing and transportation undeveloped; criticism in regard to the neglect of key social groups such as racial minorities and the aged; and increased disenchantment of youth, who resist economic materialism and favour qualitative values such as participation and openness.

The social role of management is shaped by the extent to which these broader pressures challenge the authority of the economy and force owner/shareholders to accommodate demands for change. But as Schumpeter argued, entrepreneurs are singularly ill-equipped to assume this burden and must stand back from the workforce and allow management to take up the political role of fitting the economic rationale of production to a host of new values. Efficiency now has less to do with simply converting inputs to outputs and relies instead on a far more complex mix of problems, to do with motivation, equal opportunity and external legitimacy. Managers assume the central role in this political struggle to balance or accommodate economic and social priorities.

The social construction of the management role is therefore based upon its function as a source of integration between the individual organisation and these wider pressures. Managers stand at the intersection between specific activities and general social changes. Management is in this position to both alter specific practices such as employment, training and program change, *and* identify and implement systematic strategies to transform the productive process, alter patterns of consumption, create new markets and thus steer society. Entrepreneurs and politicians may imagine the goals but theirs is not the decisive hand on the tiller.

Government and state institutions have therefore become thoroughly committed to management as the main vehicle for change and legitimation. Previous public sector strategies employed in the period up until the mid-1970s focused upon the actions of entrepreneurs through a general regime of regulation, protection and arbitration. To use the language of systems theory, this earlier approach was interested in the incentives which could influence input and output. For instance, Keynesian economics enabled the state to change the supply of key resources such as labour, education and health through the welfare state, while steering the whole productive system with activities to lift or retain consumer demand. What went on inside the organisation (throughput) was not viewed as the state's business. Neither were shareholders and entrepreneurs much interested. Differences in the work of state and private organisations were unimportant. Often the two would overlap; frequently they would compete and more often than not they pursued different logics of internal governance.

With the decline of growth the Keynesian strategy and its subset of policies to support consumption became exhausted. Previous patterns of conflict between the economic and the social re-emerged in the 1970s. Business demanded a fight-inflation-first strategy which sanctioned high unemployment and an attack on both money wages and state-provided social wage benefits, such as health services and free education. Labour retaliated with campaigns to maintain jobs and improve money and social wages.

The new role of management now formed part of a post-Keynesian compromise aimed at integrating workplace change with social and economic objectives. This can be seen most clearly in alterations to welfare programs initiated through OECD frameworks such as the Active Society model. Expressed in the United States as Workfare programs and in Australia as Newstart and Jobsearch, this model redefined the right to income outside the workplace which had been initiated by the post-war welfare state. Issues of poverty were now regarded as labour market problems, and social security payments for the unemployed and supporting parents were extensively refashioned to meet workplace requirements. Rather than concentrating upon increasing the overall level of demand for labour, governments focused attention upon altering the skills and attitudes of welfare recipients in order to tie them back to the workforce. Studies of the changing needs of employing organisations drove these welfare programs and produced new criteria for welfare assistance based largely upon the marketability of their skills and their willingness to stand ready to be re-employed when new forms of work emerged. By integrating work and welfare the state now seeks to use new policy tools based largely upon a greatly enlarged form of management. In place of equitable and legalistic systems of social security are put case management protocols through which officials negotiate welfare assistance in return for a commitment by recipients to retrain, undertake motivation programs and engage in short-term job experience activities.

Example: Newstart

The Australian scheme which best exemplifies this strategy is Newstart, announced by Treasurer Paul Keating in the Economic Statement of February 1990. Newstart replaced the social security entitlement to unemployment benefits and argued explicitly for 'reciprocal obligations' between the state and benefit recipients. Welfare bureaucrats in the Department of Social Security (DSS) were required to shift their attention from being efficient suppliers of statutory benefits to become active and decisive managers of individual cases. The criteria for case management were set by the economic imperatives of repeated recession and declining access to traditional forms of employment.

The Newstart policy required clients to accept continuous contact with the DSS, submit to regular assessments, pass work tests, attend any program deemed by the DSS to be relevant, visit the Commonwealth Employment Service (CES) at least once every fortnight, and sign an agreement with the department in regard to training and work search activities.

The range of activities deemed applicable for recipients was wide. They could be required to attend motivation workshops, psychological counselling, weight reduction clinics and rehabilitation. They could also be required to shift house or alter their attire. Those willing and able to engage in close-contact management were offered more assistance by the CES, and were rewarded by becoming more likely to be accepted into wage subsidy programs.

Further changes to the bureaucracy's role took place in 1986 with the establishment of mobile review teams to conduct audits of the individual's efforts to find work. Over the next four years the number of teams was steadily increased to sixty. This policing function was extended in 1987 to allow the teams to seek and act upon information about beneficiaries supplied by members of the general public. DSS internal policies were also changed to strengthen management's responsibility for achieving adequate results in tailoring people to jobs. The coercive powers of the program attracted criticism from welfare leaders, who attacked the punitive aspects of the benefit contract system and the inappropriateness of increasing the demands made of recipients at a time when the economy was reducing the availability of work.

A similar pattern of change is evident within the industry policy sector. Larger economic levers such as tariffs and export subsidies are being replaced by strategies for the close management of structural change. The focus is the internal organisation, and public policies of economic change depend upon new management roles undertaken jointly by the state and local private managers. These initiatives cross policy boundaries and include strategies to alter training, pay, tenure, skill development and the movement of workers between new and old industries.

The clue to the huge commitment now being made to management strategies comes from an alternative analysis of economic decline from that presented by economic liberals such as Friedman and Hayek. For these neo-classical economists the prime causes of recent problems in the world economy were seen as the inappropriate inflation of demand caused by governments expanding their programs and raising debt. These critiques were quickly turned into full-scale attacks on the welfare state by leaders such as Reagan and Thatcher, and by the general re-emergence of neo-classical ('supply side') economics among policy makers throughout the OECD countries (Beilharz, Considine and Watts 1992).

The collapse of confidence in Keynesian justifications for government intervention did more than inspire a return to hardline policies to reduce the state. They also caused rethinking on the part of those committed to intervention. They began to ponder the fact that Keynesian strategies had taken for granted the fact that once adequately stimulated, the market would become efficient. In reality what often happened was that immediate political considerations influenced the choices which politicians and managers made, leading the economy towards short-run, piecemeal responses to economic problems.

Looking to Japan and Germany, these post-Keynesians argued that under certain conditions the existence of strong non-market institutions could encourage forms of equity, employment and worker participation which contributed to economic performance. The minimal institutions recommended by hard-line economic liberals would not be capable of bringing about this level of performance, the post-Keynesians argued. Streeck (1991) provides an example of this reasoning in his study of the strategies available to countries wishing to diversify and improve the quality of their economic outputs. If they want to take advantage of the gains to be had from the world's rising demand for advanced products, countries would need to 'cultivate a rich institutional structure capable of imposing enforceable social constraints on rational market participants', and at the same time provide incentives for these actors to engage in restructure, he argued.

The advanced products these researchers have in mind are those achieved through high technology applications, quality-oriented values, using flexible non-Taylorist forms of work. One important model was the German experience, in which industrial production was able to use a strategy of highly-customised products of high quality to shield their markets from lower-priced products from developing economies.

As Hirschhorn (1984), Poire and Sabel (1984) and others have suggested, these models all assume that the state will provide a thick layer of appropriate supports for industries which are attempting to restructure. But what has this to do with management? Simply this. In virtually every case the emphasis on both the state and the corporation's side is the creation of new management skills and strategies. Streeck says that 'the conceptual emphasis on product diversity and quality. . .directs attention towards the shopfloor and the institutional and organisational forms that regulate and sustain complex manufacturing processes'.

Unlike the traditional industrial models which depended upon individual companies forging into new markets with cheap, mass produced products, these new approaches demand co-operation between firms. Governments provide a regulatory framework for this co-operation, but much of the rest is left to managers who undertake joint ventures, exchange information on foreign markets, share suppliers and co-operate in training programs. The emphasis on quality of product, on rapid shifts to new product lines as old ones are exhausted, and on close relations with one's suppliers and (government) regulators all suggest a new role for management. The old values of fixing and controlling give way to new norms associated with lateral trust among managers and incentives to reward change. This new vision of industrial production implies that the former distinction between management and the workforce will also be revised. Rapid change from one product to another, and movement out of one service to one which has only recently become known, all suggest that knowledge and initiative will need to shift down the line towards those directly responsible for operations. This is in stark contrast to service sector strategies based upon low discretion, low wage expansion of the hamburger chain type.

The tensions surrounding the new management emphasis will be obvious. Managers cannot stand free of pressures from workers and owners. Nor can they ignore their own personal interests in pay, security and long tenure. Rather than view these emerging visions of managers as statements of reality, it is possible to see their veracity in a particular kind of self-image which managers themselves are now developing and which will therefore influence their contributions to policy making.

Several implications can be identified. Management now extends across both the public and private spheres as a more unified factor and is placed at the center of *purposive* rather than merely *administrative* functions. This has the effect both of privatising the internal life of public organisations, and subjecting formerly private decisions about training and investment to social norms and demands. This homogenisation challenges the role of other interests such as politicians, professionals, community groups and citizens, who nevertheless find their futures constrained by the forms of performance defined as manageable, but who do not agree among themselves about alternative views of appropriate standards of service.

Management can no longer be considered as external to policy in the manner suggested by legal-rational models of the corporation and the bureaucracy. Instead management as a strategic factor necessary to the survival of the group is central, while boards of directors and ministers are peripheral, since neither of the latter contribute significantly to the outputs judged as critical to the organisation's performance. It may now be more appropriate to view owners and ministers as 'consumers' or 'stakeholders' rather than as integral to the work of the group. The implications of this for democratic theory and practice are dire. They suggest the need for management to develop their own forms of direct accountability to the public rather than being shielded by the notional responsibility of their legal superiors and subordinates.

At the workforce there are several other implications of this new managerialism. The politicised role of senior management may improve co-ordination between organisations by facilitating joint ventures, improved communication, and so on. But management is also apt to become more temporary and less able to look at longer-term problems. Unless the state provides institutions capable of encouraging inter-organisational planning and co-ordination, the higher profile of management may simply intensify pressures on them to become reactive, political actors. These pressures are evident in each of the major management changes introduced in the public sector in the past twenty years: program and one-line budgeting, corporate and business planning, and new performance improvement schemes. These innovations appear first as straightforward management techniques which aim to improve certain aspects of efficiency and performance. When contextualised, however, they also provide a form of dedicated systems engineering which will change the relationships between managers, experts and citizens. In some cases these changes are intended, while in others they contribute to an unplanned *configuration* which distributes new sources of power unevenly and in a form likely to provoke controversy and resistance. The policy impact must therefore by understood at three levels: the level of the actor wishing to create or consume services, the level of the organisation and its programs, and the level of society which wishes to bring about a change in itself.

Program and One-Line Budgeting

First developed by the Rand Corporation as a management tool for the American Defense Department under Robert McNamara in the early 1960s, program budgeting was originally known as the Program Priority Budgeting System (PPBS). Its great virtue was that it gave a systematic overview of the way resources were being committed. This, it was hoped, would give policy makers a better base from which to make decisions about which programs to increase or decrease.

The program budget can best be understood by contrasting it with the traditional line item budget used by organisations. Here the emphasis was on control through resource constraints. Organisations were supplied with a set amount of staff, funds for rent, materials and other fixed costs, each of which was described by a line in the budget. From this resource base the organisation was expected to maximise the services it delivered. During the budget cycle its leaders would bargain for percentage increases in all or some of the line items. Senior management took responsibility for distributing these resources internally and would make extra bids according to whether or not new demands could be met from within existing resources.

In practice the line item budget kept activities shielded from external scrutiny, and funding agencies could only guess at the extent to which current resources were being fully utilised. If they wanted to increase attention to some favoured area of the organisation's activities, these suppliers of resources could only add funds; they could do little to adjust the internal priorities from one existing area to another. Senior managers had the same problem when confronting the work of sub-units. Existing commitments were seen as fixed and change could only be achieved through increases for preferred activities. So, for example, the Minister for Health might wish public hospitals to devote more attention to geriatric medicine, but could not request that spare resources in, say, pathology be shifted. Instead these new priorities could only be achieved through budget increases.

The first step to remedy this problem was to require organisations to describe their budgets as actual programs, rather than broad line items. With the aid of new computer technology, resources were divided down into three or four levels of specificity. Basic programs described the major areas of policy such as youth services, welfare for veterans and women's health. Within these programs a series of sub-programs described the actual projects which aimed to implement the overall intentions.

For instance, a women's health program might have sub-programs dealing with specific issues such as prevention, aged services, community health and occupational health. Then, within each sub-program there would be found a range of actual activities involving the delivery of training, medical and welfare measures to specific individuals. This fan-shaped arrangement of people and resources greatly improved visibility and required the organisation to develop clear intentions. Policy makers believed they would have a much greater chance to align actual activities with what they imagined was going to occur in the field. Unlike line item and other total factor budgets, the program budget promised to allow inputs to be traced through the organisation to an eventual output.

The Australian and New Zealand public sectors invested heavily in program budgeting during the 1980s. Labor governments were particularly interested in the policy advantages of this technique and saw them in purely instrumental terms—that is, they made certain forms of control easier and this allowed centrally driven objectives to be forced through the bureaucracy.

There were several problems with these program budget models, and from the experience of using them, organisation designers developed an important modification, known as the one-line budget. Increased visibility of the flow of resources did not in itself change the way officials spent them. It had been assumed that policy issues would flow to the surface once everything was expressed in the program format and that this would enable far more sensitive changes to priorities. Each sub-program would have its own purpose and its own set of dedicated resources. If policy makers wanted more or less of those services they could simply 'phase-up or phase-down' in each specific area.

Four kinds of problems stopped this from occurring. First and most importantly, not everything that organisations were responsible for doing proved amenable to expression as a self-contained program or sub-program. Services were more complex than this and their boundaries were neither specific to one part of the organisation, nor even to the organisation itself. This made it difficult to locate a fixed set of resources and group them into a single program. When forced by decision makers to prepare program budgets for these ambiguous services, officials had to approximate. The result was the creation of categories which sometimes bore no resemblance to practice.

Second, it was assumed by the model that organisation structure would be modified to fit program and sub-program budgets. Staff and other resources ought logically to be grouped together with whatever other factors made up a given service. In other words the model required organisations to shift to the highly detailed form of the program divisional structure described earlier. This was not always possible or desirable. Often the staff of the organisation were responsible for several activities belonging to more than one sub-program. For instance, a doctor in a local health centre might provide assistance to patients from the women's health program and also see people who obtained services under a disability support project or a youth services program. Even more complex were the cases where the same client received services from a number of programs such as rental assistance, welfare counselling and home help with household maintenance. Here it made no sense to duplicate all the program systems, and nor was it time-efficient or feasible to subdivide individuals to fit organisational categories.

Third, the elaborate program descriptions and accounting systems appropriate to the more complex activities of bureaucracies could not cope well with activities which did not result in an immediate and direct product or service. Management time, capital works, co-ordination, certain forms of training and planning, the cost of communications systems and research and development were impossible to 'charge-out' to specific programs run from within the same organisation. Increasingly, organisations chose to place these outside the new format by naming them as programs in their own right, yet these internal 'programs' only made sense to the extent that they helped the organisation produce specific outputs. Once the rigours of the program budget model were amended to allow for these exceptions, it became a device which only controlled operational activities. This tended to lower both the legitimacy and the effectiveness of the system.

Finally, the program model sometimes failed adequately to deal with questions of responsibility. The point in allocating resources to specific programs and thereby making them more visible was to aid decision making at both the centre and the service delivery area. It was expected that each activity area could now be fine-tuned to achieve a more appropriate mix of resources, with arbitrary allocations at the centre declining. The slogan which best expressed this hope was 'let the managers manage'. Supporters of program budgets believed that with this model in place local managers could be released from central controls which had been developed in the days of input-oriented line budgeting. This proved difficult to achieve because the model had made no provision for significant changes in the internal authority of the organisation. Policy commitments made at the centre by senior managers and politicians still governed both the ends and means of the organisation. Managers were still required to obey personnel rules about deployment, promotions, pay and conditions. Clearance from higher authorities was still needed to spend public money. Rules of accountability and fair treatment continued to limit the nature of service delivery to clients.

One-line budgets were developed as a modification to this aspect of the technique. In essence the one-line budget promised local managers maximum flexibility in the deployment of the resources which the organisation had devoted to their program. Staff could be substituted for new technology, equipment budgets could be converted into marketing strategies, minor capital works could be put off and the funds spent on temporary staff.

To facilitate this new flexibility, organisations moved towards new personnel conditions. In place of career appointments and centrally controlled conditions of employment, they instituted more general definitions of the qualifications required for work, and took away many of the limits on who could be asked to perform certain tasks. Local managers were now able to do more hiring and firing and could shift these and other resources around their sub-unit in response to demand and their own strategies for service delivery.

This increase in the power of middle level managers has not thus far led to significant local autonomy, for two reasons. Although some prudential controls have been released at the centre, others have been substituted. Improved performance measurement systems of the type described below are one such change. Increased external accountability through public reporting requirements and client rights to information are another. In addition, as with the original program budget models, under one-line responsibility the local management only got control of a part of the organisation's resources. To retain their own control, senior managers typically held back authority over capital works, management information systems, training, and special initiatives funding. In many cases this has been supplemented by internal reorganisations which concentrate senior management control over the setting of policy related values by cutting head office functions back to a core of strategic issues deemed by the centre as most important. One such approach, termed the Strategic Core Reorganisation (SCR) effectively removes access of professionals and middle managers to these policy functions and, when combined with one-line budgets, requires local managers to limit themselves to purely operational matters.

Two other problems, which the one-line model has failed to overcome, concern demand. When they have greater flexibility over the deployment of their own resources, and when a new internal value system grants managers legitimacy which is based upon the idea that they take responsibility for their success or failure in using these resources, local managers bear the brunt of pressures to meet demand. It is no longer possible for them to pass this up the line and receive automatic funding for new clients. This issue becomes totally negotiable and those above them may wish to see them exhaust their own resources before granting new funds. School principals, for example, may be required to cut their maintenance allocation, close special programs, cancel the purchase of new computers and use up development funds to meet the costs of increased student numbers. They do not have, and in the public sector are unlikely to get, authority to turn clients away. This can have perverse effects upon the delivery of service, since it creates strong negative incentives to distract new consumers, to disinvest in more developmental strategies and to demotivate staff with declining working conditions.

Corporate Planning

Like budgets, plans are an attempt to resolve resource questions through authoritative procedures. Planning is both an operational and a strategic problem for management. Its operational aspects are those technical issues associated with co-ordinating a complex set of relationships. Staff, equipment and other materials must be in the appropriate place at the right time or services will not be delivered. The need to plan therefore increases with uncertainty and complexity. There are dozens of patent cures for the modern organisation's planning problem, the most popular of which in the last ten years has been corporate planning or business planning. Like program budgeting this is an attempt to develop a technique for bringing resource and value questions together in a single authoritative process.

During the 1980s corporate planning became a dominant methodology. Its characteristics were three-fold: the whole organisation and all of its activities would be subjected to clear, goal-driven priorities which would be expressed in the plan; these priorities would be sensitive to the needs of major stakeholders; and the organisation would be held accountable for its performance against the priorities it established. The subsequent implementation of corporate planning took different forms. The most common approach, however, was one involving two levels of analysis. At the first senior managers and consultants would take time out to write a corporate mission statement and guiding philosophy which was intended to express the identity and purpose of the organisation. The intention here was to give each component part of the plan a guiding purpose. Each sub-component would then express its goal as a derivative of the mission statement. At this first stage senior management would also provide a policy setting which reflected the political goals of the minister and the government, and here again the idea was to give a framework within which other issues could be incorporated.

At the second and most exhaustive level each of the main functions of the organisations would be expressed as policy objectives. These would be related to condition statements about the issues in the environment and the constraints which the organisation faced in bringing about change. Programs and sub-programs would have their own sets of goals to govern subsequent activity. It was intended that these would lead to clear statements by which later performance could be judged. At this second level, the participation of middle managers was invited and a range of conferences and workshops was typically used to flesh out the issues and help define local objectives. Consumers, political groups, interest associations and the community were not generally involved.

The final product in almost every case was a published plan which was part-public relations and part-representation of real issues. Two problems were encountered in most cases. They were to do with participation and political vulnerability. In Australian and New Zealand public organisations, most of this form of planning was done at the top, with relatively little attention being given to subordinates at the middle and lower levels. This not only limited the internal legitimacy of the plans, but also weakened their accuracy. Outsiders such as parliamentarians and interest groups had not been consulted and therefore important information about them was also missing.

Because the plans were to be made public, there was a strong political incentive for management and the minister to avoid any indication that significant tensions existed inside the organisation or within their own roles. Battles over how much attention a value or program should receive rarely emerged. Instead, a flat, resolved and rather colourless picture tended to emerge. Divergent values were incorporated in language which implied it was possible to give equal weight to potentially conflictual priorities. Housing departments set goals to both increase the speed of rent payments and improve customer relations. Corrections departments said they intended to both improve prison security and incorporate respect for the rights of offenders.

When it came to action, the plans were also weak. The process of their development had not been directed at new opportunities. In other words, policy was assumed to be a given. Any novelty in the plan was therefore purely operational. Hopes for new computer systems, scenarios for advanced staff training and proposals for inter-agency co-ordination figured among strategies for innovation. Far less was said about emerging community needs, social change and opportunities for new policy to be developed.

In the later part of the 1980s and the early 1990s, corporate plans gave way to business plans. This technology evidenced a far greater interest in planning operational matters, a problem which corporate plans had been unable to tackle because of their head office orientation. Business planning was far more attentive to pressures on local managers, at least in so far as resources and authority were concerned. As a result they enjoyed greater respect among practitioners. Coupled with the new forms of local responsibility already outlined (and also discussed further in the discussion of performance measurement), business planning was intended as a manager's guide to emerging demands for service. In place of the rather static picture of the environment came a recognition that new technology, changed workplace practices and budget restraint would transform the organisation. So business plans attempted to give managers an opportunity to map a path forward.

Resource questions dominated business plans. In particular, managers were asked to plot their strategies for increasing fees, contracting services and limiting demand. Critics claimed with some truth that this planning process was often based on an accountant's view of the future. Participation at the middle level of the organisation was improved, but the range of issues under consideration was much abbreviated. Despite these limits, the planning process was more genuinely dynamic, if only because the other changes occurring around the organisation required significant adjustment. The business planning process became a vehicle for managers to think about and plan their response to adversity.

Without an authentic policy development arm, however, this planning system remained a management control strategy for many organisations. Economic values and tests of efficiency predominated. Questions of consumer, client and citizen involvement were kept to the margin. Practitioner input was frequently constrained by a centrally-driven requirement that the planning process look at improvement to existing programs, not at new activities and relationships. Where this was not an explicit demand it became in implicit one by virtue of the fact that resources were not available to develop new scenarios, study alternatives used elsewhere, or make commitments to the trial of different activities. Business planning protocols assumed that some other process existed for these larger policy issues. They would become the province of the minister's office or of senior management. Only policy questions which arose from operational concerns with efficiency would be noticed in the business plan.

Performance Improvement

The two management objectives driving budget, planning and performance improvement were increased control and better resource utilisation. Although the needs of citizens and the actual impact of programs on consumers were included as official objectives, the techniques did not always enhance these values. The various performance improvement systems introduced in the past ten years show the strength of the commitment to improved resource use. They also show how much weaker these systems are as sources of policy and program improvement.

The work of Wholey (1979, 1987) is closely associated with a number of the strategies employed in the United States, Canadian, Australian and New Zealand public sectors to improve performance. To see how questions of performance became management prerogatives it is important to understand Wholey's approach, for he is one of the few advocates of these techniques to provide a reasoned defence. He developed his views during a long career in the program evaluation industry, where the chief concerns of theorists and practitioners was with testing how well programs had done in reaching their objectives.

For most evaluators the question of performance is a complex matter. A spirited debate has been carried on for thirty years or more over the way in which outcomes should be judged. Whose objectives should the evaluator take as the yardstick? Most evaluators accept that different objectives will be found among the different actors involved. Key figures such as Scriven (1976) even go as far as to insist that evaluators ought to ignore goals altogether and simply concentrate on whether or not programs deliver benefits which people need.

The point about these debates among evaluators is that they recognise certain social science problems to do with performance and ideology. Those who fund evaluations are likely to have firm ideas about their own objectives and will steer evaluation results towards consideration of these values, rather than others. Evaluation issues are simply performance issues discussed in slightly different language. So how are values dealt with in the development of these techniques for organisational performance assessment? It is here that Wholey's distinctive approach is important. He carves up the program assessment issue into three domains which he calls markets: the individual consumer market, the program management market and the policy market. He argues that the second of these is the place where performance is most critical. Good intentions by policy makers and recognised needs among consumers will not produce good programs if there is poor implementation.

Wholey developed a seven-stage process through which managers could be assisted to check and verify the performance of their programs. At the first stage they describe and define the program, distinguishing it from other activities. Next they obtain agreement in the organisation about realistic, ground-level program objectives and some indicators which would show progress towards them. The third step requires managers to set in place a mechanism to assess performance on these agreed criteria. Stage four involves the setting of targets to show what level of achievement can be considered adequate. The fifth level of his schema requires managers to develop a means to use the new information on performance to produce improvements. Stage six requires refinement of indicators and targets in response to the new information, and the final level demands that managers communicate data on performance to policy makers and the public. Wholey and his associates pioneered the use of performance indicators and also put together an impressive set of techniques to assist managers in bringing their programs to a stage where assessment could be successful. His is a far more sensitive view of the role of measurement than one finds in many of the management improvement programs initiated in the 1980s, yet the focus is the same.

Management is viewed as the primary actor and the only force capable of improving performance. Who is management? In this case it is the handful of people directly able to influence the program. This limits attention to operational managers, their direct superiors, key staff in the budget section and ministerial advisers or legislative staff with a close interest in the program. The concern to help managers to do better has the advantage of clarity and simplicity, but as critics such as Shadish, Cook and Leviton (1991) have noted, it is important to realise that this approach turns evaluation and associated policy issues into questions of information gathering and 'feedback' for one part of the public system only. Consequently, the performance improvement techniques which flow from this approach depend entirely upon the acceptance of management centrality.

This is not the same thing as assuming that managers are trustworthy. Indeed many of the techniques aim to limit the actions of local managers to defined and measured tasks in a manner which implies that the agency and transaction problems identified by economists such as Ouchi and Williamson are endemic. But even in these cases the solutions are described as problems for other managers to solve. Only at the end of the process are a wider group of policy makers and the public to be involved.

The Hawke government's Financial Management Improvement Program (FMIP) was the first comprehensive expression of these intentions in Australia. The Thatcher government's Efficiency Strategy and Financial Management Initiative (FMI), developed in Britain by Derek Raynor between 1979 and 1982, also embodied much of this logic. In New Zealand a broadly similar approach can be found in the government's Civil Service reforms of 1984.

The Australian FMIP required departments to develop new internal structures to set objectives, establish priorities and develop performance measures on a comprehensive basis. Central agencies took charge of the process and began by altering the federal Budget formulation system to make program objectives visible. An efficiency dividend was introduced to reward good performance by managers. At the organisational level a range of new structures was put in place to assist this process, ranging from new information systems to extensive management training programs. David Shand, a key player, described it neatly as a means to make 'managers manage through a greater emphasis on the reporting of performance'.

A key element in these strategies in each of the state and national government implementations was a shift in the conditions of employment of managers. From being the senior levels of a unified administrative career, management became a separate élite known as the Senior Executive Service (SES). This new structure had several functions. It gave politicians and central agency leaders such as Prime Minister's and Premiers' departments, and Treasuries and Finance bureaux a means by which to separate program managers from their own organisational interests and make them more attentive to centrally-stated objectives. It then enabled the organisation and its sponsors to attempt to reward and punish senior staff according to specific output, rather than according to general criteria such as qualification, seniority and day-to-day activity. Further, it enhanced mobility around the public sector by establishing a new form of career. Managers now became people who could use the new techniques of performance control, rather than being professionals with commitments to specific jobs or client groups.

The success of the SES officer was now to be a matter of measured output. Key Result Areas (KRAs) or defined objectives of some similar kind were developed. Each management role underwent job analysis to determine which programs were being influenced, and to tie management seniority and pay to performance indicators which reflected their contribution to output. The development of a separate SES also enabled staff from outside the public sector to be recruited more easily, since the new visibility of the tasks encouraged decision makers to see the management role as a more technical function driven from above.

Pusey's study has demonstrated that in Canberra this technocratic focus appears to have made management more vulnerable to the dominant economic values of the day. Yeatman's work has also argued that the new managers at the state level in Australia were prone to an unwarranted affection for patriarchal and private sector values. The 'people and process' concerns of staff tended to be overlooked within a new management culture which became preoccupied with economy and efficiency, Yeatman argues.

Since the introduction of the SES the application of these forms of performance measurement have been extended to other employees and to groups dependent on the state for funding. Hospitals, for example, have undergone extensive review through systems designed to separate activities into Diagnosis Related Groups (DRGs), and to set incentives and resources according to the throughput of patients in each category. Purchaser-provider relationships between Health departments and major hospitals extend this principle to a system of explicit agreements based on a bid by providers to produce a given service in a set time frame to a nominated client group. Similarly sub-units of a single organisation may now be evaluated by placing a budget 'circle' around the specific activities for which they have responsibility and then adjusting incentives such as budget, pay and staff levels according to fixed targets. The effect of these initiatives is to make the organisation more attentive to the activities being measured, in the hope that this will improve performance.

Performance Indicators

These larger initiatives to improve organisational performance rely on a common commitment to the production of measurable indicators of performance. Instead of costly evaluations of programs and their impacts on the community, these management-driven strategies seek quick, inexpensive and continuing feedback about both activities and outputs. The assessment of managers themselves will typically include such things as completion of tasks laid out in the departmental plan, achievement of budget targets, processing of a given number of transactions within their unit, and maintenance of standards set down in legislation or departmental regulations. Other staff will often have performance indicators related to cases handled, time spent on activities and production of reports or plans.

The success of these internal systems to check and then improve performance through the use of standard categories of activity cannot be judged at the general level. Evaluation of their impact must proceed with attention to their specific effect on actual programs and to their cumulative role in changing the relationships between the organisation and its environment. A number of factors should be clearly understood when considering whether or not appropriate changes in effectiveness will result.

Program Definition

The first dimension is one of program definition. Organisations undertake a wide variety of tasks in order to meet internal and external pressures. Some are more available to systems of indicator judgement than others. Very simple organisations doing regular, stable work can be evaluated with these simple devices. For example, a swimming pool operated by a local council seeks to maximise patronage across the municipality. People come, pay their entrance fee, use the facility and leave. They all get much the same service. Staff working at the pool have responsibility for a defined part of the service such as receiving fees, maintaining the facility, ensuring safety and providing information. Each of these can be described as a separate activity and there are few problems in defining contributions. In this case performance measurement would be possible without major cost, since all consumers enter at the same place, use the same service and exit with a completed transaction.

Unfortunately this simple, stable organisation is not typical of many found in the public sector. The program definition problem encountered in a welfare agency provides a more usual case. An organisation which aims to assist migrants to find appropriate housing will not find it so easy to define its programs as a fixed set of transactions. Each individual is likely to have significantly different requirements. The service they need will probably have to be tailored. Different staff input will certainly be demanded, with some migrants getting advice on housing, others also requiring income support advice, and still more needing help to locate local schools and transport facilities. The agency will require special language assistance to deal with some applicants. Even among those who simply need accommodation there will be major variations according to their age, sex or disability status.

Even more problematic for the staff responsible for this service may be the fact that they do not control the key resource being sought. Successful placement of people into houses and apartments will depend on the condition of the private property market, attitudes of landlords and the rental assistance available from other government agencies. Here there is considerable difficulty defining the fixed service to be used as the baseline for a performance indicator. It will make sense to develop a large number of standard types such as 'simple referrals', 'housing with disability', 'housing plus counselling', and so on. But the greater the number of sub-fields, the weaker the performance system becomes. This is because added complexity raises the cost of measurement and increases resistance to accurate assessment. A large numbers of boundary definition or ambiguity problems are likely to occur when a single program has a wide variety of valid implementations. Other forms of evaluation are apt to be more reliable, including client satisfaction, peer review and time series studies of outcomes.

Problems of definition suggest that programs and activities require careful description, and a regularly amended program model will be needed to keep assessment and organisational practice in balance. These are not matters which management can achieve alone. The support and commitment of staff directly involved in the service will be needed to achieve this accuracy in the analysis of the service. Some activities may not be able to be allocated to a specific program. The publicity and community relations function in the housing agency may take significant amounts of time without being attributable to a specific program output. If indicators are only produced for fixed program commitments, the organisation will not be able to assess and reward this potentially important group of activities. Indicators which measure the number of press releases issued, or the amount of time spent on liaison with local community groups, will not tell the organisation very much about effectiveness in this kind of area. Again, other evaluation strategies will be required.

Program Goals

Related to the program definition problem is the question of goal analysis. Even when a clear description of program activities is achieved, it may be quite difficult to determine program goals. There are three main types of goal problem. There may simply be no goal at all. The program may exist because spare resources needed to be used. In this case some very general statement of objectives can often be found, but this will bear no real relationship to the reason the program was initiated. More common are the second kind of goal problem, where there are several goals. This may be the case because the program is serving different interests, who each have a different purpose, or because the program is complex and has to reach more than one objective. The final form of confusion arises when there are stated goals which are no more than rationalisations for other, deeper objectives which actors may or may not be capable of acknowledging.

It will be obvious that these problems pose major obstacles to simple forms of performance measurement, such as those being discussed here. In a more detailed program, evaluation time can be spent teasing out alternative reasons for the actions of participants. However, if managers choose to select measures which seem to them to reflect the underlying purpose of the program, other participants may have no confidence in what is to be analysed or measured. If management adds to this a determination to build financial and status incentives into this system, those whose goals are unacknowledged may withdraw their support or engage in opportunistic behaviour.

Causation

The final aspect of performance which needs to be considered when examining indicators and other related management techniques is the question of causation. Causation has an internal and an external face. In complex programs being run from within large bureaucracies it will usually be difficult to attribute cause and effect to individuals or sub-groups. Is the local manager the best person to reward when the relative performance of the office she controls improves? In theory it may be possible to decompose the program into specific transactions, but it will almost always be too expensive to measure these in the performance management system. The approximations which are substituted for this level of detail will blur the line between internal contributors.

These are small problems compared to the external complexity dilemma. Even in long-term evaluations of stable programs, researchers find it difficult to disentangle program effects from other influences on outcomes. Shorthand indicators usually find it impossible. Take the example of health education programs run by agencies wishing to combat AIDS, drink driving, heart disease and the like. Their goal is presumably to lower the incidence of these illnesses or behaviours. Yet education may be one of many factors likely to influence these external conditions. Suppose education had its best effect when combined with strong legal penalties for inappropriate behaviour, and suppose that this effect was specific to some sub-cultures and not to others. The small agency responsible for education programs almost certainly does not control law enforcement, let alone the community status given to different age, ethnic or class groups. Without a thorough evaluation of the causal possibilities, no shorthand indicator will even approximate as a measure of performance, and even with a thorough evaluation there are likely to be enough sub-conditions to each issue so that the indicators will show up as wrong. If the agency is rewarded according to the rise and fall of statistics on, say, heart disease, they may reap the benefits of new fashion diets in one year, and suffer the consequences of recession-induced stress levels the next. Neither are actionable issues within the organisation's control.

This external causation question creates most concern in programs which require long periods in order to mature. A change in literacy levels, improved health and road safety are all examples of programs which may take ten or more years to achieve outcomes. But because budgets, staff appraisals and planning decisions are made on a six-monthly or annual basis, weaker, more problematic indicators will tend to be used.

The most common solution for these measurement and causation problems employed in these management systems is to abandon their stated interest in program outcomes and to substitute throughput and output measures. So instead of a health centre trying to count the improved length and quality of their patients' lives, they count the number of patients and the numbers of services given to them. If more detailed studies and evaluations provide a basis for thinking that the outputs and eventual outcomes are related, this approach may prove very effective. If not, the risks are high.

Throughput measures assist management more than any other group. Managers are responsible for the activities of the organisation, and their primary consideration is, therefore, efficiency. If a program is efficiently implemented, but has no observable effect, managers will usually be in a position to attribute responsibility for this to politicians and policy designers elsewhere. If resources are poorly administered, they will have no such option.

In considering management's need to measure throughput efficiency it is inevitable that indicators of time spent on tasks, costs-per-client and relative output compared with other units will be favoured. Management will be well placed to insist that these become standard sources of program incentives. If other goals and interests are to be considered, however, alternative measures will be demanded. In some cases these will not be compatible with the indicators technique. Time, cost and reliability issues may prevent programs from measuring such things as consumer satisfaction or real impacts in every program for every year. Internal contests over the performance measurement system will then have to consider the virtues of supplementing these with other evaluation strategies, or substituting different indicators.

It makes little difference whether the management technique is performance indicators, benchmarking or quality circles. The underlying issue is the definition of the program and its purpose. If values and purposes are taken as given and the product or service is viewed as the result of a stable 'engineered' system, management techniques will rarely move beyond gathering feedback on errors and inefficiencies which slow the engine down.

In programs which are dynamic, sensitive to external change and dependent upon less tangible factors such as motivation, commitment, reliability and quality, performance systems will need to be integrated with open learning facilities. Here, in order to improve productivity, management requires a more complex framework for assessing both contributions and outcomes. Unfortunately the resistance to achieving this from management itself will usually be significant. Managers are reluctant to assume responsibility for external factors they do not understand. To widen the net to include employee satisfaction and client goals requires forms of power sharing that many managers find threatening. Most problematic, however, is the shift in rationality which is implied by any attempt to redefine performance. Once the measured, quantitative output of defined products is challenged, and their simple comparison with labour costs or capital input has been shown to be an inadequate measure of actual performance, space for new definitions of performance may emerge. Two kinds of effects are likely. First, staff and clients will want qualitative impacts to be considered alongside quantitative ones. This will require management to initiate a range of challenging techniques such as focus groups, questionnaires and in-depth interviews.

Second, performance issues may become focused on process issues, rather than on outputs. Staff, clients and suppliers of resources may push for the program to assess how well it communicates, how well it listens, how willing it is to make changes to suit the interests of others, and how flexible it is to take up issues not previously defined as part of the program. These attempts to modify the values and power structure of the program can be expected to offend management and create resistance, because they create increased uncertainty. Their success, as in other cases of power struggles over policy making, is most likely to be governed by the extent and nature of vulnerability which management exhibits in relation to the environment external to the organisation. In other words, programs and their managers will engage in alternative performance strategies only if they have to. Predicting whether or not managers can be coerced will involve understanding whether consumers can apply effective pressure, how the views of staff may be reflected in the external leverage of unions or professional associations, and how policy making authority imposes specific limits on the way performance is understood.

References

Beilharz, P. Considine M. and Watts, R. *Arguing about the Welfare State: The Australian Experience.* Sydney: Allen and Unwin

Bell, Daniel (1976) *The Coming of Post-Industrial Society.* Harmondsworth: Penguin

Boston, Jonathon *et al.* (1991) *Reshaping the State.* Auckland: OUP

Bramley, Ailsa (1992) 'Newstart: A Policy Response To Unemployment', Unpublished dissertation, Graduate Diploma in Public Policy, University of Melbourne

Bryson, Lois (1987) 'A Game of Strategies', *Australian Society* 6 (11), November

Chandler, Alfred D. (1977) *The Visible Hand: The Managerial Revolution in American Business.* Cambridge, Mass.: Belknap Press

Considine, M. (1988) 'The Costs of Increased Control: Corporate Management and Australian Community Organizations', *Australian Social Work* 41: 3

— (1993) 'The Role and Significance of Strategic Core Reorganisations in the Australian Public Sector: Preliminary Findings', *The International Journal of Public Sector Management* 6 (1) 1993

Copeman, G., Luijk, H. and Hanika, F. (1963) *How the Executive Spends His Time*. London: Business Publications Ltd

Friedman, Milton (1977) 'Inflation and Unemployment', The 1976 Alfred Nobel Memorial Lectures, Occasional Paper 51, London: Institute of Economic Affairs

Halligan, J. and Power, J. (1992) *Political Management in the 1990s*. Melbourne: OUP

Hayek, F.A. (1984) '*Unemployment and the Union*', Hobart Paper 87, London: IEA

Hirschhorn, Larry (1984) *Beyond Mechanisation: Work and Technology in a Post-Industrial Age*. Mass.: MIT Press

Kalisch, David (1992) 'Longterm Unemployment Benefit Recipients: The Impact of Newstart and Economic Conditions', in P. Saunders and S. Encel (eds), *Social Policy In Australia: Options for the 1990s*, Social Policy Research Centre, Conference Proceedings

Minzberg, Henry (1975) 'The Manager's Job: Folklore And Fact', *Harvard Business Review* 53 (4)

— (1973) *The Nature of Managerial Work*. New York: Harper and Row

Packer, Michael B. (1983) 'Measuring the Intangible in Productivity', *Technology Review*, February-March: 48-57

Painter, Martin (1988) 'Editorial', *Australian Journal of Public Administration* XLVII (1)

Peters, T. J. and Waterman, R. H. (1982) *In Search of Excellence*. New York: Harper and Row

Piore, M. J. and Sabel, C. F. (1984) *The Second Industrial Divide: Possibilities for Prosperity*. New York: Basic Books

Pusey, Michael (1991) *Economic Rationalism in Canberra*. Cambridge: Cambridge University Press

Schon, Donald (1971) *Beyond the Stable State*. New York: Random House

Schumpeter, Joseph (1942) *Capitalism, Socialism and Democracy*. London: Allen and Unwin

— (1967) *Managers and Their Jobs*. Maidenhead: McGraw-Hill

Stewart, R. (1976) *Contrasts in Management*. Maidenhead: McGraw-Hill

—, Smith, P., Blake, J., and Wingate, P. (1980) *The District Administrator in the National Health Service*. London: Pitman

Streeck, Wolfgang (1991) 'On the Institutional Conditions of Diversified Quality Production', in Matzner, Egon and Streeck (eds), *Beyond Keynesianism: The Socio-economics of Production and Full Employment*. Aldershot: Edward Elgar

Touraine, Alaine, translated by L. F. X. Mayhew (1974) *The Post-Industrial Society*. London: Wildwood House

Tudiver, Neil (1982) 'Business Ideology and Management in Social Work: The Limits of Cost Control', *Catalyst* 13: 25

Yeatman, Anna (1990) *Bureaucrats, Technocrats and Femocrats*. Sydney: Allen and Unwin

10

Conclusions: Policy Making and Innovation

The challenges which face public policy makers have never been greater, nor the means for developing solutions more uncertain. Western societies have higher levels of economic inequality than ever before. Poverty and homelessness, especially among the young, have been increasing steadily for more than ten years. Ethnic and cultural tension has risen to the highest point since World War II, setting loose a host of conflicts and struggles over identity and political control.

During the same period, the natural environment has reached a point of degradation which even the most conservative scientists regard with great alarm. Air pollution, soil erosion, ozone layer depletion and the death of rivers and oceans each testify to this crisis. Technology has offered great gains in all areas of social and material concern, but with its discoveries have come complexities and problems. Industry, agriculture and even health services often pay for their scientific breakthroughs with a variety of pernicious environmental side effects.

The world economy has also reached a point of extreme fragility and turbulence. Economies like Australia's are more vulnerable than ever before to the shifts, small and large, which take place in Tokyo and New York. The post-war confidence that economic growth would trickle down and create jobs and opportunities has been replaced by the realities of recession. Even the more optimistic projections are fractured with doubt: growth, when it returns to the international economy may be jobless growth. In the meantime established industries such as car production, heavy engineering and clothing manufacture have been forced into rapid decline.

Those such as mining and agriculture, which produce valued export revenues, do not generate sufficient numbers of jobs.

Furthermore, the skills and career paths which once defined the route which ordinary workers might take towards economic security are no longer so highly valued. Even the concept of career has been thrown into doubt. Where once a young employee could have expected continuous employment and promotion, the pattern now is of disconituity. With these uncertainties have come profound criticisms of the education systems of contemporary societies which are now being asked to shoulder responsibility for workforce retraining. Other social institutions have been drawn into this crisis of confidence. Unemployment relief schemes, single parent benefits and age pension entitlements have been attacked as disincentives to work and a costly imposition on business.

Finally, within the personal realm, too, this process of rationalisation has taken a heavy toll. Sexuality has become the primary vehicle for the setting of commercial values. Family patterns, including the definitions of youth and old age, have splintered and fragmented under the challenge of a variety of new personal creeds and economic priorities. The implications of these changes for welfare, education, housing and employment policies are only beginning to become apparent. But it is clear that traditional forms of social support have been eroded, and no new structure has yet emerged to replace them.

At the policy making level it is all too obvious that effective responses to these radical changes and profound problems cannot succeed through occasional bursts of legislative heroism, or infrequent episodes of interest group outrage. The issues are too profoundly complex. Why should this be the case? One important reason is that it is difficult for policy makers to attack problems without putting at risk other important priorities. We understand this as a problem of complexity. In complex situations valuable increases in liberty are often interwoven with unwanted intrusions. Rising affluence is apparently paid for with new forms of economic exclusion. Gender equality is accompanied by greater levels of violence against women and—serious difficulties in regard to the care of children. Solutions to ecological problems frequently threaten the jobs, opportunities and prosperity of vulnerable rural communities—and so on.

How then can change be achieved? None of these problems is a simple matter of finding the right leader or empowering the best expert. Nor are these the kinds of problems which revolve around straightforward questions of individual choice. There is no defined menu of reliable solutions ready to be evaluated and selected.

Even if there were, no informed citizen would have the time or knowledge to perform the calculations needed. The development of answers to major policy issues of this type therefore begins with a recognition that they have some things in common. In addition to value complexity, in each of the fields we have identifed problems arise from an intersection of material, social and cultural facts. We might think of this as contingent complexity. It is not possible to tackle the material problems without also considering the cultural and political issues which are involved. This also generally means that no single actor has the authority or resources to effect solutions.

Moreover, in each area where we find this kind of complexity there is frequently significant policy inertia. An already existing regime of policies and practices creates a dominant mind-set and a pattern of vested interests which must be confronted in any strategy for change. What these three conditions—value complexity, contingent complexity and inertia—suggest is that problems of this type require systematic, institutional responses. These are processes in which both the policy development and policy implementation aspects of the problem are vested in a process which empowers each key actor in the system, in order to achieve commitment to continuing action.

The argument which this suggests is that these contemporary policy predicaments have in common the need for a particular type of policy response where the complexity of the problem is matched by the complexity of the solution. In effect this means that solutions must come through continuing, institutional mechanisms which link values, authority and resources. The broad outline of this approach may be characterised as a form of structured innovation in which there is:

- a systematic application of human ingenuity and democratic values
- a recognition of the key role of social conflict
- concerted negotiation among all those affected
- reorganisation of public and private resources, and
- reconsideration of the values which determine the allocation of those resources.

The Policy Innovation Model

In this chapter we bring together the main themes of the book in order to focus attention upon this final problem of how to effect major policy change in these complex and uncertain policy systems. The innovation model which will be outlined here defines policy change as a form of intentional action in which new ideas are socially cultivated and refined into negotiated strategies. Innovation, therefore, is not merely the production of clever proposals. Nor is it just the application of good solutions to new problems. Inspiration and implementation are viewed as a part of a single cultural process.

This model rests upon the other main claims of the book, in particular the propositions that: policy is the outcome of particular kinds of system; systems are built from material and cultural interdependence; institutions do the 'thinking' for these policy systems; key actors are linked through learning networks; and participation defines the dominant forms of economic and social capital in a system.

In this concluding chapter we add to these propositions two final arguments which will be discussed in the following pages. The first is that **policy innovation occurs when there is an institutional system for increasing cultural value**. Second, **this occurs through the expert networking of key social interests**.

Innovation is a subject which encompasses a formidable terrain. Scientific discovery, technological change and shifts in types of organisation may all be considered part of this area. Using the insights from these fields to develop particular frameworks for public sector change is therefore a challenging task. It may be argued that the Public Service is not the same as a commercial research and development company. This is certainly true. Some common mechanisms in the linking of innovation and institutional structure can, however, be identified and adapted for particular use in the public sector. After all, many public organisations have extensive experience in this area. Public hospitals combine service delivery and research, state conservation departments run laboratories and other research programs, and the cultural creativity of symphony orchestras and theatre companies depends heavily upon structured government support. These are only the most spectacular cases. Every public organisation entails developmental action which can contribute to innovation. Our purpose here is to distil some common understandings of how this might be adapted and applied to the special problems we face in contemporary public policy.

One of the first things to note about the existing scholarly research on innovation is that it is split between studies and accounts of the origins of innovations, and those which investigate how innovations are passed from system to system. For ease of discussion we can term these theories of invention and theories of diffusion. For reasons which we will examine below, much of the public sector literature has tended to concentrate on issues of diffusion (Walker 1969, Gray 1973, Savage 1978). This division of attention is unhelpful. It encourages a false view of the relationship between those who 'invent' and those who capitalise on such breakthroughs.

The second general point to note is that this research literature is also polarised according to the weight given to the economic basis of innovation, and that given to its social determinants. In the first case, it is said that new ideas are developed when there are clear, rational incentives for individuals to develop them (Schumpeter 1939). In the second type new products or processes come into being when there is a particular social system of learning, communication and recognition. These nourish the creative interests of individuals and groups (Callon 1980). Following the themes of the rest of the book, the argument here will be that economic approaches can only be understood through sociological constructs. The quickest route to this point is through a recognition of the inadequacies of dominant economic approaches.

Economic Approaches to Innovation

The most common economic model of innovation conforms closely to neo-classical ideas about the importance of informed choice and efficiency. Many scholars and officials work within this framework of assumptions and take the view that innovation is the result of market forces which produce a 'demand' or 'pressure' for the development of new ideas and techniques (Mowery and Rosenberg 1979: 104). According to this model, new ways of solving problems and meeting needs come about because those with the potential to develop such ideas come to know that there is demand, and realise that they can get some direct personal benefit from meeting it.

This economic logic produces a linear model of innovation starting with:

- visible consumer needs
- incentives for producers to meet needs
- incentives for producers to commission experts
- incentives for experts to develop new products or processes
- responses by consumers to these products
- returns to the organisation for its efforts, and
- rewards to those involved in securing these returns.

This is the logic of what is called the demand-pull or demand-led account of innovation. For more than thirty years it has been the centre of debate. Langrish *et al.* (1972), in one of the most widely

demand-pull / demand-led model

quoted studies of industrial innovation, examined eighty-four cases of successful innovation. They concluded that the linear model is inadequate. There are a variety of other similar studies which contradict important aspects of the neo-classical view (David 1975, Pavitt 1971, Von Hippel 1988). Quite simply, the innovation which finally produces benefits for producers and consumers is often a different outcome from the one which was originally planned (Langrish *et al.* 1972). The chief problem with this model is that in practice innovation is frequently supply-led, not demand-driven.

It is not difficult to see why this might be. It is practically impossible for anyone to know that a demand exists before there is a successful product there to prove it. Hunches, inspired guessing and market pretesting cannot provide information on consumer needs for a product as yet undeveloped. Service innovation provides the analyst with much the same problem. It might be possible to identify a gap or a space in the market or system, but knowledge about what will fill that gap can only come through detailed interaction between service users and different groups of suppliers.

This suggests that all research and development systems face risks of failure. Reducing these risks turns out to be a key part of the strategy for sucessful innovation. The first and most important part of the risk problem is the nature of the environment in which the potential innovator works. The more stable the environment, the more likely it is that good guesses can be made about the likely success of innovations. But the minute we accept that organisations are forced to act within highly uncertain environments, the less credible is the demand-pull model's confidence that producers will successfully match their efforts to the needs of consumers, new suppliers or new social conditions.

The second, related problem with the demand-pull model is that consumers may not have solitary, independent needs, tastes or preferences. In the literature this issue is subject to extensive dispute. The dominant neo-classical position, put by Stigler and Becker (1977), regards tastes as explained by prices or personal endowments. Other than that, they argue, individuals do not vary. In other words, apart from what they are born with, individuals are much the same when it comes to what they need or want. The rest is up to the market, which is thought to stimulate consumption through offering opportunities which are attractively priced. This approach rests upon the related neo-classical argument that individuals are primarily self-interested actors who seek to expand the range and level of their satisfactions (Frank 1988). The origins of preferences of these individuals, however, cannot be explained within the confines of an economic approach.

Feminists, among others, dispute this idea of the solitary, undifferentiated individual. They rightly point out that gender is always present and if it is deleted from the vocabulary this is probably because the author believes that dominant male characteristics can be generalised to all individuals. There are also problems with the solitary nature of the individual, whether that person is a consumer or producer. As England (1993: 44) argues: 'Are most individuals so impervious to their surroundings that they can hold a job for years without their preferences being affected by the routines they get used to in this job?' The same could be said for the experience of being married, living in a particular neighbourhood, or being a member of a racial or ethnic community (Ferber and Nelson 1993).

But what do these issues have to do with the problem of policy innovation? First, as we have seen, it is necessary to challenge the notion that ideas flow primarily from an economic demand system. Second, it is important to avoid the problems created by viewing needs, tastes and preferences as solitary properties. And third, it is helpful to recall that both 'consumers' and 'producers' are actually involved in a system of relations with each other. This requires that we find sociological explanations of economic actions, rather than the reverse. Wildavsky (1987: 4) acknowledges this point by showing that neither preferences nor interests are independent of the world they help create: 'Instead of this phenomenological understanding—[that] interests are self-evident—we would rely on the convergence of certain strands of work in social science, according to which *meanings are shared*; they are conferred on objects or events through social interaction.'

This has presumably been the case throughout history for every social group or community. What is different about the present condition which policy makers face? The argument here is that current conditions challenge many of the underpinnings of liberal capitalist societies, preventing their policy makers from resorting to established routines. Whole sets of institutional practices must be changed in order to create new methods for dealing with these highly complex problems. This is also Touraine's (1974: 5) point:

> The individualised features of private life, as well as local societies and their ways of life have been profoundly affected—even destroyed—by ever growing geographic and social mobility, by the massive diffusion of information and propaganda, and by broader political participation than ever before. Precisely these factors make it impossible for exclusively economic mechanisms to be maintained any longer at the centre of social organisation and activity.

Social Approaches to Innovation

These criticisms of the neo-classical economic model open the door to alternative accounts of the means by which the genesis of successful programs and services might be better understood. The key to that critique is that both service users (consumers, actual and potential) and providers (present and future) often discover their needs through continuing interaction. And demand will therefore often be stimulated by supply, rather than the reverse. Public policy has long been aware of this potential, and 'garbage can' theories (Cohen, March and Olsen 1972) show how often solutions seek problems to solve, rather than the reverse. What the 'garbage can' accounts regard as a form of potential pathology, innovation theory might merely regard as an investment-oriented approach. In other words, existing systems of expertise may be used as a base from which to attract new services, clients and so on.

When we view the standard models of policy making we find that the demand-led account is manifested in its intellectual sibling, the rational action models of policy development (Allison 1971, Lindblom 1977, Steinbrunner 1974). These also have a linear view of the way actors deal with problems, and also take the view that goals (preferences) come first.

In practice we know from numerous case studies that policy makers do not stand back and contemplate specific problems in order to match them with dispassionate solutions (Lindblom 1959, Laver 1986, Wildavsky 1987, Davis and Weller 1987). Rather they engage in an endless process of action, consideration and reaction which is quite unlike the measured, linear view which textbooks take of rational deliberation. The two things which are wrong with the standard rational action approach are thus that it presumes clear goals which are thought to direct attention and resources, and assumes that policy occurs in neat episodes. It is worth pausing for a moment to explore these two problems in order to show how social innovation models differ.

The goal problem, as it impacts upon our understanding of organisations, has already been discussed in Chapter 7. As with the economist's confidence in the existence of 'demands', the goal problem has to do with the actual practices by which actors reach conclusions. They rarely start by having clear, unambiguous preferences. Usually they refine their preference in collaboration with others, and keep modifying what they think as new issues and opportunities emerge. Larger sets of values may be more stable over time, but here again actors often defer to the strong groups with whom they are associated in order to locate guiding principles. They do not make utility calculations in advance of each problem or issue (Evans-Prichard 1971, Douglas 1987). So it makes little sense to design a policy making system around the idea that goals are independent, that they precede choices, or that institutional behaviour is a result of their logical implementation.

Nor does consideration of policy issues usually take place in self-contained episodes. There is no definite start and finish to policy action. Instead, the problem may pass from one hand to another, may slip from public view for long periods, and might be frozen and unfrozen by nearby crises and shifts of attention. But it remains within the policy system, fixed there by continuing relationships between dependent groups of actors. Further, each instance of deliberation occurs within a history of previous commitments and interests, in the manner already discussed in the chapters on policy systems earlier in this book. For analytic purposes and to construct a narrative from which lessons may be learned, we often speak as if policy did occur in self-contained cases. Once this is challenged we can pay attention to the underlying processes, which may be chaotic and conflict-ridden, but are nevertheless recurrent, not episodic.

The innovation framework being sketched here suggests that specific actions by protagonists and the individual decisions of organisations serve to punctuate the flow of work and interaction. They do not complete or finish the job. Nor can they, by themselves, adequately define what has taken place nor predict what will happen next. When considered from the vantage point of this social imperative, policy making can be viewed as the attempts of several kinds of social actors to learn new ways to involve themselves in social innovation, while also stabilising or regulating those things which they wish to preserve. In other words, policy is what occurs at regulated traffic intersections when social institutions attempt simultaneously to manage the problems of current crowding, and also deal with emerging problems. Holding social systems together in the face of immediate threats, while also changing them to meet new challenges, is therefore a highly complicated achievement.

This implies a model of social learning in which systematic appreciation of the new takes place alongside the re-evaluation of the skills and knowledge embedded in the old. Both imperatives, regulation and learning, can be acknowledged in the analysis of policy making only if it is viewed as a structured system of innovation devised not simply to produce and consume resources, but more importantly to alter and revise the sets of relationships, rules and resources which prefigure the future.

The policy studies literature unfortunately provides a problematic account of this conceptual traffic snarl. The technicians recommend better signalling devices, the economists advise a means to assure that drivers and pedestrians pay an adequate price, while the managers and politicians are typically consumed with the immediate interest conflicts of commuters, residents and environmentalists. All too often this literature paints a picture of fragmentation and gloom in which idealism and expertise fall victim to local self-interest and élite compromise.

In the account of innovation given here, a different, anthropological view is taken of these matters. The policy making process and its programs are returned to the social context from which they first emerged. The politics of the court, the board room and the Cabinet are viewed as part only of a larger pattern of social investment in regulation and learning. Rulers and vested interests do not play their parts in isolation from other participants, but in direct response to their manoeuvres, whether actual or potential.

Social groups or formations are seen as being composed of several kinds of actors who seek to influence and direct the future through policy making and who, even as the objects of attention, retain a critical capacity to influence the course of events. The various élites who populate most policy case studies undoubtedly play a key role. But the existence of a leadership group is only significant to the degree that others accept their roles as followers. Immediately this fact is recognised, policy necessarily becomes a form of communication between one part of the group and the rest of its number. No matter how seemingly compliant or disinterested, the behaviours and views of this larger membership form a vital part of the action. Their willingness to work, their propensity to migrate and their capacity to co-operate are just the most obvious manifestations of the power they retain over the bigger patterns of social investment.

Regulation and Autonomy

Policy is therefore viewed as always being conditional on the gaining and securing of this wider investment of effort. With each episode of policy making, a new or revised social configuration emerges or an established one is re-invented. To achieve such an investment of effort it is necessary to create institutions which allow autonomy and discretion, yet focus efforts on a common project. This tension over regulation and autonomy is endemic to the policy maker's world.

Lipsky (1976) describes one important example of this unresolved struggle to both confine the actor's behaviour and accommodate the complex capacities of subjects to introduce novelty and chaos. Even in the most heavily-regulated policy systems, subjects prove resistant to simple control. The result is a continuing series of negotiations between the structure of rules and resources on one hand, and the individuality and contingency of actors on the other. Lipsky examined the work of local police who are responsible for the implementation of one of society's most extensively structured means of regulation. The ordinary constable walking the beat or crusing the streets appears at first glance to be the ultimate approximation of an instrument for the implementation of a fixed set of rules. But Lipsky's study shows that police are actually autonomous agents who make important choices about the rules they are required to enforce. These choices are far from being random selections or willful acts of rebellion. The variations of practice they exhibit are in fact a required part of a strategy to survive the turbulence and complexity of real world police work.

Because resources are limited and because the situations police face are frequently chaotic and dangerous, various forms of local practice develop. This is encouraged by the fact that the criminal justice system has contradictory expectations about the way police should behave—best expressed by the requirement that police be simultaneously friendly and helpful, suspicious and vigilant. At the policy level, police are required to treat all citizens equally and at the same time to take special care to allow for differences due to ethnicity, age and economic circumstances. Pressures on the job result in police making critical choices about whether or not to arrest offenders, who to regard as a potential assailant, and what facts will constitute evidence of misbehaviour. As Lipsky points out, these critical forms of discretion are not the result of police corruption, although they make corruption possible. They are instead the consequences of the incapacity of even very comprehensive sets of rules to express the conditions likely to prevail in real life situations. Consequently actors retain the capacity to use their discretion not only to choose what to do in non-rule situations, but also to use their power to interpret, bend or ignore the rules themselves.

This struggle over the capacity to regulate and the practical demand for autonomy is one of the central issues in debates on policy innovation. Critics of government action frequently complain that bureaucrats exercise far too much power over their clients and, following Weber (1968), over the political system. This central ambivalence about state policy making runs through most contemporary strategies of the political Left and the re-emergent Right. Bureaucrats and their budgets have become the targets of both democrats and demagogues. Importantly, discussions about the means that might be used to control bureaucracy reveal the assumptions which actors make about policy itself. The control issue can be thought to have two different dimensions—responsibility and effectiveness (Rourke 1969). Policy makers, including ordinary citizens, seek to use the state and its offices as a means to express their views and, in turn, to have these views expressed in laws and programs. To achieve this close relationship the bureaucrat is tied to various forms of accountability and required to obey certain rules.

If they can be made to work, these constraints prevent bureaucrats ignoring the demands of the democratic process, and allow the public's elected representatives to use state organisations in a manner sanctioned by the electoral process. This creates an instrumental relationship between officials and their organisations, and between public organisations and their governors. But it is now easy to see that this might well lead to threats to democractic values, as well as to problems of effectiveness.

Popular interests are plainly not served by state officials and organisations doing as they please. If such agents do only what their political masters specifically tell them to do, however, the state may become hopelessly myopic. Programs may go only to electorally sensitive constituents; the friends and associates of those in power will be needed to take key jobs in the Public Service in order to make them secure; and the bureaucracy may well lose any independent obligation to serve the general public. If this notion that state officials have only an accountability upwards to their political masters is successfully criticised, the instrumental account of regulation will have to be challenged as an insufficient rationale. Forms of 'downward or 'outward' accountability must then be institutionalised, and a means sought to resolve the inevitable clashes which will occur between the rights of those above and below.

These problems of responsibility are matched by dilemmas in regard to policy effectiveness. Three common problems are found. In the first, political leaders and senior bureaucrats may give the wrong instructions to subordinates because they are ignorant. For example, they instruct employment agencies to provide training in computing skills when there is no market for them. Staff in the agencies may know, through their closer contact with the field and their expertise in labour market economics, that this is mistaken, but their upward accountability requires them to obey. A second common problem occurs when officials are held responsible for results they do not control. Local police may have their performance measured against local crime statistics, because it is thought that an effective police presence reduces crime. However reasonable, this notion ignors all the other causes of crime which lie outside the control of the police. A third inappropriate form of accountability is the use of the wrong measures and incentives. This frequently occurs when those wishing to assert control do not know what results will constitute success. Instead of an outcome standard they choose to control activities. So, in the police example cited above, the outcome being sought is reduced crime rates and the activity measured is some specific task police perform to achieve it, such as the number of arrests made. When, in cases like this, those in control reward and punish officials according to their arrest record, serious perversions may result. Staff may find it rational to ignore other important activities which are not being measured or rewarded. They may engage in opportunistic behaviour to put their activities in the best light. For example, if schools are financed according to the final test scores of their graduating students, they may choose to screen out low performing students or coerce them into taking the courses most likely to advantage the school's overall performance.

The means available for policy makers wishing to avoid these kinds of control problems are many, but in each case a degree of uncertainty and risk is evident. Too tight a restraint, or the wrong control, and the effectiveness of the program is sacrificed. Too loose a connection between policy making and its implementations and officials may lose their way. Regulation and autonomy must therefore be carefully negotiated. As a general rule, the more individual or variable the needs of the client, the greater the need for operational autonomy by local officials. The greater the level of operational autonomy, the more the regulatory system must rely on input controls such as training and trust, rather than activity or output controls.

From Demand to Supply: Industry Policy

The focus upon innovation models implies a fundamental shift in the strategy of governance from instrumental power directed to production and consumption towards strategic investments in highly differentiated, flexible service systems. To understand the nature of the shift involved, it is helpful to contrast the old episodic/demand models of policy development to this alternative.

This is nowhere more obvious than in approaches to the regulation of the economy. Until recently the standard responses by governments facing problems of unemployment and international vulnerability have consisted of various forms of demand management. Tariffs, public works programs and centralised wage controls were the favoured instruments of those wanting to stimulate production and sponsor economic expansion. The industrial 'growth machine' (Molotch 1976) promised to increase the size of the national economic pie, enabling diverse social groups to benefit from either their privileged positions as producers or as recipients of 'trickle down' prosperity.

Private enterprise was, in this view, the best vehicle for decisions about exactly what would be produced. A standard education and basic levels of income defined government obligations to ordinary participants in this system. Although some regarded this as a form of advanced market allocation, in practice the decisions which most influenced outcomes were taken by the managers of large and small corporations, and consumers (including governments), were content to accept the choices made.

During the 1970s, this model began to fail. Globalised economic activity enhanced the power of international corporations and trading blocs largely outside governmental control. Environmentalists demonstrated that resulting industrial growth was often achieved at a huge, possibly terminal, cost to the local environment. Aid agencies and economists identified increasing disparaties between the life options of industrial élites and the dependent poor.

Even among beneficiaries a disappointment with the results of industrial growth grew more and more obvious. Hirsch (1978) complained that the driving force of inequality and envy was creating a cycle of dependence and dissatisfaction. Economic expansion had become a means to deliver the required goods, but by the time they were available for mass consumption, the original attraction had been overshadowed by a new set of problems and demands:

> the family in the tail end...that acquires its automobile after the luxury of pleasure driving has been qualified by congestion and parking restrictions—while the necessity of car ownership has been established by the decay of public transport and by the switching of the channels of physical communication between home, work and social facilities—for this family passing the once-vaunted milestone of car ownership, the passage may appear less a release from its old subordinate position than as a new facet of an unchanged subordinate reality. (Hirsch 1978: 167)

The other overpowering problem with the demand-driven growth model was its fiscal cost. If Keynes had been right and governments had been able to correct slumps through spending and flatten booms via spending restraint, investment problems might have been left to the private economy. Instead, the world economy experienced a 'double blow' recession in the mid-1970s in which high inflation was accompanied by high unemployment. In this situation increased government spending simply led to greater inflation and increased debt. A decade later, governments and markets around the world had all but abandoned their faith in these demand-side strategies. In their place there has begun to grow a new generation of strategies which eschew tactical intervention in favour of continuous involvement in workplace change, retraining, research and development and other 'supply side' solutions. The dominant characteristic of this new approach to economic steering is its heavy reliance upon a new system of soft structures linking state and private actors. Authoritative plans, state-sponsored producer networks, industry training strategies, research and development authorities and other such initiatives have multiplied. Although often directed and sponsored by governments, they are not controlled by them. Instead, they typically have a negotiated governing structure which includes employers, unions, educational institutions, professional groups, consultants and marketing companies.

The motive for such arrangements is clear. The major problems of economic and social change cannot be approached by any one social actor alone. None holds sufficient power or resources to oblige co-operation from the others. Were it simply a matter of taxing and spending, governments might have proceeded alone. But many of the new problems concern issues which lie outside the easy reach of legislators. Convincing employees to undertake retraining, developing programs of urban renewal, or penetrating foreign markets are only possible through local initiatives supported by central co-ordination. Soft structures, or supply side institutions, attempt to create new forms of authority to undertake these negotiated changes. As they proliferate, such arrangements begin to alter the character of the governmental role, drawing officials away from older models of episodic intervention towards a recurring commitment to knowledge sharing and interdependence.

Lazonick (1991) provides a compelling analysis of the institutional basis of previous forms of economic transformation, showing the inadequacy of Adam Smith's model of innovation through the market. British domination of the nineteenth century international economy cannot be explained through the private decisions of entrepreneurs. Instead, historians give credit to government-enacted changes in the regulation of capital, new rules for the employment of labour, and military support for monopoly trading companies such as the East India and the Royal Africa Companies. When these insights are placed alongside research into the German and Japanese economic miracles, a consistent picture emerges:

> For the sake of the creation of value, organisational co-ordination is continually superseding market co-ordination, and substituting privileged for equal access to resources, in key areas of economic activity. (Lazonik 1991: 61)

The account of policy making which can be derived from these insights and which underpins the innovation model presented here differs from traditional theories by regarding policy as both a regulatory and a learning system directed at the creation of institutionally-based innovation. In place of episodic attention to correcting disequilibria, with its focus on élite intelligence and instrumental action, this framework seeks an understanding of the contributions which governments and other actors make to continuing forms of knowledge generation, privileged access to resources, and the collaborative formulation of authoritative plans.

These systems of organisational interdependence are qualitatively different for both markets and hierarchies, both of which betray what Landau and Chisolm (1985) call an 'arrogance of optimism', because of their inherent interest in short-term efficiency and their structural blindness to long-run problems of reliablity.

Knowledge Communities

Innovation systems clearly depend upon the development of public intelligence and skill. Episodes of investigation and implementation contribute one set of actions to this process, but they do so on terms which are defined by the continuing character of the system of applied knowledge available in any field such as health, transport or education. Policies therefore result from, and contribute to a particular knowledge community. To develop a new health care arrangement, policy makers must engage in strategies of change which seek to alter the contributions of doctors, nurses, administrators, taxpayers and patients, all of whom have existing roles and interests. Indeed, such a policy will inevitably spring from problems or tensions within this existing field. To succeed, this new policy or innovation must accomplish a revision of the skills which these participants possess, based upon new information and knowledge. Governments, no matter how powerful, do not control this information, and nor can they achieve new skills without the active compliance of many other groups of actors.

It is assumed that these actors are incapable of generating knowledge and deploying these new skills without the strategic intervention of other actors, including governments. The reasons for this can vary a great deal, but for the most part they are a consequence of individual difference, isolation and market failure. New knowledge and the skills which it makes possible are only generated collectively. Left to their own devices, particular actors, whether they are individuals or organisations, do not have the resources or incentives to make significant investments in major new products or services. Nor do they have enough certainty about what others may do to predict the effects of any changes they might instigate. In other words, their isolation increases the risks they face in the future. Arrow (1974) defines this chronic uncertainty as the plain fact that 'we do not have a complete description of the world which we fully believe to be true'. In place of this state of doubt, potential innovators require collective efforts to spread information, share insights and perfect techniques. If they take a private and locally rational view of their individual chances of benefiting from these innovations, they will regularly choose to persist with current practices rather than risk scarce resources on changes which may either fail or give ground to competitors. Arrow (1962) has formulated the economic logic of this problem in so far as individual firms are concerned, although he did so without challenging the economists' commitment to market competition. Lundvall (1988) has developed this insight in relation to the necessary interactions and the cumulative character of learning systems. Kodama (1992: 71) explains the implications of this shift as one in which firms move from 'breakthrough' approaches to technological change, towards a recognition of the power of 'technology fusion'. In this, a 'non-linear, complementary, and co-operative' blending of improvements from several previously separate fields is used.

> Relying on breakthroughs alone fails because it focuses the R&D effort too narrowly. . .Yet many Western companies still rely almost exclusively on the breakthrough approach. The reasons are complex: distrust of outside innovations, a not-invented-here engineering arrogance, and aversion to sharing results.

De Gues (1988) argues that for large organisations such as Royal Dutch Shell, this problem amounts to a choice between planning systems which focus upon crisis and the responses which can be made to it, or to 'planning as learning', in which the ability to institutionalise information generation, the systematic imagination of alternative scenarios and a willingness to abandon autocracy are paramount. Elam (1993) has extended this understanding of knowledge generation and its transfer with the observation that 'where learning to innovate is a priority, information may even be regularly understood as the "perfect gift" rather than a saleable commodity'.

Policy making, when considered as a system of innovation among linked or interdependent actors, becomes a learning and regulating web based upon continuous exchanges of information and skill. Learning occurs through regulated exchange, rather than through heroic acts of individual insight or special legislative feats of the kind regularly described in newspapers. Interactive learning about new ways to confront the future come to depend upon the existance of alliances, obligatory ties and other continuing forms of co-operation between suppliers of raw materials, processors, producers, consumers and authorities—including citizens.

The dynamics of this institutional system can be demonstrated in complex policy making areas such as environmental planning, where governments face diverse and conflictual values and unpredictable political agendas. Successful institutions such as the Victorian government's Land Conservation Council (LCC), and the Australian government's Resource Assessment Commission (RAC), have common characteristics. They draw protagonists into continuing research consultations which aim to stabilise value disputes, obtain consensus data concerning environmental problems, hear complaints from affected parties, and consider new arrangements in the light of both scientific and political imperatives. All those involved are drawn into continuing roles as producers, regulators and policy makers (Considine 1992, Economou 1993). It is also clear that such approaches rely upon lateral forms of organisation rather than traditional forms of hierarchy. Project teams with clear mandates, adequate resources and scope to trial novel proposals are regularly seen to be the institutional form most likely to nourish innovation (Katzenbach and Smith 1993).

The underpinnings of innovation systems include rich information exchanges, collaborative investigations and implementations, a common perception of the risks of failure and an ideology or culture of trust and commitment. Benveniste (1987) shows how existing forms of professional discipline may, under the right circumstances, contribute one important form of collaborative commitment. Groups of experts such as engineers, lawyers and doctors frequently establish their own forms of knowledge transfer and enrichment, which cross the boundaries of key organisations and persist beyond specific problem encounters. They also link service provider organisations with educational institutions through alumni groupings and career advancement training programs. Von Hippel (1988) defines this critical contribution as 'know-how trading' and rates it highly as a source of innovation in industry: 'Informal know-how trading is essentially a pattern of informal co-operative R&D. It involves routine trading of proprietary information between engineers working at different firms—sometimes direct rivals.' There is no reason to expect a lesser role in the public sphere.

A second aspect of this innovation system is the forms of moral regulation which are created by participants wishing to deal with their common predicament of risk and vulnerability. Elam (1993) shows how this generalised form of valuation and virtue is necessary to the establishment of trust among participants. The honest communication of new information and the continuation of reliable forms of giving prove essential to any system's ability to manage its ignorance about the future. Elam borrows Beck's (1987) insight regarding the effect of uncertainty upon notions of individual responsibility:

> Our notions of individuality, of 'self-determination', of 'one's own life', are founded upon personal access to reality. To the extent that we are cut off from this access, we are driven—in the full flower of individualism—into a *collective existence* at the height of modernity.

According to this view the technological problems of the present are profoundly more complex than those of the past. Issues such as environmental contamination and biotechnological interventions into the nature of life impose challenges which individuals (be they scientists or not) cannot comprehend or control through their ordinary sensory faculties. They cannot investigate these problems through recourse to personal experience because to do so involves waiting until it is too late. Consequently they become more and more reliant upon collective information and shared perceptions.

The policy-as-learning perspective is therefore an inevitably shared experience in which actors require continuing opportunities to develop joint strategies. The practical possibilities of this model are easily seen in the product and process innovation theories which have developed to explain the German, Italian and Japanese manufacturing successes of the past ten years. Von Hippel's work on American product and process innovations in the semiconductor, circuit board, plastics and scientific instruments industries also supports this account.

All such accounts point to the particular social-institutional configurations which underpin the highly successful experiences of firms in these countries. In place of the more common models of individual management responsibility for innovation, these studies point to highly integrated forms of intevention by state and sector-wide industry bodies which steer firms towards co-operative forms of product and process development. These institutions seek to regulate the supply side, or investment dimension, of the production system through training programs, skill sharing, joint marketing arrangements and strategic alliances among suppliers and co-producers.

Those who have examined these institutions argue convincingly that the high risk associated with investments in new technology, together with market demands for greater reliability and quality of products, force individual actors to seek the security of collective effort. Hirshhorn (1984) has extended this analysis to include new demands for learning inside the firm. High technology enables a rapid shift to new products and processes, but it does so at the cost of making the firm more dependent upon the commitment and skill of a technically trained workforce. Quality circles, Total Quality Management (TQM) techniques and other systematic attempts to secure this new form of workforce reliability have in common a recognition that without these forms of internal learning employers cannot guarantee appropriate deployments of new machines and a regular flow of mistake-free production. But left to its own logic, the labour market will neither encourage the formation of these skills, and nor will it reward individual employers who invest heavily in the necessary forms of worker involvement. Only social institutions beyond the firm are able to mobilise and spread this set of skills and commitments and prevent destabilising episodes of 'poaching' and competition by opportunistic employers.

Conclusions

The general features of these forms of institutional support have a common character which can now be appropriated into an account of policy making as innovation. The state's role is focused first and foremost upon the establishment of organisations for system-wide information exchange and knowledge transfer. This is supported by mechanisms which attach these sectoral objectives to educational efforts within the mainstream educational system and the labour market. Various applied skill development programs are also typically involved, with governments acting as the key source of authority to make such endeavours a permanent source of tranferable skill. These institutions also include marketing and promotional activities designed to inculcate new values which reward innovative behaviour by workers and by individual organisations. Such a system of pre-production engineering is also directed at obliging these critical agents—workers, unions, employers, scientists, educators, government regulators—to commit to a collective or shared view of their own best interests.

Innovation strategies which have worked in industry and in public sector settings such as health and conservation have the following common characteristics:

- Authoritative agreements regarding the nature of the problems and issues to be tackled;
- Willingness to reform processes as well as specific programs or products;
- Clear leadership roles for key experts and managers;
- Use of existing professional and ideological commitments to achieving change;
- Supported networks for links between organisations and the knowledge community;
- Continuous links between suppliers, providers and consumers;
- Team work through project-based institutions;
- Priority attention to using the knowledge of staff at the front line;
- Disciplined project management;
- Practical material and status incentives for employees and citizens/community interests to contribute;
- Political recognition of successful efforts and achievements.

These constitute something less than a blueprint. They point to an anthropology of policy change, in which deliberate alterations in institutional practices rebound and ricochet through countless smaller policy transactions. These cultures do not presume consensus or demand uniformity. They are only necessary, in fact, because difference and conflict are ever-present. But when the clash and clamour of alternative perspectives interrogate new policy problems, potential solutions may begin to multiply. From there it is a shorter step to finding feasible solutions.

References

Allison, G. (1971) *Essence Of Decision*. Boston: Little, Brown

Arrow, Kenneth (1962) 'Economic Welfare and the Allocation of Resources for Invention', in 'The Rate and Direction of Inventive Activity: Economic and Social Factors', Conference of the Universities—National Bureau Committee for Economic Research and the Committee on Economic Growth, Social Science Research Council, Princeton University Press, Princeton

— (1974) *The Limits of Organisation*. New York: Norton

Beck, Ulrich (1987) 'The Anthropological Structure of the Firm', *American Economic Review Proceedings* 75: 156

Benveniste, Guy (1987) *Professionalising the Organisation: Reducing Bureaucracy to Enhance Effectiveness*. San Francisco: Jossey-Bass

Cohen, Michael D., March, James G. and Olsen, Johen P. (1972) 'A Garbage Can Model of Organisational Choice', *Administrative Science Quarterly* 17: 1–25

David, P. A. (1975) *Technical Choice, Innovation and Economic Growth* Cambridge: Cambridge University Press

Davis, G. and Weller, P. (1987) 'Negotiated Policy or Metanonsense? The Policy Prescriptions of Murray Frazer', *Australian Journal of Public Administration* 25 (4): 380–87

De Gues, Arie P. (1988) 'Planning as Learning', *Harvard Business Review*, March-April: 70–74

Douglas, Mary (1987) *How Institutions Think*. London: RKP

Evans-Prichard, E. A. (1971) *The Azande: History and Political Institutions*. Oxford: Clarendon Press

Ferber, Marianne A., and Nelson, Julie A. (eds) (1993) *Beyond Economic Man: Feminist Theory and Economics*. Chicago: University of Chicage Press

Frank, Robert (1988) *Passions Within Reason: The Strategic Role of the Emotions*. New York: W. W. Norton

Gray, Virginia (1973) 'Innovation in the States: A Diffusion Study', *American Political Science Review* 67, December: 1,174–85

Hirsch, Fred (1978) *Social Limits to Growth*. Cambridge, Mass.: Harvard University Press

Hirschhorn, Larry (1984) *Beyond Mechanisation*. Cambridge: MIT Press

Katzenbach, Jon and Smith, Douglas (1993) *The Wisdom of Teams: Creating the High-Performance Organisation*. Boston: Harvard Business School Press

Kodama, Fumio (1991) *Analysing Japanese High Technologies: The Techno-Paradigm Shift*. London: Pinter Publishers

— (1992) 'Technology Fusion and the New R&D', *Harvard Business Review*, July-August: 70–78

Kosik, Karel (1983) *Fourth Congress of the Czech Writers Union* (1967), quoted in Alain Touraine, Francois Dubet, Michael Wieviorka and Jan Strezelecki, *Solidarity: Poland 1980–81*. London: Cambridge University Press

Landau, Martin and Chisolm, Donald (1985) 'The Arrogance of Optimism', Working Paper 88–16, Institute of Governmental Studies, University of California, Berkeley, CA, October

Langrish, J., Gibbons, M., Evans, W. G. and Jevons, F. R. (1972) *Wealth From Knowledge: A Study of Innovation in Industry*. New York: John Wiley and Sons

Laver, Michael (1986) *Social Choice and Public Policy*. Oxford: Blackwell

Lazonick, William (1991) *Business Organisation and the Myth of the Market*. New York: Cambridge University Press

Lindblom, C. E. (1959) 'The Science of Muddling Through', *Public Administration Review* 19: 79–88

— (1977) *Politics and Markets*. Basic Books

Lipsky, Michael (1976) 'Towards a Theory of Street-Level Bureaucracy', in W. D. Hawley and Michael Lipsky (eds), *Theoretical Perspectives on Urban Politics*. Englewood Cliffs, NJ: Prentice-Hall

Lundvall, B-A. (1988) 'Innovation as an Interactive Process: From User-Producer Interaction to the National System of Innovation', in G. Dosi, C. Freeman, R. Nelson, G. Silverberg and L. Soete (eds), *Technical Change and Economic Theory*. London: Printer Press

Mannheim, K. (1936) *Ideology and Utopia*. New York: Harcourt Brace

Pavitt, K. (1971) *The Conditions for Success in Technological Innovation*. Paris: OECD

Rourke, F. E. (1969) *Bureaucracy, Politics and Public Policy*. Boston: Little Brown

Savage Robert (1978) 'Policy Innovativeness as a Trait of American States', *The Journal of Politics* 40, February: 212–24

Schumpeter, J. A. (1939) *Business Cycles*, 1. New York, McGraw-Hill

Stigler, George and Becker, Gary (1977) '*De Gustabus Non Est Disputandum*', *American Economic Review* 67: 76–90

Steinbrunner, J. D. (1974) *The Cybernetic Theory of Decision: New Dimensions of Political Analysis*. Princeton, NJ: Princeton University Press von Hippel, Eric (1988) *The Sources of Innovation.* New York: Oxford University Press

Walker, Jack L. (1969) 'The Diffusion of Innovations Among American States', *American Political Science Review* 63, September: 880–99

Wildavsky, A. (1987) 'Choosing Preferences by Constructing Institutions: A Cultural Theory of Preference Formation', *American Polictical Science Review* 81: 3–21

Index